Shaheed Bhagat Singh

Shaheed Bhagat Singh

Dr. C.P. Raj
Dr. Ved Prakash

AMIGA PRESS. INC
Delhi -110051

AMIGA PRESS. INC
H.O :- 28-A, Indra Park, Chander Nagar
Delhi :- 110051 (India)
Tel :- 011-22504028, +91-98736-57000
Email :- amigapress@gmail.com
amigaeditorial@gmail.com
Website :- www.amigapress@co.in

This edition is published by Amiga Press.Inc

ISBN : 978-93-84533-22-9

First Published 2018

PRINTED : THOMSON PRESS INDIA

Preface

Bhagat Singh is considered to be one of the most influential revolutionaries of Indian Nationalist Movement. He became involved with numerous revolutionary organizations and played an important role in the Indian National movement. He died a martyr at the age of just 23 years. Following his execution, on March 23, 1931, the supporters and followers of Bhagat Singh regarded him as a "Shaheed"

The legend of Bhagat Singh, a valiant fighter of freedom, will continue to inspire the youth of our country forever. His spirit of self-sacrifice and the fearless manner in which he faced death are unparalleled in the annals of the freedom struggle of India.

Bhagat Singh is often termed as the 'youth icon' or the 'revolutionary of the youth' but his stature is one that equals some of the prominent names in the Indian freedom struggle. His patriotism was not restricted to the strong violent outburst against the British; he rather had a mind and intellect of a genius who could foresee division of India on communal lines which many of the much esteemed leaders of the time were unable to see. Keeping the cause of country ahead of the religion was another signs of his mature and rational mind. His educational qualifications establish the fact that his opinions and ideas were well thought and not just a product of hysterical mass movements.

In March 1925, inspired by European nationalist movements, the Naujawan Bharat Sabha was formed with Bhagat Singh, as its secretary. Bhagat singh also joined the Hindustan Republican Association (HRA), a radical group, which he later rechristened as the Hindustan Socialist Republican Association (HSRA) along with fellow revolutionaries Chandrashekhar Azad and Sukhdev. He returned to his home in Lahore after assurances from his parents that he would not be compelled to get married. He established contact with the members of the Kirti Kisan Party and started contributing regularly to its magazine, the "Kirti". As a student, Bhagat Singh was an avid reader and he would read up about European nationalist movements. Inspired by the writings of Friedrich Engels and Karl Marx, his political ideologies took shape and he became more inclined towards a socialist approach. He also wrote in newspapers like "Veer Arjun" "under several pseudonyms.

In response to the formulation of Defence of India Act, the Hindustan Socialist Republican Association planned to explode a bomb inside the assembly premises, where the ordinance was going to be passed. On April 8 1929, Bhagat Singh and Batukeshwar Dutt threw a bomb onto the corridors of the assembly, shouted 'Inquilab Zindabad!' and threw pamphlet outlining their missive into the air. The bomb was not meant to kill or injure anyone and therefore it was thrown away from the crowded place, but still several council members were injured in the commotion. Following the blasts both Bhagat Singh and Batukeshwar Dutt courted arrest.

In this book the authors have tried to explore all the related aspects of Bhagat Singh's life and his participation in Indian freedom struggle.

—*Editor*

Contents

1

Biography

Bhagat Singh was an Indian freedom fighter, considered to be one of the most famous revolutionaries of the Indian independence movement. For this reason, he is often referred to as Shaheed Bhagat Singh (the word shaheed means "martyr"). He is also believed by some historians, such as K. N. Panikkar, to be one of the earliest Marxists in India. Singh was also one of the leaders and founders of the Hindustan Socialist Republican Association (HSRA).

Born to a family which had earlier been involved in revolutionary activities against the British Raj in India, Singh, as a teenager, had studied European revolutionary movements and was attracted to anarchism and communism. He became involved in numerous revolutionary organizations. He quickly rose through the ranks of the Hindustan Republican Association (HRA) and became one of its leaders, converting it to the HSRA. Singh gained support when he underwent a 63-day fast in jail, demanding equal rights for Indian and British political prisoners. He was hanged for shooting a police officer in response to the killing of veteran social activist Lala Lajpat Rai. His legacy prompted youth in India to begin fighting for Indian independence and also increased the rise of socialism in India.

CHILDHOOD

Singh was born into a Jat Sandhu family to Sardar Kishan Singh Sandhu and Vidyavati in the Khatkar Kalan village near Banga in the Lyallpur district of Punjab. Singh's given name of Bhagat means "devotee". He came from a patriotic Sikh family, some of whom had participated in movements supporting the independence of India and others who had served in Maharaja Ranjit Singh's army. His grandfather, Sardar Kishan Singh, was a follower of Swami Dayananda Saraswati's Hindu reformist movement, Arya Samaj, which would carry a heavy influence on Singh. His uncles, Ajit Singh and Swaran Singh, as well as his father were members of the Ghadar Party, led by Kartar Singh

Sarabha Grewal and Har Dayal. Ajit Singh was forced to flee to Persia because of pending cases against him while Swaran Singh was hanged on December 19, 1927 for his involvement in the Kakori train robbery of 1925.

Unlike many Sikhs his age, Singh did not attend Khalsa High School in Lahore, because his grandfather did not approve of the school officials' loyalism to the British authorities. Instead, his father enrolled him in Dayananda Anglo Vedic High School, an Arya Samajist school. At age 13, Singh began to follow Mahatma Gandhi's Non-Cooperation Movement. At this point he had openly defied the British and had followed Gandhi's wishes by burning his government-school books and any British-imported clothing.

Following Gandhi's withdrawal of the movement after the violent murders of policemen by villagers from Chauri Chaura, Uttar Pradesh, Singh, disgruntled with Gandhi's nonviolence action, joined the Young Revolutionary Movement and began advocating a violent movement against the British.

In 1923, Bhagat famously won an essay competition set by the Punjab Hindi Sahitya Sammelan. This grabbed the attention of members of the Punjab Hindi Sahitya Sammelan including its General Secretary Professor Bhim Sen Vidyalankar. At this age, he quoted famous Punjabi literature and discussed the Problems of the Punjab. He read a lot of poetry and literature which was written by Punjabi writers and his favourite poet was an Indian freedom fighter Allama Iqbal from Sialkot.

In his teenage years, Bhagat Singh started studying at the National College in Lahore, but ran away from home to escape early marriage, and became a member of the organization Naujawan Bharat Sabha ("Youth Society of India").

In the Naujawan Bharat Sabha, Singh and his fellow revolutionaries grew popular amongst the youth. He also joined the Hindustan Republican Association at the request of Professor Vidyalankar, which was then headed by Ram Prasad Bismil and Ashfaqulla Khan. It is believed that he had knowledge of the Kakori train robbery. He wrote for and edited Urdu and Punjabi newspapers published from Amritsar.

In September 1928, a meeting of various revolutionaries from across India was called at Delhi under the banner of the Kirti Kissan Party. Bhagat Singh was the secretary of the meet.

His later revolutionary activities were carried out as a leader of this association. The capture and hanging of the main HRA Leaders also allowed him to be quickly promoted to higher ranks in the party, along with his fellow revolutionary Sukhdev Thapar.

BIOGRAPHICAL PROFILE

Born as Bhaganwala on the 26th September, 1907, Bhagat Singh grew up in a petty-bourgeois family of Sandhu Jats settled in the Jullunder Doab district of the Punjab. He belonged to a generation that was to intervene between two decisive phases of the Indian national movement-the phase of the 'Extremism' of Lal-Bal-Pal and the Gandhian phase of nonviolent mass action.

In the first decade of the 20th century, the Punjab had a broad spectrum of popular leaders working in the state. Two such leaders were Sardar Ajit Singh and Sardar Kishen Singh, Bhagat Singh's paternal uncle and father. Interestingly, although middle class, both leaders were in great opposition to the mainstream leadership of the Indian National Congress and particularly Lala Lajpat Rai. Both brothers were consistently radical in attempting to mobilise the masses to oppose the British at every opportunity that arose.

In an article called 'Emergence of the Punjab in the freedom movement', Bhagat Singh traces their inspiration to the extremist leader, Bal Gangadhar Tilak. 'Having seen their enthusiasm at the 1906 Congress Convention in Calcutta, Lokmaniya was pleased and in bidding them adieu, gave them the responsibility of strengthening the movement in the Punjab.' On returning to Lahore, both brothers 'started a monthly newspaper called Bharat Mata to propagate their ideas'. Since they had no money and no influence among the rich, says Bhagat Singh, they had to collect everything necessary for propaganda work themselves. This they did by attracting a crowd in the market by ringing a bell and giving a lecture 'on how foreigners had destroyed India's industry and commerce'. This was followed by an announcement that an important meeting would be held within the week at the Bharat Mata office. After the first two meetings held on two consecutive Sundays, a decision was taken to hold a meeting every Sunday. Many people joined the group including Lala Lalchand 'Phalak', the 'national poet' of the Punjab, Lala Pindidas, Dr. Ishwari Prasad and Sufi Amba Prasad. Sardar Ajit Singh and Mahant Nandkishore were elected the President and Secretary of the group now organised as the 'Bharat Mata Society'.

In 1887, the Punjab government created the Chenab Colony, by diverting the Chenab river into a system of perennial canals rapidly turning the barren wasteland of the central Punjab into fertile farmland. The colony was to be a model for the rest of Punjab, supervised by a paternalistic administration. 'Healthy agricultural communities of the "best Punjabi type" would be established... (which would) in turn demonstrate to other Punjabis how proper sanitation, careful economic planning and cooperation with the government could result in a higher standard of living'.

In October 1906 the government introduced the Punjab Colonisation of Land Bill in the local Legislative Council. This Bill established retroactive conditions concerning sanitation, tree planting and construction in the Chenab Colony. In case of breach of the conditions, fines would be collected in the same fashion as revenue. Section 31 ruled that courts would have no jurisdiction in the Colony.

In November, the government announced a drastic increase in the occupier rate (charge on canal water). In the Bari Doab canal area running through the districts of Amritsar, Gurdaspur and Lahore, rates had been lower because the government had hoped that a leniency in revenue would ensure the loyalty of the Sikh Jats who supplied recruits for the Indian Army. The yeomen farmers of the Colony were already discontented over the maladministration in the Colony and opposed the extra legal fees that the Bill sought to legitimise. Graft and corruption had galvanised the whole Colony into opposition to the entire system of interference and paternalism. From 1903, Sifaj-ud Din Ahmed, a retired postal officer, started the Zamindar, a newspaper, to publicise the colonists' plight. It was only a matter of time for discontent to turn into political opposition.

Bhagat Singh's grandfather, Sardar Arjan Singh, had migrated to the canal area and settled at Banga, Lyallpur. It is therefore not surprising that Sardar Ajit Singh was able to articulate so clearly the problems of the colonists and the objection to the Bill.

On 22nd and 23rd March, 1907, the Zamindar held a public meeting to protest against the bill. Although this was a platform for the rich yeomanry, Ajit Singh sent delegates from the 'Bharat Mata Society' to launch an agitation against the British. Lala Lajpat Rai was asked by the newspaper to give a speech. Bhagat Singh in his article on the national movement in the Punjab, shows how Lajpat Rai and Ajit Singh differed on this issue.

'Before leaving (for Lyallpur) Lalaji sent a message to Sardar Ajit Singh saying that the government should be thanked for (a previous) amendment and then asked to repeat the law'. To this Ajit Singh is said to have replied 'we shall prepare the masses for a no revenue campaign. Also we can never thank the government'.

The meeting itself is described by Bhagat Singh thus, 'Lalaji was received by a large rally and consequently reached the pandal two hours late... In the meanwhile, Sardar Ajit Singh gave a speech. He was an impressive speaker.

His tireless style of speech made the audience enthusiastic and by the end he had a large following of people. By the time Lalaji reached the pandal, the masses were with the Bharat Mata Society;... Lalaji was Punjab's finest orator but the style, the fearlessness and determination with which he spoke was something else. He received an ovation after every line.

After the meeting many people dedicated their lives to the motherland'. This account is also corroborated by N. Gerald Barrier, 'Lajpat Rai attempted to be moderate, but as happened frequently with his speech making, the crowds' frenzy drove him to use phrases and ideas verging on what the British termed 'sedition'.

After the meeting, Lajpat Rai went on a lecture tour in the United Provinces, while Ajit Singh began to organise the farmers of Amritsar and Lahore. Under Ajit Singh's leadership the colonists passed a resolution supporting a boycott of British goods and started a campaign to ensure that nobody paid the new water rate.

The price of disobedience was social ostracism by the offender's caste or a fine of Rs. 500. The Lieutenant Governor of the Punjab, Denzil Ibbetson believed sedition in the province to be taking two directions. First Ajit Singh was trying to spread disaffection among the troops and the students and secondly the 'fomenters of unrest' were corrupting the yeomanry. He asked the Government of India for permission to deport Ajit Singh and Lajpat Rai so as to be able to 'strike terror into the minds of those concerned'. Ajit Singh was deported to Mandalay. Sardar Kishen Singh though less prominent than his brother was also part of this agitation and was put into jail.

In 1907 the Bill was repealed and soon Ajit Singh and Kishen Singh were released. Bhagat Singh, born in September that year, was called Bhaganwala (the child of God) by his grandmother. Bhagat Singh began his primary education at the District Board Primary School in Banga. In 1916-17, his father moved to Lahore to be able to organise relief work for the victims of a severe earthquake in Kangra. Bhagat Singh was now shifted to the D.A.V. High School, Lahore. Writing about these years, Bhagat Singh said, 'It was through his (father's) teachings that I aspired to devote my life to the cause of freedom'.

In his first letter, written to his grandfather at the age of 12, Bhagat Singh reassures him that he has passed his school exam comfortably and the latter need not worry on that count. Two years later he wrote again to tell his grandfather that 'railway men are planning to go on strike. Hopefully they will start by the next week'. This letter is dated the 12th of November 1921 and shows that he was aware of the Non Cooperation Movement that Gandhi had launched. Both letters are in fluent Urdu.

In 1923, Bhagat Singh joined the National College, Lahore. It was affiliated to the Punjab Quami Vidya Pith and was founded and managed by Lala Lajpat Rai and Bhai Parmanand. The College was set up as an alternative to the institutions run by the Government, bringing to the field of education the idea of Swadeshi. The philosophy behind the establishment of such a College was to produce 'self reliant, aggressive (in order to be progressive) men and women that new India wants'.

Bhagat Singh seems to have had an impressive academic record in College. The Principal of the College, Chhibil Das wrote in his memoirs, 'There were no books at hand. So it was for the teachers to select books from the libraries and give the relevant portions to the students... in our National College, we used to talk about Mazzini and Garibaldi. We used to talk about Ireland, about Sinn Fein movement of De Valera and other movements and about the Russian revolution'. The Russian Narodniks seem to have been discussed with the history professor, Jai Chandra Vidyalankar.

Bhagat Singh was also a member of the College dramatics society and seemed to have 'gained much prominence amongst the students and teachers, not only of his own college but other local colleges'. 'He was particularly impressive because of his youthful physique and commanding voice', one of his biographers, S.R. Bakshi tells us. Bhagat Singh was fluent in Urdu, Hindi, Gurmukhi, English and Sanskrit. In the pamphlet, 'Why I am an Atheist' Bhagat Singh writes about his days in college. 'Though a favourite with some professors and disliked by certain others, I was never an industrious or studious boy. I could not get any chance of indulging in such feelings as vanity. I was rather a boy with a shy nature, who had certain pessimistic dispositions about (my) future career'.

By the age of 16, Bhagat Singh was completely dedicated to the cause of national liberation. Nothing illustrates this better than his attitude to marriage.

In 1924, Bhagat Singh was pressurised to get married. Unable to convince his parents of his determination not to marry, Bhagat Singh left his house in Lahore and reached Kanpur armed with an introduction by Jai Chandra Vidyalankar for Ganesh Shankar Vidyarthi.

In the note left behind for his father Bhagat Singh said, 'my life has been dedicated to the noblest cause, that of the freedom of the country. Therefore there is no rest or worldly desire that can lure me now. If you remember, when I was small, Bapuji (Arjun Singh) declared at my thread ceremony that I had been dedicated to the service of my country. I am, thus waiting to fulfil that commitment. I hope you will forgive me'. On being asked why he did not want to get married, Bhagat Singh told Jaidev Gupta, his classmate and friend, that he had chosen a path which was full of many possibilities. His two uncles had gone that way and they had left two widows. Should he also leave another widow? Chhabil Das has left us an account of how when he was to get married, Bhagat Singh came and reproached him on getting married.

'Besides them being my students we had good personal relations too... when Bhagat Singh heard that I was going to be married... he insisted that I should not marry. I said, if I could get a really good life companion who, instead of retarding my activities, would invigorate them, what would be your view? In the same breadth I quoted three concrete examples of Mrs. Sun Yat Sen,... wife of Lenin and... companion of Karl Marx. (At this) Bhagat Singh replied "Guruji who can vanquish you in any argument". So he yielded.'

From 1923-24, Bhagat Singh worked with Ganesh Shankar Vidyarthi in Kanpur. Vidyarthi brought out a weekly nationalist newspaper called the Pratap. Here Bhagat Singh worked under the alias, Balwant. It was here that he met people like B.K. Dutt, Shiv Venna, B.K. Sinha etc. with whom he would share a close camaraderie. Ajoy Ghosh who was fifteen at the time wrote about his first meeting with Bhagat Singh thus, 'I believe it was sometime in 1923 that I met Bhagat Singh... he was introduced to me by B.K. Dutt in Cawnpore. Tall and thin, rather shabbily dressed, very quiet, he seemed a typical village lad lacking smartness and self confidence. I did not think very highly of him and told Dutt so when he was one'.

This was the first time that Bhagat Singh had left his house and the Punjab for a new city and new people. Ganesh Shankar Vidyarthi attempted to get Bhagat Singh a job as a headmaster of a National school near Aligarh, a post he did eventually accept. 1924 was perhaps the most important year in Bhagat Singh's life. In Kanpur he became a member of the Hindustan Republican Association, started by Sachindranath Sanyal a year earlier. The main organiser of the Association was Chandra Shekhar Azad and Bhagat Singh became very close to him. It was as a member of the HRA that Bhagat Singh began to take seriously the philosophy of the Bomb. Armed revolution was understood to be the only weapon with which to fight British imperialism. Bhagat Singh went from village to village recruiting people and to activate the villages in the United Provinces. Propaganda attracted police work but it had now become easy to escape unnoticed.

In 1925, Bhagat Singh returned to Lahore and within the next year he and his colleagues started a militant youth organisation called the Naujawan Bharat Sabha. In April 1926, Bhagat Singh established contact with Sohan

Singh Josh and through him the 'Workers and Peasants Party' which brought out the monthly magazine Kirti in Punjabi. For the next year Bhagat Singh worked with Josh and joined the editorial board of Kirti. In 1927, he was first arrested on charges of association with the Kakori Case accused for an article written under the pseudonym Vidrohi (Rebel). He was also accused of being responsible for a bomb explosion at Lahore during the Dussehra fair. He was let off for good behaviour against a heavy security of Rs. 60,000.

In 1928, Bhagat Singh and Chandra Shekhar Azad were the sole absconders of the Kakori case and the other leaders being put behind bars meant that they were the leaders of the Hindustan Republican Association. 'One day in 1928 I was surprised when a young man walked into my room' Ajoy Ghosh remembers, 'and greeted me. It was Bhagat Singh but not the Bhagat Singh that I had met... before. Tall and magnificently proportioned, with a keen, intelligent face and gleaming eyes, he looked a different man altogether. And as he talked I realised that he had grown not merely in years.... All those who met Bhagat Singh then and afterwards have testified to his remarkable intelligence and to the powerful impression he made when talking. Not that he was a brilliant speaker. But he spoke with such force, passion and earnestness that one could not help being impressed. We talked the whole night and as we went out for a stroll... it seemed to me that a new era was dawning for our party. We knew what we wanted and we knew how to reach our goal'.

LATER REVOLUTIONARY ACTIVITIES

Lala Lajpat Rai's Death and the Saunders Murder

The British government created a commission under Sir John Simon to report on the current political situation in India in 1928. The Indian political parties boycotted the commission because it did not include a single Indian as its member and it was met with protests all over the country. When the commission visited Lahore on October 30, 1928, Lala Lajpat Rai led the protest against the commission in a silent nonviolent march, but the police responded with violence. The police chief beat Lala Lajpat Rai severely and he later succumbed to his injuries. Bhagat Singh, who was an eyewitness to this event, vowed to take revenge.

He joined with other revolutionaries, Shivaram Rajguru, Jai Gopal and Sukhdev Thapar, in a plot to kill the police chief. Jai Gopal was supposed to identify the chief and signal for Singh to shoot. However, in a case of mistaken identity, Gopal signalled Singh on the appearance of J. P. Saunders, a Deputy Superintendent of Police. Thus, Saunders, instead of Scott, was shot. Bhagat

Singh quickly left Lahore to escape the police. To avoid recognition, he shaved his beard and cut his hair, a violation of one of the sacred tenets of Sikhism.

Bomb in the Assembly

In the face of actions by the revolutionaries, the British government enacted the Defence of India Act to give more power to the police. The purpose of the Act was to combat revolutionaries like Bhagat Singh. The Act was defeated in the council by one vote. However, the Act was then passed under the ordinance that claimed that it was in the best interest of the public.

In response to this act, the Hindustan Socialist Republican Association planned to explode a bomb in the assembly where the ordinance was going to be passed. Originally, Azad attempted to stop Bhagat Singh from carrying out the bombing; however, the remainder of the party forced him to succumb to Singh's wishes. It was decided that Bhagat Singh and Batukeshwar Dutt, another revolutionary, would throw the bomb in the assembly.

On April 8, 1929, Singh and Dutt threw a bomb onto the corridors of the assembly and shouted "Inquilab Zindabad!" ("Long Live the Revolution!"). This was followed by a shower of leaflets stating that it takes a loud voice to make the deaf hear. The bomb neither killed nor injured anyone; Singh and Dutt claimed that this was deliberate on their part, a claim substantiated both by British forensics investigators who found that the bomb was not powerful enough to cause injury, and by the fact that the bomb was thrown away from people. Singh and Dutt gave themselves up for arrest after the bomb. He and Dutt were sentenced to 'Transportation for Life' for the bombing on June 12, 1929.

Trial and Execution

Shortly after his arrest and trial for the Assembly bombing, the British came to know of his involvement in the murder of J. P. Saunders. Bhagat Singh, Rajguru, and Sukhdev were charged with the murder. Bhagat Singh decided to use the court as a tool to publicize his cause for the independence of India. He admitted to the murder and made statements against the British rule during the trial. The case was ordered to be carried out without members of the HSRA present at the hearing. This created an uproar amongst Singh's supporters as he could no longer publicise his views.

While in jail, Bhagat Singh and other prisoners launched a hunger strike advocating for the rights of prisoners and those facing trial. The reason for the strike was that British murderers and thieves were treated better than Indian political prisoners, who, by law, were meant to be given better rights.

The aims in their strike were to ensure a decent standard of food for political prisoners, the availability of books and a daily newspaper, as well as better clothing and the supply of toilet necessities and other hygienic necessities. He also demanded that political prisoners should not be forced to do any labour or undignified work. During this hunger strike that lasted 63 days and ended with the British succumbing to his wishes, he gained much popularity among the common Indians. Before the strike his popularity was limited mainly to the Punjab region.

Bhagat Singh also maintained the use of a diary, which he eventually made to fill 404 pages. In this diary he made numerous notes relating to the quotations and popular sayings of various people whose views he supported. Prominent in his diary were the views of Karl Marx and Friedrich Engels. The comments in his diary led to an understanding of the philosophical thinking of Bhagat Singh. Before dying he also wrote a pamphlet entitled "Why I am an atheist", as he was being accused of vanity by not accepting God in the face of death.

On March 23, 1931, Bhagat Singh was hanged in Lahore with his fellow comrades Rajguru and Sukhdev. His supporters, who had been protesting against the hanging, immediately declared him as a shaheed or martyr. According to the Superintendent of Police at the time, V.N. Smith, the hanging was advanced:

Normally execution took place at 8 am, but it was decided to act at once before the public could become aware of what had happened...At about 7 pm shouts of Inquilab Zindabad were heard from inside the jail. This was correctly, interpreted as a signal that the final curtain was about to drop.

Singh was cremated at Hussainiwala on banks of Sutlej river. Today, the Bhagat Singh Memorial commemorates freedom fighters of India.

IDEALS AND OPINIONS

Marxism

Bhagat Singh's political thought evolved gradually from Gandhian nationalism to revolutionary Marxism. By the end of 1928, he and his comrades renamed their organization the Hindustan Socialist Republican Association. He had read the teachings of Karl Marx, Friedrich Engels, and Vladimir Lenin and believed that, with such a large and diverse population, India could only survive properly under a socialist regime. These ideals had been introduced to him during his time at the National College at Lahore and he believed that India should re-enact the Russian revolution.

In the case that India were not socialist, he believed that the rich would only get richer and the poor would only get poorer. This, and his militant methods, put him at odds with Gandhi and members of the Congress. He became the first socialist leader in India to make any gain. Even today, socialist leaders sometimes refer back to him as the founder of Indian socialism.

Atheism

During his teenage years, Singh was a devout Arya Samajist. He began to question religious ideologies after witnessing the Hindu-Muslim riots that broke out after Gandhi disbanded the Non-Cooperation Movement. He did not understand how members of these two groups, initially united in fighting against the British, could be at each others' throats because of their religious differences.

At this point, Singh dropped his religious beliefs, since he believed religion hindered the revolutionaries' struggle for independence, and began studying the works of Bakunin, Lenin, Trotsky-all atheist revolutionaries. He also took an interest in Niralamba Swami's book Common Sense, which advocated a form of "mystic atheism".

While in a condemned cell in 1931, he wrote a pamphlet entitled Why I am an Atheist in which he discusses and advocates the philosophy of atheism. This pamphlet was a result of some criticism by fellow revolutionaries on his failure to acknowledge religion and God while in a condemned cell, the accusation of vanity was also dealt with in this pamphlet. He supported his own beliefs and claimed that he used to be a firm believer in The Almighty, but could not bring himself to believe the myths and beliefs that others held close to their hearts. In this pamphlet, he acknowledged the fact that religion made death easier, but also said that unproved philosophy is a sign of human weakness.

Death

Bhagat Singh was known for his appreciation of martyrdom. His mentor as a young boy was Kartar Singh Sarabha. Singh is himself considered a martyr by many Indians for acting to avenge the death of Lala Lajpat Rai, also considered a martyr. In the leaflet he threw in the Central Assembly on 8th April 1929, he stated that It is easy to kill individuals but you cannot kill the ideas.

Great empires crumbled while the ideas survived. After engaging in studies on the Russian Revolution, he wanted to die so that his death would inspire the youth of India to unite and fight the British Empire.

While in prison, Bhagat Singh and two others had written a letter to the Viceroy asking him to treat them as prisoners of war and hence to execute them by firing squad and not by hanging. Prannath Mehta, Bhagat Singh's friend, visited him in the jail on March 20, four days before his execution, with a draft letter for clemency, but he declined to sign it.

Conspiracy Theories

Many conspiracy theories exist regarding Singh, especially the events surrounding his death.

Mahatma Gandhi

One of the most popular ones is that Mahatma Gandhi had an opportunity to stop Singh's execution but did not. This particular theory has spread amongst the public in modern times after the creation of modern films such as The Legend of Bhagat Singh, which portray Gandhi as someone who was strongly at odds with Bhagat Singh and did not oppose his hanging.

A variation on this theory is that Gandhi actively conspired with the British to have Singh executed. Both theories are highly controversial and hotly contested. Gandhi's supporters say that Gandhi did not have enough influence with the British to stop the execution, much less arrange it. Furthermore, Gandhi's supporters assert that Singh's role in the independence movement was no threat to Gandhi's role as its leader, and so Gandhi would have no reason to want him dead.

Gandhi, during his lifetime, always maintained that he was a great admirer of Singh's patriotism, but that he simply disapproved of his violent methods. He also said that he was opposed to Singh's execution (and, for that matter, capital punishment in general) and proclaimed that he had no power to stop it. On Singh's execution, Gandhi said, "The government certainly had the right to hang these men. However, there are some rights which do credit to those who possess them only if they are enjoyed in name only." Gandhi also once said, on capital punishment, "I cannot in all conscience agree to anyone being sent to the gallows. God alone can take life because He alone gives it."

Gandhi had managed to have 90,000 political prisoners who were not members of his Satyagraha movement released under the pretext of "relieving political tension," in the Gandhi-Irwin Pact. According to a report in the Indian magazine Frontline, he did plead several times for the commutation of the death sentence of Bhagat Singh, Rajguru and Sukhdev, including a personal visit on March 19, 1931, and in a letter to the Viceroy on the day of their execution, pleading fervently for commutation, not knowing that the letter would be too late.

Lord Irwin, the Viceroy, later said:

As I listened to Mr. Gandhi putting the case for commutation before me, I reflected first on what significance it surely was that the apostle of non-violence should so earnestly be pleading the cause of the devotees of a creed so fundamentally opposed to his own, but I should regard it as wholly wrong to allow my judgment to be influenced by purely political considerations. I could not imagine a case in which under the law, penalty had been more directly deserved.

Saunders Family

On October 28, 2005, a book entitled Some Hidden Facts: Martyrdom of Shaheed Bhagat Singh--Secrets unfurled by an Intelligence Bureau Agent of British-India [sic] by K.S. Kooner and G.S. Sindhra was released. The book asserts that Singh, Rajguru, and Sukhdev were deliberately hanged in such a manner as to leave all three in a semiconscious state, so that all three could later be taken outside the prison and shot dead by the Saunders family. The book says that this was a prison operation codenamed "Operation Trojan Horse." Scholars are skeptical of the book's claims.

LEGACY

Indian Independence Movement

Bhagat Singh's death had the effect that he desired and he inspired thousands of youths to assist the remainder of the Indian independence movement. After his hanging, youths in regions around Northern India rioted in protest against the British Raj.

Modern Day Legacy

The Communist Party of India (Marxist) itself acknowledges Bhagat Singh's contribution to Indian society and, in particular, the future of socialism in India. To celebrate the centenary of his birth, a group of intellectuals have set up an institution to commemorate Singh and his ideals.

Several popular Bollywood films have been made capturing the life and times of Bhagat Singh. The oldest was Shaheed in 1965, starring Manoj Kumar as Singh. Two major films about Singh were released in 2002, The Legend of Bhagat Singh and 23rd March 1931: Shaheed. The Legend of Bhagat Singh is Rajkumar Santoshi's adaptation, in which Ajay Devgan played Singh and

Amrita Rao was featured in a brief role. 23 March 1931: Shaheed was directed by Guddu Dhanoa and starred Bobby Deol as Singh, with Sunny Deol and Aishwarya Rai in supporting roles.

The 2006 film Rang De Basanti (starring Aamir Khan) is a film drawing parallels between revolutionaries of Bhagat Singh's era and modern Indian youth. It covers a lot of Bhagat Singh's role in the Indian freedom struggle. The movie revolves around a group of college students and how they each play the roles of Bhagat's friends and family.

The patriotic Urdu and Hindi songs, Sarfaroshi ki Tamanna (translated as "the desire to sacrifice") and Mera Rang De Basanti Chola ("my light-yellow-coloured cloak"; Basanti referring to the light-yellow colour of the Mustard flower grown in the Punjab and also one of the two main colors of the Sikh religion as per the Sikh reheat meryada (code of conduct of the Sikh Saint-Soldier)), while created by Ram Prasad Bismil, are largely associated to Bhagat Singh's martyrdom and have been used in a number of Bhagat Singh-related films.

In September 2007 the governor of Pakistan's Punjab province announced that a memorial to Bhagat Singh will be displayed at Lahore museum, according to the governor "Singh was the first martyr of the subcontinent and his example was followed by many youth of the time."

CRITICISM

Bhagat Singh was criticized both by his contemporaries and by people after his death because of his violent and revolutionary stance towards the British and his strong opposition to the pacifist stance taken by the Indian National Congress and particularly Mahatma Gandhi.

The methods he used to make his point-shooting Saunders and throwing non-lethal bombs-were quite different to the nonviolent non-cooperation used by Gandhi. He was accused of having knowledge of the Kakori train robbery by the British.

Bhagat Singh has also been accused of being too eager to die, as opposed to staying alive and continuing his movement. It has been alleged that he could have escaped from prison if he so wished, but he preferred that he die and become a legacy for other youths in India. Some lament that he may have done much more for India had he stayed alive.

QUOTATIONS

Wikiquote has a collection of quotations related to:

Bhagat Singh

- "The aim of life is no more to control the mind, but to develop it harmoniously; not to achieve salvation here after, but to make the best use of it here below; and not to realise truth, beauty and good only in contemplation, but also in the actual experience of daily life; social progress depends not upon the ennoblement of the few but on the enrichment of democracy; universal brotherhood can be achieved only when there is an equality of opportunity-of opportunity in the social, political and individual life." -from Bhagat Singh's prison diary, p. 124
- "Inquilab Zindabad" (Long live the revolution)

WHAT IF BHAGAT SINGH HAD LIVED?

Surely there are umpteen very important contemporary issues on which follow-ups can be presented before you dear readers. But today let us walk together to follow into the life of a hero, who had sacrificed his life literally and willingly for our sake.

An enigma, obsessed with passion for his country's freedom, he had achieved rare clarity of thought, sharpened his intelligence and conquered the fear of death in his teens. And that death was inflicted upon him at the age of 23, for he was fighting for you and me, to enable us to live with dignity in a free homeland.

This unparalleled hero was Bhagat Singh whose death anniversary falls on March 23. He was born on September 26, 1907, in the family of freedom fighters. His uncle, Ajit Singh, and father, Kishan Singh, were known as radicals and had successfully mobilised masses to oppose the British at every step under an organisation called "Bharat Mata Society".

Today 70 years later we ought to pause and review how Bhagat Singh was different from Mahatma Gandhi? Though both had fought for the freedom of India yet both vehemently adopted routes totally different in nature.

While Bhagat Singh was merely 20 years old in 1928, Mahatma Gandhi was already a mature person of 59 years. Yet both were into the movement in full swing with matching intensity, dedication, conviction and above all passion. What was it between the two that presents a very uneasy historical record ? Before we delve into that aspect let us have a brief life sketch of Bhagat Singh as his life actually was.

Bhagat Singh studied at D.A.V. High School and later at National College, Lahore. He acted in plays and became fluent in Urdu, Hindi, Gurmukhi, English and even Sanskrit.

By the age of 16, Bhagat Singh had of his own choice dedicated his life to achieve freedom for his country. How firm and full of conviction he was about this goal can be gauged from the fact that a year later, in 1924, when his family pressurised him to get married, he categorically refused.

Immediately after this Bhagat Singh left for Kanpur and worked for Ganesh Shankar Vidyarthi in his weekly called Pratap.

In the same year he became a member of the Hindustan Republican Association.

Merely 17 and his life got moulded into a revolutionary from here onwards. By 1925 he had founded "Naujawan Bharat Sabha" in Lahore. Soon he worked for Sohan Singh Josh in his monthly called Kirti.

Bhagat Singh's first direct encounter with the British came in 1927, when he was arrested on charges of having links with the accused in the Kakori case for an article written under the pseudonym "Vidrohi" which meant "rebel". However, he was let off on grounds of good behaviour but on a heavy security bond of Rs 60,000.

Bhagat Singh came under the influence of Marx, Lenin, Trotsky, Bakumin besides thoroughly studying the history of the revolutionary movement in India, which included the Bahhar Akali Movement too.

Amongst his contemporary living legends the person who succeeded in occupying the seat of "mentor, friend and brother" in Bhagat Singh's own words was Kartar Singh Sarabha, who fought racial discrimination in San Francisco, USA.

Bhagat wrote many articles in a very short span of his life. These writings speak volumes about his astonishingly clear and focused thinking despite his rather young age. All the brilliantly written articles reveal his own depth, seriousness of purpose, truthful accounts and of course a targeted mission.

There were a series of barbarous authoritarian, dictatorial and atrocious actions of the British Government besides daily display of injustice and discrimination towards Indians that outraged the impressionable but extraordinary intelligent mind of young Bhagat Singh.

Saunders' cruel assault on the forehead of Lala Lajpat Rai with a baton during the anti-Simon Commission demonstration which took his life, the Nankana Sahib massacre (six Sikhs were executed by the British), Kartar Singh Sarabha's execution when Bhagat Singh was just a child, Jatin Das's death in jail during a hunger strike and endless atrocities on freedom fighters led Bhagat Singh to give a befitting reply to the British.

Soon followed the murder of Saunders in Lahore in December, 1928, and bombs were thrown in the Legislative Assembly on April 8, 1929. It is important to note the self-confession that the bombs were carefully thrown behind the chairs so as no innocent was physically hurt.

"Revolution to me is not the cult of bomb and pistol but a total change of society culminating in the overthrow of both foreign and Indian capitalism and the establishment of the dictatorship of the proletariat." Bhagat Singh himself expressed these profound views during his own trial.

It may also be mentioned here that it was Bhagat Singh and all his contemporary radicals alone who insisted that freedom fighters should continue their struggle for "Puran Swaraj".

It is a historical fact that Mahatma Gandhi and his associates in the face of British cunning were willing to adopt the middle path.

The bombs were clearly meant to be purely demonstrative. It is noteworthy that the occasion was the anti-Labour Trades Disputes Bill. The year 1928-29 had witnessed a massive labour upsurge in India.

Finally, awaiting his own execution for the murder of Saunders, Bhagat Singh at the young age of 23 studied Marxism thoroughly and wrote a profound article, "Why I am an atheist".

It was at this juncture that many organisations of the times fervently appealed to Mahatma Gandhi to save the life of Bhagat Singh.

The Yuva Vahini of Jawaharlal Nehru, the Naujawan Bharat Sabha, Aruna Asaf Ali, all the known radical revolutionaries, pleaded with Mahatma Gandhi to save Bhagat Singh and his associates Sukhdev and Rajguru.

The Gandhi-Irwin talks were on and political observers were confident that a word from Gandhi will certainly commute hanging to life imprisonment.

The historical records of the dialogue between Gandhi and Irwin in the series of crucial meetings that took place pretty close to the hanging of Bhagat Singh reveal a dismal picture.

Mahatma Gandhi spoke for everyone and every issue but did not utter a single word to bargain for Bhagat Singh's life. Hence his statement after the hanging of martyr Bhagat Singh, "the Congress made many attempts to save the lives of Bhagat Singh and his two associates", is not a substantiated fact.

Historian Dr. Rajiv Lochan whose major research work revolves around Mahatma Gandhi puts this whole historical perspective in the following observations: "From all events and records available it is quite obvious that Gandhiji perceived both Subhas Chander Bose and Bhagat Singh as potential threats to his own highly acclaimed position". At Hussainiwala in Ferozepore the place where Bhagat Singh's samadhi has been built to keep his memories alive, the scene fills you with tears flowing from your heart. B.K.Dutt's samadhi as per his last wish has also been made in the lap of Bhagat Singh's own samadhi. Amidst silence, flowers and water flows a question which will never get answered: "What if Bhagat Singh had lived ?".

REALISATION OF THE NEED FOR ARMED STRUGGLE

The founders of the HSRA fully grasped the basis and essence of British state power in India. The leadership of the HRSA, fully realising that the British had conquered India with the sword and the gun, and maintained their oppressive and exploitative subjugation of the Indian people primarily by force of arms, they could not be "persuaded' to leave India by peaceful protests (satyagrahas), noncooperation, civil disobedience and other such methods advocated by Gandhi to stunt the development of a mass revolutionary movement capable of sweeping the British and the Indian exploiting classes alike from the face of India. Hence the mobilisation of the masses and the organisation of armed struggle against the British rule was an integral part of the programme and practical activity of the HRSA, which at its 1928 Conference established an armed wing, the Hindustan Socialist Republican Army, with Chandar Shekhar as its Commander in Chief.

BHAGAT SINGH'S VISION OF A FUTURE INDIA

Bhagat Singh, his close comrades and the new generation of national revolutionaries were determined to make revolution by relying on the masses and learning from the most advanced science of revolution. This is clearly revealed by the fact that, after throwing bombs in the Central Assembly on 8 April 1929, an act for which they were to pay with their lives, Bhagat Singh and his comrades made sure that the Assembly hall was strewn with red leaflets ending with the slogans Long live revolution and Long live the dictatorship of the proletariat.

In their statement, prepared by Bhagat Singh and read by their lawyer Asif Ali on 6 June 1929 before the court trying them, Bhagat Singh and his co-accused explained that they had thrown the bombs to protest against the arrest of communists and other members of the labour movement, resulting in the Meerut Conspiracy case, and against the

Trades Disputes Act which sought to prevent a general strike by industrial workers. Having made it clear that no plethora of Safety Bills, no amount of ordinances, no trumped up conspiracy cases, could snuff out the flames of revolution and stand in the way of its onward march, the statement went on to explain the reorganisation of society on a socialistic basis, saying that "unless this thing is done and exploitation of man by man and of nations by nations is brought to an end, suffering and carnage with which humanity is threatened cannot be prevented.

All talk of ending war and ushering in an era of universal peace is undisguised hypocrisy."

Repudiating all notions of individual terrorism, isolated from the mass movement of the working class and peasantry, the statement went on to portray Bhagat Singh's vision of revolution thus:

> *"Revolution does not necessarily involve sanguinary strife, nor is there any place in it for individual vendetta. It is not the cult of the bomb and the pistol. By 'Revolution' we mean that the present order of things, which is based on manifest injustice, must change. Producers or labourers, in spite of being the most necessary element of society, are robbed by their exploiters of their labour and deprived of their elementary rights. The peasant who grows corn for all, starves with his family; the weaver who supplies the world market with textile fabrics, has not enough to cover his own and his children's bodies; masons, smiths and carpenters who raise magnificent palaces, live like pariahs in the slums. The capitalists and the exploiters, the parasites of society, squander millions on their whims. These terrible inequalities and forced disparity of chances are bound to lead to chaos. This state of affairs cannot last long, and it is obvious that the present order of society in merry-making is on the brink of a volcano.*
>
> *"By 'Revolution' we mean the ultimate establishment of an order of society which may not be threatened by such breakdowns, and in which the sovereignty of the proletariat should be recognised and a world federation should redeem humanity from the bondage of capitalism and misery of imperial wars."*

On 21 January 1930, the death anniversary of V I Lenin, the accused in the Lahore conspiracy case appeared in the court sporting red scarves and shouting slogans: Long live the socialist revolution, Long live the Communist International, Lenin's name will never die, and Down with imperialism. Bhagat Singh read out this message to the Comintern and, with characteristic audacity, asked the trial judge to pass it on to that body: "On Lenin day we send hearty greetings to all who are doing something to carry forward the ideas of the great Lenin. We wish success to the great experiment which Russia is carrying out. We join our voice to that of the international working class. The proletariat will win. Capitalism will be defeated. Death to imperialism."

BHAGAT SINGH'S CONTEMPT FOR THE COMPROMISING INDIAN BOURGEOISIE

These ideas of the national revolutionaries were an anathema to the cowardly and compromising leadership of the Indian bourgeoisie. Bhagat Singh understood the class character of this leadership as clearly as he understood the revolutionary potentialities of the masses.

He contrasts the two, and exposes the utter wretchedness of the bourgeois leadership of the Indian freedom movement in a letter addressed to Young Political Workers, written from his prison cell on 2 February 1931:

> *"The real revolutionary armies are in the villages and in factories, the peasantry and the labourers. But our bourgeois leaders do not and cannot dare to tackle them. The sleeping lion once awakened from its slumber would become irresistible even after the achievement of what our leaders aim at. After his experience with Ahmedabad labourers in 1920, Mahatma Gandhi declared: 'We must not tamper with the labourers. It is dangerous to make political use of the factory proletariat.' ('The Times', May 1921). Since then, they never dared to approach them. There remains the peasantry. The Bardoli resolution of 1922 clearly defines the horror these leaders felt when they saw the gigantic peasant class rising to shake off not only the domination of an alien nation but the yoke of the landlords.*

"It is there that our leaders prefer a surrender to the British than to the peasantry... That is why I say they never meant a complete revolution." As if anticipating a sustained slander campaign by the Gandhite bourgeois leadership against himself and his fellow revolutionaries, and so as to leave no one in doubt on this score, Bhagat Singh, in this letter too returns to the question of individual terrorism, stating:

> *"Let me announce with all the strength at my command, that I am not a terrorist and I never was, except perhaps in the beginning of my revolutionary career. And I am convinced that we cannot get anything through these methods... I do not mean that bombs and pistols are useless, rather the contrary. But I mean to say that mere bomb-throwing is not only useless but sometimes harmful. The military department of the party should always keep ready all the war-material at its command for any emergency. It should back the political work of the party. It cannot and should not act independently."*

And a few lines earlier: "Apparently I have acted like a terrorist. But I am not a terrorist. I am a revolutionary who has got such definite ideas of a lengthy programme as is being discussed here."

Even in their conduct during the Lahore conspiracy trial and in the tactics they adopted in the court, Bhagat Singh and his comrades were just the opposite of the treacherous, cowardly and pusillanimous bourgeois followers of Gandhi. Gandhi had advised the fighters for Indian independence not to defend themselves before a British court, saying that the refusal to recognise the jurisdiction of the courts established by the British, the refusal to enter a legal defence and the readiness to face any sentence would strike at the prestige of British rule.

Such a course of action could not, and did not, satisfy the revolutionaries who were determined to turn their trial into a trial of British rule, with the Indian masses acting as judges. Just a few days before his execution, Bhagat Singh sent a letter to the authorities demanding that he and his condemned comrades, since they were prisoners of war, be executed by a firing squad instead of being hanged.

Thus it can be seen that Bhagat Singh and his comrades were the product of their time and circumstances-a time when the economic and political development in the domestic and international arena were thrusting the masses into the whirlpool of revolutionary politics, radicalising the petty bourgeoisie and obliging the latter to adopt Marxism as the only weapon for the liberation of the masses from subjugation, oppression, misery, squalor and hunger. No one better symbolised this process than Bhagat Singh; no one better articulated the new socialist ideals than he did. Precisely for that reason he emerged as the most representative spokesman of this new vision of society, and, in the process, from being a mere youthful individual, he became a phenomenon.

IMPACT OF LENIN

Bhagat Singh was born in Punjab on September 28, 1907, and was hanged by the British on March 23, 1931. So it may be said that in his short life-span of 24 years political activities covered at the most a period of seven to eight years. The young Indian revolutionary was sentenced to death before he could reach his thirties. It should not be expected that his concepts regarding revolution were full-fledged and mature and had taken definite shape at such an early age. Yet, his short political career which came to an abrupt end gave remarkable and significant colour to his thought and actions.

Bhagat Singh did not come from a mere nationalist background. His family had a distinct revolutionary heritage. His father, Sardar Kishan Singh, and his uncles, Sardar Ajit Singh and Sardar Swaran Singh, were all connected with the Bharat Mata Samiti, the oldest revolutionary organisation in Punjab. They had to suffer greatly at the hands of the British. Ajit Singh, who was initially exiled to Burma in 1907, had to escape from his motherland to Iran, Turkey, Germany, and ultimately to Brazil.

Coming as he did from such a family, in his childhood and adolescent years Bhagat Singh naturally came in close contact with well-known revolutionaries like Lala Pindi Das, Ananda Kishore Mehta and others.

To young Bhagat Singh, Kartar Singh Sarava, the Ghadr Party leader, was like a mythical hero. In 1916 young Sarava had become a martyr at an even younger age than Bhagat Singh. So in his formative years his family and environment had left a deep nationalist and revolutionary impact on Bhagat Singh. While studying in the National College he had met Professor Jaychandra Vidyalankar and students like Bhagwaticharan, Sukhdev, Yashpal and Ramkishen who later earned fame as prominent revolutionaries.

Bhagat Singh went to Kanpur in 1924 and was introduced to Batukeshwar Dutta, Bejoy Kumar Sinha, Jogesh Chattopadhyay and other revolutionaries of the region by Ganesh Shankar Vidyarthi, the famous Congress leader of UP. (It may be mentioned that this is also the 50th year of Ganesh Shankar Vidyarthi's martyrdom. He died while participating in the anti-comunal movement.) Bhagat Singh became a member of the group known as the Hindustan Republican Association (HRA) because of his intimate ties with these revolutionaries.

In the constitution of the revolutionary group it was declared that the ultimate aim of the organisation was to establish a federal republican form of government in India through organised and armed revolution.....The fundamental principles of this Republic would be establishing universal suffrage and eradicating the social system in which there is class-exploitation.

The programme of the HRA also spoke of 'organising workers and peasants'. In spite of the close watch by the imperialist guardians of India, some news of the remarkable success of Soviet society and communism reached India. It seems all these revolutionaries were greatly influenced by those developments.

BHAGAT SINGH returned to Lahore early in 1925. He worked for some time on the editorial staff of Kiriti-a communist journal edited by Sohan Singh Josh. Meanwhile, after the Kakori Railway Raid in August 1925, HRA members were arrested and harassed. Bhagat Singh became involved in a plan to release the arrested leaders. Side by side, in March 1926, he established a young revolutionary group known as the 'Naojawan Bharat Sabha'. The President of this organisation was Comrade Ramkishan, the well-known revolutionary of Punjab, and Bhagat Singh was its Secretary. The 'Naojawan Bharat Sabha' went ahead of the HRA and declared that its objective was to establish "a completely independent Republic of Workers and Peasants in India".

The transformation of the Hindustan Republican Association (HRA) into the Hindustan Socialist Republican Association (HSRA) in August-September 1928, at a meeting in Delhi's Ferozeshah Kotla Ground, was a natural consequence of this process. According to Dr. Deol, the biographer of Bhagat Singh, the motion for renaming the Association was moved by Bhagat Singh. (Shahid Bhagat Singh-A Biography, p. 27) So Bhagat Singh not only wanted to establish an independent Republic based on universal franchise or a sketchy society devoid of exploitation. He clearly aimed to establish a completely independent socialist Republic.

But old forms of thinking and practice persisted in the struggle for independence and socialism. According to Ajoy Ghosh, a colleague of Bhagat Singh who later became the General Secretary of the Communist Party of India, As for the most important question, however, the question in what manner the fight for freedom and socialism was to be waged, armed action by individuals and groups was to remain our immediate task. Nothing else, we held, could smash constitutionalist illusions, nothing else could free the country from the grip in which fear held it.

When the stagnant calm was broken by a series of hammer blows delivered by us at selected points and on suitable occasions, against the most hated officials of the Government, and mass movement unleashed, we would link ourselves with the movement, act as its armed detachment and give it a socialist direction.... Such was our socialism in those days. (Bhagat Singh and his Comrades)

In 1927 a prominent Communist leader of the time, Shaukat Usmani, had connections with Bhagat Singh, Batukeshwar Dutta, Bejoy Kumar Sinha, and other revolutionaries. Usmani wrote:

> *Now I don't exactly remember when I first met Sardar Bhagat Singh. Either I met him in Lahore or in Kanpur....At that time HRA was being transformed into HSRA and it was decided that the new organisation would work in cooperation with the Communist International. At the same time I was informed that before they drop armed action by individuals they would complete some important actions which were in their list...I told Bejoy Babu (Bejoy Kumar Sinha), 'Come on, let's go to Moscow.' Personally I believed that Bhagat Singh and Bejoy Sinha's presence in Moscow would mean active armed assistance from the Soviet Union.*

Bejoy Kumar Sinha also informs us that he was elected by Bhagat Singh and his party to visit Moscow.

But due to the pressure of the ensuing jobs they could not accomplish this project. Meanwhile circumstances changed. It may be recalled here that Asfakullah, the distinguished member of the HRA who was later sentenced to death in the Kakori Conspiracy Case, was arrested in the Tribal Area near Peshwar while he was on his way to Moscow. Before Shaukat Usmani returned to India from Moscow in December 1928 the situation here had changed sharply.

The Police Commissioner, Saunders, was killed by Bhagat Singh and his group in Lahore, and to avoid arrest, Bhagat Singh and several other HSRA members had to abscond. At that time Bhagat Singh came to Calcutta secretly and established contact with the All-India Workers-Peasants Conference which was being held in the city, and with its President, Comrade Sohan Singh Josh.

A remarkable incident that next demanded attention was the throwing of bombs in the Central Assembly on April 8, 1929, by Bhagat Singh and Batukeshwar Dutta.

They courted arrest on the spot. A few days earlier, on March 20, 1929, there were countrywide arrests of Communists in connection with the Meerut Conspiracy Case. Moreover the amendment of the Public Security Bill and Trade Security Bill, after being rejected in the Central Assembly, was again forwarded to the Assembly as directed by the Governor-General. Both the Bills aimed at repressing communism and the working-class movement. Singh and Dutta wanted to protest against these measures by hurling bombs in the Central Assembly.

That is clear from the leaflets distributed in the Assembly by the two revolutionaries: The Government is imposing the Public Security Bill and Trade Security Bill upon us, while it has kept away the important Sedition Bill regarding newspapers for the next Assembly session. The indiscriminate arrest of working class leaders also clearly indicates the attitude of the Government...Let the mass representatives return to their electorates and prepare the people for the future revolution. Let the Government also know that while protesting against the repressive Bills and the brutal assassination of Lala Lajpat Rai we want to stress again the established truth that it is easy to kill a person but it is not easy to destroy one's ideology. Empires crumble. The Bourbons and Tsars are thrown away. The true ideology of the people survives.

On June 6, 1929, the statement of Bhagat Singh and Dutta also referred to the two Bills. Their explanation of the term "Revolution" would be pertinent in this respect. Revolution is not necessarily connected with a bloody struggle. It has no place for personal grievances. Nor is it a game of bombs and pistols.

By the term Revolution we mean dismissing the prevalent social system which is established on evident impropriety. Though the producers and workers are the most important component of society they are...deprived of the products of their labour and even of their fundamental rights. The farmer who produces corn for everybody has to starve with his family; the weaver who makes garments for all does not get enough clothing for himself. So until and unless this exploitation is prevented, the entire civilisation would crumble down. The cry of the day is absolute transformation and those who realise it bear the responsibility to reorganise society on the basis of socialism...By Revolution we understand the establishment of such a social system.... dictatorship of the proletariat and Communist internationalism which would save humanity from Capitalism and Imperial Wars. If the British Government pay no heed to our warning and continue with the old measures of repression, a mighty struggle would start which would sweep away all obstacles and ultimately establish the dictatorship of the proletariat for the fulfilment of the Revolutionary ideology.... Every-one has a birth right to independence. Labour controls society. The future of the labourer lies in the sovereignty of the people.

Ajoy Kumar Ghosh wrote that Bhagat Singh spent most of his time in prison studying socialist literature and during this time came very close to the communist ideology. Dr. Deol refers to Bhagat Singh studying the life of Lenin and the Communist Manifesto. Gopal Tagore, another biographer of Bhagat Singh, relates that a few days before his death when asked what was his last wish, he replied that he was studying the life of Lenin and he wanted to finish it before his death. (Bhagat Singh-The Man and His Ideas, p. 30)

When he was in prison he wrote two hundred pages of notes regarding capitalism, socialism, the origin of state, communism, religion, sociology, and also many facts regarding India, the French Revolution, Marxism, governmental structures, family, Communist International etc. (Shahid Bhagat Singh-A Biography, p. 30) The pamphlet Why I am an Atheist shows that Singh was very clear in his stand on religion. It is also seen in one of his letters written to his friend Joydeb that he requested him to sent books like Civil War in France by Marx, Left Wing Communism and Collapse of the Second International by Lenin. (Ibid., pp. 29-30)

It is further known from Ajoy Ghosh that Bhagat Singh and his colleagues sent a telegram to the Soviet Union on November 7, 1930, greeting the Great Russian Revolution. Dr. Deol says that in Janaury 1930, to commemorate "Lenin Day", they entered the Court Room wearing red scarfs and demanded that their greetings should be intimated to the President of the Third

International. (Ibid., pp. 69-70) Hearing about the martyrdom of Bhagat Singh, Rajguru and Sukhdev, the convicts of the Meerut Conspiracy Case sent a letter of condolence to Sardar Kishan Singh. They also demanded adjournment of the hearing that day. The organ of the Third International, International Correspondence, the organ of the British Communist Party and that of the American Communist Party, Daily Worker, also denounced the judicial murder (Ibid., pp. 77 and 90)

Bhagat Singh wrote to Sukhdev a few days before his death:

> *You and I may not live but the people of our country would. The ideology of Marxism and Communism would definitely triumph.-(Introduction, Gopal Tagore's Biography)*

I would like to mention another incident which I have come across in the book Prithvi Singh Azad in Lenin's Land written by Prithvi Singh Azad, the 88-year-old revolutionary. In the latter half of 1930 Bhagat Singh and his comrades were in Lahore Jail. CID officials came to Bhagat Singh to interrogate him. During the interrogation they mentioned the name of Prithvi Singh Azad a number of times to find out whether Bhagat Singh knew his whereabouts or had any secret contacts with him. On the other hand, Bhagat Singh was keen to know about Azad's activities and whereabouts. So he chalked out a plan. He utilised this opportunity and said that he knew nothing about Azad's whereabouts. In fact he believed that Azad had died while underground. Thus he wanted to get information, about Azad from the police officials. The CID officials divulged they had definite information that Prithvi Singh was alive and was somewhere in Bombay or Gujarat. This bit of information was enough for Bhagat Singh to make arrangements to contact Azad. When his comrades went to meet him in prison he told them to contact Azad somehow and give him a message.

Dhanwantari, who later became a prominent Communist leader, volunteered to perform this job. He managed to meet Prithvi Singh in a house in Allahabad and told him that he was a member of the HSRA and Chandra Shekhar Azad had brought a message for Prithvi Singh from Bhagat Singh. It was decided that Prithvi Singh would meet Chandra Shekhar Azad and Dhanwantari in Alfred Park at 8 pm that very night (it was here that Chandra Shekhar Azad died after a few days fighting gallantly with the British police) and get from them the message of Bhagat Singh. Azad met the two as decided. They informed him that Bhagat Singh had asked them to contact Prithvi Singh as a member of the HSRA. Moreover he ardently wanted the HSRA to send Prithvi Singh to the Soviet Union to study the nature and process of the Revolution. This should be done for the benefit of Indian revolutionaries and the Indian Revolution. Prithvi Singh was highly moved by the request of Bhagat Singh. He had never expected such a message from him. So without hesitation he said he was ready to accept this responsibility. Though Prithvi Singh was much older than Bhagat Singh, he was touched by the earnestness and sincerity of Bhagat Singh. When Prithvi Singh reached the Congress session in Karachi secretly, Bhagat Singh had already been hanged.

How Azad ultimately managed to reach the Soviet Union is another story, but what fascinates me is Bhagat Singh's greatness. Even when he was on the threshold of death he wanted that the project of freeing the country from the imperialists must be accomplished. Moreover, the revolutionary movement should take a proper course enlightened by the Marxist and communist doctrine.

On the occasion of the fiftieth anniversary of the martyrdom of Chandra Shekhar Azad, Bhagat Singh, Rajguru and Sukhdev and Harkishan Talwar (and also of Ganesh Shankar Vidyarthi), this humble tribute to their immortal memory is being paid.

ON BHAGAT SINGH

The bombs in the Assembly episode set into motion a train of events that were to haul Bhagat Singh and his comrades before a specially constituted tribunal in Lahore in the famous Second Lahore Conspiracy trial and send them to the gallows. Bhagat Singh was suspected of being implicated in the killing of Saunders. The pistol from which he fired two unaimed shots in the Assembly gave him away, as did the posters strewn across the floor of the Assembly chamber, identified to be in his handwriting-the same handwriting which bore its imprint on the posters pasted on the walls of Lahore in the evening following Saunders' killing.

The police raided several premises used by the HSRA [Hindustan Socialist Republican Association] revolutionaries in Lahore, Agra and Saharanpur, resulting in the arrest of several revolutionaries and the capture of literature, bomb-making equipment and other incriminating material. Two of them-Jai Gopal and Hans Raj Vohra-made confessions, which resulted in further arrests of revolutionary activists in Punjab, UP and Bihar. Depressingly, unable to stand torture, seven of them turned approvers. Two of these seven were members of the Central Committee. The trial of Bhagat Singh, Rajguru, Sukhdev and many other revolutionaries commenced on 10 July 1929 and came to a close on 7 October 1930. The accused turned the tables on the colonial authorities, using the court for propagating their revolutionary programme, laying bare the outrages of the alien rulers and putting them in the dock for their crimes against the Indian masses. While in jail they undertook a lengthy hunger strike to press their claim to be treated as political prisoners, rather than as common criminals, and for improved facilities such as proper food, availability of literature, as well as the right not to be subjected to forced labour. The authorities refused to budge, with the result that on the sixty-fourth day of the hunger strike, on 13 September 1929, Jatin achieved martyrdom. Huge crowds lined the streets of Lahore as his mortal remains were carried along the main roads of the city, ending in a mammoth public meeting. Following this, Durga Bhabi (wife of Bhagwati Charan Vohra and a real revolutionary in her own right) took Jatin Das's body by train from Lahore to Calcutta. At every station along the route masses of people turned up to pay their homage to a dear and departed hero. In Calcutta, an unprecedented crowd of 600,000 followed his coffin to the crematorium.

Even the Government Advocate, Carden Noad, felt obliged to pay a glowing, even if hypocritical, tribute to Jatindra Nath Das. "I desire on behalf of all", he told the Court on 24 September 1929, "to express the sincere regret and genuine sorrow we feel on account of the untimely death of Jatindra Nath Das. There are qualities which compel admiration of all men alike, and pre-eminent among them are the qualities of courage and consistency in the pursuit of an ideal. Although we do not share ideals which he followed, we cannot but admire the unwavering fortitude and firmness of the purpose he displayed" (Tribune, 26 September 1929).

The most meaningful and touching tribute came from Mary, widow of Terence McSwiney, Lord Mayor of Cork, who had been martyred in Ireland in similar circumstances: "Family of Terence McSwiney unites with patriotic Indians in grief and pride in the death of Jatindra Nath Das. Freedom will come." The proceedings before the Special Magistrate, whose remit was limited to determining whether the evidence disclosed that a prima facie case existed to warrant the committal of the accused for trial to the Court of Session, were a mockery of all norms of justice. The accused were routinely handcuffed, subjected to regular beatings, roughed up in court right before the magistrate; while the relatives and friends of the accused had every obstacle put in their way to prevent them from entering the Court and viewing the proceedings, most of the space there was occupied by the police and detectives in plain clothes, who could listen in to every word between the accused; while the Public Prosecutor and the Government Advocate were treated with courtesy bordering on subservience, with every one of their requests readily granted, the defence had to struggle for the rights of the accused, only to be met with refusal and obstruction by the magistrate, whose actions were controlled by the police and the government. The general public were denied entry into the Court; often even the press had restrictions imposed on it.

It is to the undying credit of the accused that, even in these trying circumstances, they behaved with dignity, courage, fortitude and, above all, with unswerving and irrepressible revolutionary determination and enthusiasm, remaining faithful to their ideals and cheerfully optimistic as to their realisation. On entering and leaving the Court, it was their practice to shout "Long Live Revolution!", "Long Live the Proletariat!", and "Down with Imperialism!".

On 24 January 1930, the accused, wearing red scarves, entered the Court shouting appositely the slogan "Long Live Lenin!" Characteristically, Bhagat Singh passed on to the magistrate a message with the request that it be telegraphed to the President of the Communist International. The message read. "On the occasion of the Lenin Day, we express our hearty congratulations on the triumphant and onward march of Comrade Lenin's success for the great experiment carried on in the Soviet Russia. We wish to associate ourselves with the world revolution movement. Victory to the workers' regime. Woe to capitalism. Down with imperialism" (The Tribune, 26 January 1930).

On 29 January 1930, after the Court refused permission to Bhagat Singh's legal adviser, Lala Duni Chand, to witness the proceedings, the accused unanimously decided to withdraw from these farcical proceedings. Bhagat Singh addressed the Court thus: "I am instructed by my comrades to request you [the magistrate-LALKAR] to send us back to jail and proceedings may be carried on in our absence. Let us sit in peace in jail and let the proceedings also go on here in peace".

After the government made a conciliatory gesture on 19 February 1930, the accused resumed their cooperation and the trial proceeded smoothly between 8 March and 3 May-the last day of the proceedings before the magistrate. Meanwhile, two days earlier (on 1 May) an ordinance had been promulgated to set up a Tribunal to try the case. Noad, the government prosecutor, had good reason to thank the magistrate, Rai Saheb Pandit Sri Krishen, for his "impartiality". Bhagat Singh, who had received horrible treatment from the magistrate, too, spoke without rancour. Polite in the extreme, and as free from personal hatred as he was from fear, he thanked the magistrate on behalf of his comrades and himself, telling the magistrate that although they had often to defy the bureaucracy, whose representative the magistrate was, they held nothing against him personally.

He added that the magistrate was too polite and lenient, of which leniency the prosecution, unlike the accused, had taken advantage. He proceeded to say that the appointment of the Tribunal was a clear victory for the accused who from the outset desired nothing more than to expose the government's lawless conduct in the eyes of the public. Through the appointment of the Tribunal, the government had revealed its true colours.

THE TRIBUNAL

The Lahore Conspiracy Case ordinance, under which the Tribunal was established, was promulgated by the Governor-General Lord Irwin allegedly in exercise of the power conferred by S.72 of the Government of India Act, 1919. The said Act, however, stipulated that the Governor-General's Ordinance could not have a life of more than six months and that it could only be made in "cases of emergency".

There was no such emergency. But, in the light of the tremendous and growing popularity of Bhagat Singh and his comrades and the infectious example which they set for others, the colonial authorities were determined on a course of reckless haste and securing a shortcut to the gallows, especially for Bhagat Singh. There was to be no jury and no appeal against the Tribunal's decision, whose members were removable at will-as indeed two of them were within two months of its being constituted. If the accused were too weak to attend (as for instance consequent upon hunger strike) or would not attend as a political protest against unreasonable police or court behaviour, the trial could proceed in absentia.

This was no judicial tribunal. It was a political court, blatantly used as a political weapon by the autocratic alien authorities to snuff out the finest sons of India-in defiance of all norms of justice and fairness.

The Tribunal began its proceedings on 5 May 1930. After the accused were badly treated and handled roughly in the court on 12 May, they participated no further in the proceedings, which were 'continued' in their absence. The requests of the defence for cross examining all the prosecution witnesses and for more time to enable the defence to go through the evidence were rejected by the Tribunal-all in the rush to conclude the case before the 6-month period after which the appointment of the Tribunal would lapse, and with it the Tribunal itself, thus invalidating the entire proceedings. So the prosecutor abruptly closed his case before the Tribunal on 26 August so as to bring it to completion before the 31 October 1930 deadline. On 10 September, Carden Noad finished his concluding speech. Less than a month later, on 7 October 1930, the Special Tribunal to try the Lahore Conspiracy Case delivered its judgement, acquitting three and convicting all others. While Bhagat Singh, Sukhdev and Rajguru were sentenced to death, seven were transported for life, the remaining two were given rigorous imprisonment terms of seven and five years.

Even Nehru, whose attitude, for reasons of class and self interest, as well as the malign influence of Gandhi's one-sided nonviolence, with its insistence of nonviolence by the masses in the face of the brutality of the exploiting classes, was always marked by ambivalence, reacted to the Court's verdict with considerable anger and aguish. In a speech at Allahabad on 12 October 1930, he said: "If England were invaded by Germany..., would Lord Irwin go about advising the people to refrain from violence against the invader? If he is not prepared to do that, let him not raise the issue. It is for Mahatma Gandhi and others, who believe with him, to do so.... But let there be no mistake about it. Whether I agree with him or not, my heart is full of admiration for the courage and self-sacrifice of a man like Bhagat Singh. Courage of the Bhagat Singh type is exceedingly rare. If the Viceroy expects us to refrain from admiring this wonderful courage and the high purpose behind it, he is mistaken. Let him ask his own heart what he would have felt if Bhagat Singh had been an Englishman and acted for England."

BHAGAT SINGH'S LAST DAYS

Meanwhile, as the judgment day neared, unable to contain his paternal feelings, Bhagat Singh's father, Kishen Singh, petitioned the Tribunal in a last desperate effort to save his son's life. On hearing of his father's petition, Bhagat Singh was incandescent with rage and wrote to his father a remonstrative letter, which brings out clearly Bhagat Singh's exacting standards of conduct-standards which he followed and expected others, including those he dearly loved and respected, to abide by. Bhagat Singh's letter, published in full by The Tribune on 4 October, just three days before the Tribunal's judgement, reflects not only his legendary courage, fidelity to principle and indomitable spirit of self-sacrifice, but also the deeply-felt injury to his feelings inflicted on him by the father that he loved and respected. This is what, inter alia, Bhagat Singh wrote to his father on this occasion:

"My dear father,

"I was astounded to learn that you had submitted a petition to the members of the Special Tribunal in connection with my defence. This intelligence proved to be too severe a blow to be borne with equanimity. It has upset the whole equilibrium of my mind. I have not been able to understand how you could think it proper to submit such a petition at this stage and in these circumstances. In spite of all the sentiments and feelings of a father, I don't think you were at all entitled to make such a move on my behalf without even consulting me.

"My life is not so precious, at least to me, as you may probably think it to be. It is not at all worth buying at the cost of my principles. There are other comrades of mine whose case is as serious as that of mine. We had adopted a common policy and we shall stand to the last, no matter how dearly we have to pay individually for it.

"Father, I am quite perplexed. I fear I might overlook the ordinary principle of etiquette and my language may become a little but harsh while criticising or censoring this move on your part. Let me be candid. I feel as though I have been stabbed in the back. Had any other person done it, I would have considered it to be nothing short of treachery. But in your case, let me say that it has been a weakness-a weakness of the worst type.

"This was the time when everybody's mettle was being tested. Let me say, father, you have failed. I know you are as sincere a patriot as one can be. I know you have devoted your life to the cause of Indian independence, but why, at this moment, have you displayed such a weakness? I cannot understand.

"In the end, I would like to inform you and my other friends and all the people interested in my case that I have not approved of your move.

"I want that the public should know all the details about this complication, and therefore, I request you to publish this letter.

"Your loving son, Bhagat Singh"

On 3 March 1931, Bhagat Singh saw his family for the last time. Distressed by the tearful sight of his younger brother Kultar in tears, Bhagat Singh wrote to him a letter-at once moving and inspiring. The original, written in Urdu, is reproduced here in Roman alphabet with a translation. The reason for this is that as the English translation does not do justice to the powerful verses that Bhagat quoted in the original, those of our readers who have some knowledge of the Urdu language might thus be enabled to gauge in full the depth of ideas and powerful emotions expressed by Bhagat Singh in his very concise letter.

"3 March 1931

"Aziz Kultar,

"Aaj tumhari aankhon mein aansu dekh kar bahut ranj hua. Aaj tumhari baat mein bahut dard tha. Tumhare aansu mujh se bardasht nahin huye.

"Barkhurdar, himmat se taalim hasil karte jana aur sehat ka khayal rakhna.

"Hausla rakhna. Aur kya... (likhun?)... Shaer main kya kahun suno:

Usay yeh fikr hardam naya tarze jafa kya hai,

Hamen yeh shauq hai dekhen sitam ki intiha kya hai.

Dair se kyun khafa rahen aur kyun gila Karen,

Hamara jahan hai sahi, ao muqabla Karen.

Koi dam ka mehman hoon ai ahle mehfil,

Chiraghe sahar hoon, bujha chahta hoon.

Mere hawa mein rahegi khayal ki khushboo,

Yeh mushte khaq hai, fani rahe na rahe.

"Achha rukhsat.

Khush raho ahle watan hum to safar karte hain.

"Hausle se rehna

"Namaste.

"Tumhara Bhai, Bhagat Singh"

English translation of the original letter:

"3 March 1931

"Dear Kultar,

"It made me very sad to see tears in your eyes today. There was deep pain in your words today. I could not bear to see your tears.

"My boy, pursue your studies with determination and look after your health.

"Be determined. What else... (can I write?)... What couplets can I recite? Listen:

They are ever anxious to devise new forms of treachery,

We are eager to see what limits there are to oppression.

Why should we be angry with the world... and complain,

Ours is a just world (ideal), let us fight for it.

I am a guest only for a few moments, my companions,

I am the lamp that burns before the dawn and longs to be extinguished.

The breeze will spread the essence of my thoughts,

This self is but a fistful of dust, whether it lives or perishes.

"Well, goodbye.

Be happy, countrymen, I am off to travel.

"Live courageously.

"Namaste.

"Your brother, Bhagat Singh".

Whereas the first eight lines are from a poem by Mohamed Iqbal, one of the greatest poets of the Indian sub-continent, the last line, appearing just after the words, "well, goodbye", is from Wajid Ali Shah, which the latter recited when the British East India Company evicted him from Lucknow after deposing him from the throne and the annexation of Oudh. The original reads thus:

"Dar-o-deewar pe hasrat se nazar karte hain

Kush raho ahle watan hum to safar karte hain".

"I cast my eyes longingly at the doors and the walls

Be happy, countrymen, I am off to travel."

Bhagat Singh deliberately omitted the first line of the above couplet. A.G. Nourani, the author of the excellent book, The Trial of Bhagat Singh, makes the correct observation that this studious omission "... speaks a lot for Bhagat Singh's refinement of feeling as well as courage", for "Bhagat Singh felt no longing for the world from which he was about to depart. He did not care to cast his eyes back. He left the world cheerfully fortified in the knowledge that he would live as a symbol of integrity and courage in the hearts and minds of his countrymen" (pp. 231-232).

As the end of life approached nearer and nearer, Bhagat Singh's firm belief in a socialist and communist future became ever more ardent. Just a few days prior to his judicial murder, in his March 1931 letter to the Governor of Punjab, he expressed himself thus: "Let us declare that the state of war does exist and shall exist so long as the Indian toiling masses and their natural resources are being exploited by a handful of parasites.

They may be purely British capitalists, or mixed British and Indian, or even purely Indian. They may be carrying on their insidious exploitation through mixed or even purely Indian bureaucratic apparatus. All these things make no difference.... This war shall continue.... It shall be waged with new vigour, greater audacity and unflinching determination till the socialist republic is established".

At a time when all seems to have been lost, to have written the above lines showed a remarkable degree of knowledge and understanding of the laws of history, not to speak of the determination and cheerful optimism and audacity that is expressed in them At a time when the alien rulers of India were universally hated by the Indian masses, to have expressed the idea that the struggle to overthrow the system of exploitation would continue its relentless march even if the place of the British exploiters was taken by Indian exploiters, was remarkable for its time in India and revealed an ability to see well beyond the struggle for freedom from alien subjugation and oppression. Alluding to the unrivalled sacrifices of Jatin Das, Bhagwati Charan Vohra and Chandrashekar Azad, Bhagat Singh concluded his letter by telling the Punjab Governor that, since the court in its verdict had emphasised that he and his fellow revolutionaries had waged war against the British Crown, they were prisoners of war and, therefore, entitled to "... claim to be shot instead of being hanged". Bhagat Singh went on to say that it "... rests with you [the Governor] to prove that you seriously meant what your court has said and prove it through action. We very earnestly request you and hope that you will very kindly order the Military Department to send a detachment or a shooting party to perform our execution" (A.G. Nourani, p.227).

To the very end of his life Bhagat Singh remained thoughtful and incisive in the extreme. On 22 March, one day before he was hanged, his fellow revolutionaries in jail sent him a note in which they asked the question if he would desire to live. His answer, as ever sagacious, portrays the following picture of the relation between his desire to live and the purpose of that life, as well as the relation between the sacrifices of the revolutionary party and the heights to which he had been elevated: "The desire to live is natural. It is in me also. I do not want to conceal it. But it is conditional. I don't want to live as a prisoner or under restrictions. My name has become a symbol of the Indian revolution. The ideals and the sacrifices of the revolutionary party have elevated me to a height beyond which I will never be able to rise if I live... Yes, one thing pricks me even today. My heart nurtured some ambitions for doing something for humanity and for my country. I have not been able to fulfil even one thousandth part of those ambitions. If I live I might perhaps get a chance to fulfil them. If ever it came to my mind that I should not die, it came from this end only. I am proud of myself these days and I am anxiously waiting for the final test. I wish the day may come nearer soon. Your comrade, Bhagat Singh"

Just as in questions of politics, so in questions of religion-Bhagat Singh's fidelity to his principles and system of beliefs did not desert him even in the face of immediate death. Manmathnath Gupta, convicted in the Kakori case, has reconstructed the events of 23 March 1931, the last day in the lives of Bhagat Singh, Rajguru and Sukhdev. On receiving the order that the hanging was to take place the same evening, the chief warder of the jail, a god-fearing man by the name of Chatar Singh, approached Bhagat Singh with a scripture and pleaded with him to pray. Polite as ever, Bhagat Singh declined the request, saying that he had been an atheist all his life and had no wish to depart from that stance on the last day of his life. Instead, he spent the entire day reading a biography of V.I.Lenin that had been sent to him at his request. At about seven in the evening, an official of the jail came over to accompany him to the gallows. Bhagat Singh, engrossed in the biography, said: "wait a minute, one revolutionary is busy meeting another". After reading a few more pages, he got up to undertake the final journey of his life. With the shouts of 'Long live revolution!' and 'Down with imperialism!', the three great revolutionaries-Bhagat Singh, Rajguru and Sukhdev-faced the hangman's noose. They were hanged while singing the following lines, which have since been repeated by the masses of Indian people and which have become a symbol of the revolutionary immortality of Bhagat Singh and his comrades:

"Dil se niklegi na marker bhi watan ki ulfat,
Meri mitti se bhi khushbue watan aaegi".
"Love for the motherland will not leave my heart even after death,
Its fragrance will still be there in my dusty remains."

Rightly fearing public anger and outpouring of grief over the murder of three of the finest sons of India and apprehending public disorder over this outrage, the colonial authorities, instead of handing over the bodies to the families of these revolutionaries, in great secrecy and with indecent haste, cremated them near Ferozepur on the banks of the river Sutlej.

The reaction of the Indian people following the news of the hanging was predictable. The whole country went into mourning. Towns and villages across the vast territory of the sub-continent witnessed condolence gatherings and demonstrations. Even those who earlier had stood aside, participated in these manifestations of anger and grief.

At several places, angry crowds clashed with the police, braving firing and baton charges, which claimed more than one hundred lives. Hundreds of schools and colleges closed as a mark of respect for the departed heroes, while hundreds of thousands observed fast.

On 24 March, the day following the execution of Bhagat Singh and his comrades, in a carefully drafted statement to the press in New Delhi, Nehru stated: "I have remained absolutely silent during their last days, lest a word of mine may injure their prospect of commutation. I have remained silent, though I felt like bursting and now all is over.

"Not all of us could save him, who was so dear to us and whose magnificent courage and sacrifice have been an inspiration to the youth of India. India cannot even save her clearly loved children from the gallows.

"There will be hartals and mournings, processions everywhere. There will be sorrow in the land at our utter helplessness but there will also be pride in him who is no more, and when England speaks to us and talks of settlement there will be the corpse of Bhagat Singh between us lest we forget" (A. G. Noorani, pp. 228-229)

Nehru was doubly wrong. His silence had been unhelpful; silence, especially in the councils of the Congress Party. And, at no time in the talks between England and the Congress was the corpse of Bhagat Singh allowed to get in the way. After Indian independence and the departure of the British from India, the Indian ruling classes and the Congress Party have done their best to turn Bhagat Singh into a non-entity, a figure of peripheral significance in the Indian liberation struggle. They have failed in this mean attempt. The credit for keeping the memory of Bhagat Singh and his comrades, of keeping alive their revolutionary tradition belongs solely to the broad masses of the Indian people and the communist movement of that country.

All the same, under the pressure of the flood of sympathy, admiration and adoration for Bhagat Singh and his co-accused during their trial, and the mass outpouring of grief and volcanic eruption of popular anger following the execution of the three of them, even the leaders of the Congress Party felt obliged to swim with the tide and heap praises on Bhagat Singh. They could hardly do otherwise in view of the fact that, at that time, Bhagat Singh enjoyed far greater popularity, prestige and respect among the Indian masses than Gandhi, whose reputation lay in ruins in view of his complicity in the execution of Bhagat Singh and his comrades (of this more anon). Patibhi Sitaramyya, the historian of the Congress Party, testifies to Bhagat Singh's popularity with this understatement: "It is no exaggeration to say that at that moment Bhagat Singh's name was as widely known all over India and was as [nay, much more] popular as Gandhi's" (A. G. Noorani)

Nehru, albeit in his characteristic contradictory and confused style, emanating from a mixture of admiration and disapproval at the same time for Bhagat Singh, portrays the following picture of Bhagat Singh's popularity: "Bhagat Singh did not become popular because of his act of terrorism [Nehru is not alone in characterising all violence as terrorism-even some would-be communists are guilty of that], but because he seemed [only seemed?] to vindicate, for the moment, the honour of Lala Lajpat Rai, and through him of the nation. He became a symbol; the act was forgotten [was it really?], the symbol [symbol unrelated to the act?] remained, and within a few months each town and village of the Punjab and to a lesser extent in the rest of northern India [nay, the whole of India], resounded with his name. Innumerable songs grew up about him, and the popularity that the man achieved was something amazing" (A. G. Noorani p.3)

A.G Noorani must have had the likes of Nehru in mind when he concluded his book with the observation: "On his [Bhagat Singh's] death, Indian leaders vied with one another in lavishing praise on him. One wonders how many of them knew then that they had lost in him a man who, had he lived, might have had an incalculable impact on the course of India's politics". Gandhi was certainly an exception to this, for he knew full well that Bhagat Singh, had he but lived, was destined to have an incalculable impact on the course of India's political development-in a direction diametrically the opposite of that desired and accomplished by the Congress under Gandhi's leadership. It was precisely for this reason that Gandhi (except once under extreme popular pressure) never lavished any praise on Bhagat Singh and played the role of an accomplice to the colonial authorities' successful efforts in sending him and his comrades to the gallows.

Four years after his execution, Bhagat Singh received a tribute from a most unlikely but most authoritative source-the Director of the Intelligence Bureau, Sir Horace Williamson. In his study India and Communism, he wrote: "Bhagat Singh made no mistake. The prisoners' dock became a political forum and the countryside rang with his heroics. His photograph was on sale in every city and township and for a time rivalled in popularity even that of Mr Gandhi himself" (Editions Indian, Calcutta, p.275, cited by A G Noorani).

2

The Revolutionary Movement and Ideology of Bhagat

Bhagat Singh was an outstanding revolutionary and martyr of the Indian anti-colonial movement. He represented the youth who were dissatisfied with Gandhian politics and groped for revolutionary alternatives.

Bhagat Singh studied the European revolutionary movement and was attracted to anarchism and communism. He became a confirmed atheist, socialist and communist. He realised that the overthrow of British rule should be accompanied by the socialist reconstruction of Indian society and for this political power must be seized by the workers. Bhagat Singh and B.K. Dutt enunciated their understanding of revolution in a statement made in connection with the Assembly Bomb case on 6th June, 1929:

> *'By Revolution we mean that the present order of things, which is based on manifest injustice must change. Producers or labourers, in spite of being the most necessary element of society, are robbed by their exploiters of their labour and deprived of their elementary rights. The peasant who grows corn for all, starves with his family; the weaver who supplies the world market with textile fabrics, has not enough to cover his own and his children's bodies; masons, smiths and carpenters who raise magnificent palaces, live like pariahs in the slums. The capitalists and exploiters, the parasites of society, squander millions on their whims.'*

They argued that a 'radical change' was necessary 'and it is the duty of those who realise it to reorganise society on the socialistic basis'. For this purpose the 'establishment of the dictatorship of the proletariat' was necessary (ed. Shiv Verma, Selected Writings of Shaheed Bhagat Singh, New Delhi, 1986, pp. 74-75).

That Bhagat Singh and his comrades had passed over to the positions of Communism is also apparent from their actions and slogans in the Lahore

Conspiracy Case on January 21, 1930. The accused appeared in court wearing red scarves. As soon as the magistrate took the chair they raised the following slogans: 'Long Live Socialist Revolution', 'Long Live the Communist International', 'Long live the people', 'Lenin's name will never die', and 'Down with Imperialism.' Bhagat Singh then read the text of the following telegram in the court and asked the Magistrate to transmit it to the Third International:

'On Lenin Day we send hearty greetings to all who are doing something for carrying forward the ideas of the great Lenin, we wish success to the great experiment Russia is carrying out. We join our voice to that of the International working class movement. The proletariat will win. Capitalism will be defeated. Death to Imperialism'. (Ibid., p. 82)

Bhagat Singh was critical of the individual terrorism which was prevalent among the revolutionary youth of his time and realised the need for mass mobilisation by the Communist Party. In his final writings he argued that the party had to organise the workers and the peasantry. The fight around the small economic demands through the labour unions were the best means to educate the masses for a final struggle to conquer political power. Apart from this work it was necessary for the Communist Party to organise a military department. He stated: 'I am not a terrorist and I never was, except perhaps in the beginning of my revolutionary career. And I am convinced that we cannot gain anything through these methods.

One can easily judge it from the history of the Hindustan Socialist Republican Association. All our activities were directed towards an aim, i.e., identifying ourselves with the great movement as its military wing. If anybody has misunderstood me, let him amend his ideas. I do not mean that bombs and pistols are useless, rather the contrary. But I mean to say that mere bomb throwing is not only useless but sometimes harmful. The military department of the party should always keep ready all the war-material it can command for any emergency. It should back the political work of the party. It cannot and should not work independently' (Ibid. p. 138).

'WHAT IS REVOLUTION?'

The hearing of the Assembly Bomb Case began on May 7, 1929. Entering the court, Bhagat Singh and Batukeshwar Dutt raised slogans of 'Long Live Revolution', 'Long Live the Proletariat' and 'Down With Imperialism'. These three slogans were to be repeatedly raised by the HSRA revolutionaries in British courts and jails over the next two years. They were to be repeated by millions across the land and were to become an integral part of the heritage of the freedom movement. Through these three slogans, Bhagat Singh and his comrades succinctly summed up their entire programme.

In their historic statement before the court on June 6, 1929, Bhagat Singh and B K Dutt, while defending their action of throwing bombs in the Central Assembly, also gave a lucid and inspiring account of what they meant by the word 'Revolution'. It clearly revealed the growing influence of Marxism and is quoted here in full:

Revolution does not necessarily involve sanguinary strife, nor is there any place in it for individual vendetta. It is not the cult of the bomb and the pistol. By 'Revolution' we mean that the present order of things, which is based on manifest injustice must change. Producers or labourers, in spite of being the most necessary element of society, are robbed by their exploiters of their labour and deprived of their elementary rights. The peasant who grows corn for all, starves with his family; the weaver who supplies the world market with textile fabrics, has not enough to cover his and his children's bodies; masons, smiths and carpenters who raise magnificent places, live like pariahs in the slums. The capitalists and exploiters, the parasites of society, squander millions on their whims. These terrible inequalities and forced disparity of chances are bound to lead to chaos. This state of affairs cannot last long, and it is obvious that the present order of society in merry-making is on the brink of a volcano.

The whole edifice of this civilization, if not saved in time, shall crumble. A radical change, therefore, is necessary and it is the duty of those who realize it to reorganize society on the socialistic basis. Unless this thing is done and the exploitation of man by man and of nations by nations is brought to an end, suffering and carnage with which humanity is threatened today, cannot be prevented. All talk of ending war and ushering in an era of universal peace is undisguised hypocrisy.

By 'Revolution', we mean the ultimate establishment of an order of society which may not be threatened by such breakdown, and in which the sovereignty of the proletariat should be recognized and a world federation should redeem humanity from the bondage of capitalism and misery of imperial wars. This is our ideal and, with this ideology as our inspiration, we have given a fair and loud enough warning.

If, however, it goes unheeded and the present system of government continues to be an impediment in the way of the natural forces that are swelling up, a grim struggle will ensue involving the overthrow of all obstacles and the establishment of the dictatorship of the proletariat to pave the way for the consummation of the ideal of revolution. Revolution is an inalienable right of mankind. Freedom is an imperishable birthright of all. Labour is the real sustainer of society. The sovereignty of the people is the ultimate destiny of the workers.

For these ideals, and for this faith, we shall welcome any suffering to which we may be condemned. At the altar of this revolution we have brought our youth as an incense, for no sacrifice is too great for so magnificent a cause. We are content, we await the advent of Revolution. Long Live Revolution!

REVOLUTIONARY BATTLES IN COURT AND JAIL

On June 12, 1929, the court sentenced Bhagat Singh and Batukeshwar Dutt in the Assembly Bomb Case to transportation for life in the Andamans. But in the meanwhile the police had uncovered the details of Saunders' assassination. Bhagat Singh, Rajguru, Sukhdev and several others were tried in the historic second Lahore Conspiracy Case. The trial started on July 10, 1929 and continued for over a year up to October 7, 1930.

Bhagat Singh and his comrades turned the court into a forum for revolutionary propaganda, just as the Communist undertrials were doing in the Meerut Conspiracy Case, which, significantly, was proceeding simultaneously with the Lahore Conspiracy Case. Both cases drew nationwide attention, but the Lahore Case was more in the limelight.

The revolutionaries began a prolonged hunger strike in jail to protest against the terrible jail conditions, to demand that they be treated not as ordinary criminals but as political prisoners, for necessities like proper diet, supply of books and newspapers and against forced labour.

The jail authorities did not relent and on September 13, 1929, on the 64th day of the hunger strike, Jatin Das died a martyr. A huge procession with his body was taken through the main roads of Lahore, culminating in a massive public meeting. His body was taken by train by Durga Bhabhi from Lahore to Calcutta and all along the route, thousands gathered at every station to pay him homage. In Calcutta itself, an unprecedented procession of more than six lakhs carried Jatin Das' coffin to the cremation ground.

Later, on May 17, 1933, Mahavir Singh, another comrade of Bhagat Singh who was transported for life in the Lahore Conspiracy Case, was martyred in the indefinite hunger strike in the Andaman Cellular Jail.

On October 19, 1929, the second Punjab Students' Conference was held at Lahore under the presidentship of Subhash Chandra Bose. From jail, Bhagat Singh sent a short message to the Conference which was read out and received thunderous response. In this message Bhagat Singh said, "Comrades, Today, we cannot ask the youth to take to pistols and bombs. Today, students are confronted with a far more important assignment. In the coming Lahore Session the Congress is to give a call for a fierce fight for the independence of the country. The youth will have to bear a great burden in this difficult time in the history of the nation...The youth will have to spread this revolutionary message to the far corners of the country. They have to awaken the crores of slum-dwellers of the industrial areas and villagers living in worn-out cottages, so that we can become independent and the exploitation of man by man will become an impossibility." Students and Politics and Youth were two other articles written by Bhagat Singh, who always set great store by the youth.

The HSRA revolutionaries observed memorable days in the court itself. On December 19, 1929, they observed 'Kakori Day' and paid homage to their hanged comrades. On January 21, 1930, they appeared in the court wearing red scarves to celebrate Lenin Day. Bhagat Singh read out a telegram and asked the magistrate to send it to the Third International. The text was: "On Lenin Day we send hearty greetings to all who are doing something for carrying forward the ideas of the great Lenin. We wish success to the great experiment Russia is carrying out. We join our voice to that of the international working class movement. The proletariat will win. Capitalism will be defeated. Death to Imperialism." On May 1, 1930, they celebrated May Day and on November 7, 1930, they sent greetings to the Soviet Union on the anniversary of the Revolution.

The year 1930 saw several historic events in the freedom struggle. At the call of the Lahore Congress in December 1929, that for the first time belatedly adopted the goal of complete independence, January 26, 1930 was celebrated throughout the country as Independence Day by raising the national flag. The mass civil disobedience movement began with the Dandi March and Salt Satyagraha of Mahatma Gandhi from March 12 to April 6, 1930. Millions participated in spontaneous demonstrations all over the country. This time, again, the movement did not always follow the Gandhian guideline of non-violence. More than 50 cases of 'terrorist' activities were registered in 1930. Some were extremely prominent.

On April 18, 1930, Surya Sen alias Masterda and his comrades Tarakeshwar Dastidar, Nirmal Sen, Ganesh Ghosh, Ananta Singh, Ambika Chakravarty, Loknath Bal, Kalpana Dutt, Pritilata Waddedar and the tiny Subodh Roy, of the Indian Republican Army (IRA) conducted the historic Chittagong Armoury Raid in Bengal and fought a pitched armed battle against the British. On April 23, 1930, Chandra Singh Garhwali and his Garhwali regiment, comprising

Hindu soldiers, refused to fire on their Muslim Pathan brethren at Peshawar in the North-West Frontier Province. On May 7, 1930, the textile workers of Solapur in Maharashtra launched a general strike, drove out the British, took over the city and ran a parallel government for ten days up to May 16, when the British imposed Martial Law.

These acts met with fierce British repression. Surya Sen and Tarakeshwar Dastidar were hanged on January 12, 1934. Chandra Singh Garhwali was court-martialled and sentenced to death. His sentence was then commuted and he was sent to transportation for life along with many others. Four leaders of the Solapur revolt-Jagannath Shinde, Qurban Hussein, Malappa Dhanshetty and Srikisan Sarda were hanged on January 12, 1931.

May 28, 1930 was a tragic day for the HSRA. One of its tallest leaders and ideologues, Bhagwati Charan Vohra, was killed in an accident while testing a highly powerful bomb on the banks of the Ravi river. He was manufacturing these bombs to rescue Bhagat Singh and his comrades from jail. Before he died his last words to those accompanying him were, "Do not grieve over this accident. Remember, the task of rescuing Bhagat Singh and others still remains incomplete."

The death of Bhagwati Charan had a shattering effect on his wife, who was called Durga Bhabhi. Along with other HSRA comrades, she had herself earlier taken part in the daring Lamington Road police station shooting episode in Bombay. She continued her revolutionary activities for many more decades. Shiv Verma wrote in 1986, "Much of the work on this volume (Selected Writings of Shaheed Bhagat Singh) was done at Lucknow at Durga Bhabhi's place. The care, love and affection I received from her was another source of courage and inspiration."

When the case was in its final stage, on September 20, 1930, Bhagat Singh's father Kishan Singh made a written request to the Tribunal, saying that there were many facts to prove his son was innocent of Saunder's murder and that his son be given an opportunity to prove his innocence. Bhagat Singh was infuriated and wrote an open letter to his father on October 4, 1930, which was printed in the Tribune. The letter is historic and throws light on Bhagat Singh's revolutionary character:

My life is not so precious, at least to me, as you may probably think it to be. It is not at all worth buying at the cost of my principles. There are other comrades of mine whose case is as serious as that of mine. We had adopted a common policy and we shall stand to the last, no matter how dearly we have to pay individually for it. Father, I am quite perplexed. I fear I might overlook the ordinary principles of etiquette and my language may become a little bit harsh while criticizing or censuring this move on your part. Let me be candid. I feel as though I have been stabbed in the back. Had any other person done it, I would have considered it to be nothing short of treachery.

But in your case, let me say that it has been a weakness-a weakness of the worst type. This was the time when everybody's mettle was being tested. Let me say, father, that you have failed. I know you are as sincere a patriot as one can be. I know you have devoted your life to the cause of Indian independence, but why, at this moment, have you displayed such a weakness? I cannot understand. In the end, I would like to inform you and my other friends and all the people interested in my case, that I have not approved of your move. I want that the public should know all the details about this complication, and therefore, I request you to publish this letter. Your loving son, Bhagat Singh.

On October 7, 1930, the Special Tribunal in the Lahore Conspiracy Case delivered judgement convicting all the accused except three who were acquitted-Ajoy Kumar Ghosh, Jatindra Nath Sanyal and Des Raj. Bhagat Singh, Rajguru and Sukhdev were sentenced to death. Kishori Lal, Mahavir Singh, Bejoy Kumar Sinha, Shiv Verma, Gaya Prasad, Jaidev Kapur and Kamalnath Tewari were sentenced to transportation for life. Kundan Lal Gupta was sentenced to seven years; Prem Dutt, to five. Almost all these revolutionaries were in their twenties. The nation was stunned. It reverberated with the demand for the commutation of the death sentences on the heroic youth.

'OUR UNDISPUTED IDEOLOGICAL LEADER'

Before and after the judgement, Bhagat Singh's reading and writing in jail continued unabated. As he declared before the Lahore Court, "The sword of revolution is sharpened on the whetstone of ideas." Shiv Verma, in an interview given to the present writer in Mumbai on March 5, 1991, replied to a question as to what set Bhagat Singh apart from the others, as follows, "I can tell you that in just one sentence: Bhagat Singh was our undisputed ideological leader. I do not remember a single moment when Bhagat Singh did not have a book in his pocket. The other virtues of Bhagat Singh like tremendous courage and so on were there in the other revolutionaries amongst us also. But his uniqueness lay in his great studiousness. The degree of clarity and integrity that he had about the aims of our movement, was not there in any one of us at that time." Bipan Chandra wrote that, "Bhagat Singh was already at a young age a giant of an intellectual and thinker." Chaman Lal wrote that, "Bhagat Singh had command of four languages, without much formal training or education. He wrote in Punjabi, Hindi, Urdu and English. His jail notebooks collect excerpts from 108 authors and 43 books including prominently Marx, Engels and Lenin, but also many others."

There are various volumes of the writings of Bhagat Singh compiled by Shiv Verma, Chaman Lal and Bhagat Singh's nephew Jagmohan Singh and his niece Virender Sindhu. They are a treasure house. There are also several meaningful letters written by him. For instance, he wrote a letter reprimanding Sukhdev who had said that if he did not get the death sentence, he would rather commit suicide than face life imprisonment. A month after he was given the death sentence, in November 1930 he wrote a letter to Batukeshwar Dutt in which he gave an idea of what he expected from comrades who had escaped capital punishment. 'Why I Am An Atheist' and 'Introduction to Dreamland' were two seminal tracts written by him in jail. It is the greatest of misfortunes that four other books written by Bhagat Singh in jail, viz. The Ideal of Socialism, Autobiography, History of Revolutionary Movement in India and At the Door of Death, although they were smuggled out of jail, were later destroyed. The Statement of the Undefended Accused, drafted by Bhagat Singh, launched this scathing attack on imperialism, which can well apply even to the present situation in the world: "We believe that imperialism is nothing but a vast conspiracy organized with predatory motives. Imperialism is the last stage of development of insidious exploitation of man by man and of nation by nation. The imperialists, with a view to further their piratical designs, not only commit judicial murders through their law courts but also organize general massacres, devastations and other horrible crimes like war. They feel no hesitation in shooting down innocent and unarmed people who refuse to yield to their depredatory demands or to acquiesce in their ruinous and abominable designs. Under the garb of custodians of 'law and order', they break peace, create disorder, kill people and commit all conceivable crimes."

Summing up his political thought, Bhagat Singh said in a message sent from prison in October 1930: "We mean by revolution the uprooting of the present social order. For this capture of state power is necessary. The state apparatus is now in the hands of the privileged class. The protection of the interests of the masses, the translation of our ideal into reality, that is, laying the foundation of society in accordance with the principles of Karl Marx, demand our seizure of this apparatus."

On February 2, 1931, less than two months before his martyrdom, Bhagat Singh wrote the remarkable appeal To Young Political Workers, which is his last testament. After analyzing the prevailing conditions and the tactics of the Congress, he advised youth to adopt Marxism as their ideology, work among the people, organize workers and peasants and join the Communist Party. He wrote: "We require-to use the term so dear to Lenin-the 'professional revolutionaries'. The whole time workers who have no other ambition or life-work except the revolution. The greater the number of such workers organized into the Party, the greater the chances of your success...The name of the Party should be the Communist Party. This Party of political workers, bound by strict discipline, should handle all other movements. It shall have to organize the peasants' and workers' parties, labour unions, and may even venture to capture the Congress and kindred political bodies. And in order to create political consciousness, not only of national politics but class politics as well, the Party should organize a big publishing campaign."

In the same appeal, renouncing terrorism, he wrote, "Apparently I have acted like a terrorist. But I am not a terrorist. I am a revolutionary who has got such definite ideas of a lengthy programme as is being discussed here...Let me announce with all the strength at my command, that I am not a terrorist and I never was, except perhaps in the beginning of my revolutionary career. And I am convinced that we cannot gain anything through those methods."

REVOLUTIONARY IMMORTALITY

On February 27, 1931, Chandrashekhar Azad, the Commander-in-chief of the HSRA, who was still at large, went to the Alfred Park at Allahabad. Along with Bhagat Singh, Chandrashekhar Azad was the most respected figure in the ranks of the revolutionaries. His courage and daring were legendary, and so also were his organizational skills. His classic marksmanship made him a terror for the British police. Despite the fact that he was not too well-educated, his political sharpness was amazing. With uncommon skill, he had eluded arrest by the police for years. But now he was betrayed by a traitor from within his own ranks and was surrounded. A fierce gun-fight with the police ensued in which Chandrashekahar Azad was killed. The life of another great revolutionary was snuffed out.

One of the negative features of the HSRA, which was common in most such underground revolutionary bodies, was the presence of traitors and approvers, who caused untold damage to the cause. In his pamphlet Bhagat Singh and his Comrades written in 1945, Ajoy Ghosh, one of the colleagues of Bhagat Singh who later became the General Secretary of the CPI from 1951-62, wrote of the time when several of them were arrested in the Lahore Conspiracy Case: "It all seemed over, our dreams and our hopes. More depressing than anything else was the shocking fact that, unable to stand police torture, no less than seven, two of them members of our central committee, had turned approvers."

One of these approvers and a former central committee member of HSRA was Phanindranath Ghosh. Since he had the most knowledge, his testimony proved to be the most damaging to Bhagat Singh and his comrades. As revenge, Phanindranath Ghosh was killed by Vaikuntha Shukla and Chandrama Singh on November 9, 1932. Shukla was hanged and Singh was consigned to long years of imprisonment.

A few days before his execution, in a letter written in March 1931 to the Punjab Governor, Bhagat Singh wrote, "Let us declare that the state of war does exist and shall exist so long as the Indian toiling masses and their natural resources are being exploited by a handful of parasites.

They may be purely British capitalists, or mixed British and Indian, or even purely Indian. They may be carrying on their insidious exploitation through mixed or even purely Indian bureaucratic apparatus. All these things make no difference...This war shall continue...It shall be waged with new vigour, greater audacity and unflinching determination till the socialist republic is established."

Referring to the unparalleled sacrifices of Jatin Das, Bhagwati Charan Vohra and Chandrashekhar Azad, he ended his letter pointing out to the Punjab Governor that since the verdict of the court was that they had waged war against the British empire, they were war prisoners; therefore "we claim to be shot dead instead of being hanged."

On March 22, the day before Bhagat Singh's execution, his comrades in jail sent him a slip asking if he would like to live. He wrote back: "The desire to live is natural.

It is in me also. I do not want to conceal it. But it is conditional. I don't want to live as a prisoner or under restrictions. My name has become a symbol of the Indian revolution. The ideals and the sacrifices of the revolutionary party have elevated me to a height beyond which I will never to be able to rise if I live...Yes, one thing pricks me even today. My heart nurtured some ambitions for doing something for humanity and for my country. I have not been able to fulfil even one thousandth part of those ambitions. If I live I might perhaps get a chance to fulfil them. If ever it came to my mind that I should not die, it came from this end only. I am proud of myself these days and I am anxiously waiting for the final test. I wish the day may come nearer soon. Your comrade, Bhagat Singh."

Manmathnath Gupta, who was sentenced in the Kakori case, has reconstructed the events of March 23, 1931, the last day in the life of Bhagat Singh, Rajguru and Sukhdev. The Chief Warder of the jail, one Chatar Singh, got the order in the afternoon that the hanging was to take place the same evening.

The God-fearing man approached Bhagat Singh and pleaded with him to pray and read a holy book that he had brought along. Bhagat Singh politely refused, saying that he had been an atheist all his life and would remain so even on this last day.

The whole day, Bhagat Singh was reading a biography of Lenin that had been sent to him at his express wish. When, at around seven in the evening, a jail official came to take him to the gallows, Bhagat Singh, still engrossed in reading Lenin's biography, said, "Wait a minute, one revolutionary is busy meeting another." After reading for a while, he got up and embarked on his final journey. Amidst slogans of 'Down With Imperialism' and 'Long Live Revolution', the three martyrs-Bhagat Singh, Rajguru and Sukhdev-attained revolutionary immortality. The final song on their lips was:

Dil se niklegi na markar bhi watan ki ulfat,
Meri mitti se bhi khushbue watan aaegi.
(Love for the motherland will not leave my heart even after death,
Its fragrance will still be there in my dusty remains.)

Drawing lessons from the massive crowds that had gathered for Jatin Das' funeral earlier, and apprehending an immeasurably greater uproar this time, the British authorities secretly took away all three bodies. Without handing them over to the relatives of the martyrs, the jail authorities hurriedly cremated them near Ferozepur on the banks of the Sutlej.

Bipan Chandra recounts: "The entire country went into mourning on hearing the news of their martyrdom. Angry condolence meetings and demonstrations were held in cities and towns, in which many who had earlier stood aside participated. In many places, demonstrators clashed with the police and faced firing and lathi charges in which over a hundred people died. Hundreds of schools and colleges observed hartals; lakhs fasted on that day."

Soon after the martyrdom of these three heroes, in the last week of March 1931 a serious communal riot broke out in Kanpur. The senior Congress leader Ganesh Shankar Vidyarthi, who was one of the mentors of Bhagat Singh and his comrades, was killed by fanatics while he was boldly trying to save the lives of innocents from communal wrath. This tragedy underlined Bhagat Singh's constant warnings against the grave danger of communalism.

AS REVOLUTIONARY

Bhagat Singh was just 23 years and a few months when he was hanged by British colonialists on March 23, 1931. By the time Bhagat Singh went to the gallows, he had entered the hearts and minds of all Indians, some of whom later became Pakistanis and Bangladeshis. With the publication of Bhagat Singh's writings largely after 1947 and more in the last few decades of twentieth century (complete documents in Hindi are now available in one volume), the martyr became known as a revolutionary socialist thinker as well. This year not only happens to be Bhagat Singh's 75th year of martyrdom but will also mark the beginning of his birth centenary year on September 28. Bhagat Singh was born on September 28, 1907, in Lyallpur Banga. His ancestral village, however, is Khatkarkalan near Banga in Nawanshahar district. Bhagat Singh spent most of his childhood in Pakistan's Punjab, particularly Lahore. He was also martyred in Lahore.

Bhagat Singh is revered not only in India but also in Pakistan and Bangladesh, while people in countries like Nepal, Sri Lanka also respect this great revolutionary from India.

Even in international arena, if Mahatma Gandhi has become a symbol of Indian nonviolent struggle for freedom, Bhagat Singh's name comes close to great revolutionaries like Che Guvera, Simon Bolivar and Nelson Mandela.

There is a need to propagate Bhagat Singh's ideas by translating his documents in all Indian languages. A picture of Bhagat Singh should be hung in Parliament. His writings against communalism and untouchability could be introduced in school curricula. This freedom fighter is a symbol of unity for the people of India, Pakistan and Bangladesh, and his ideas can be a beacon of light for them.

It is suggested that Bhagat Singh's martyrdom day should be observed as "Anti-Colonialism/Anti-Imperialism Day" in the subcontinent. It should be observed in a big way at Lahore by Indians and Pakistanis jointly. The main function should be held at Lahore Jail on March 23 at 7 pm, when 75 years ago he along with two other patriots Rajguru and Sukhdev were hanged by the British. Artists, activists and writers of both countries should hold a weeklong event, which could include seminars, street and stage plays and film shows. This would help revive the memories of the martyrs and spread their ideas among the youth

In fact, it is felt that Pakistan should enter into a healthy competition with India in claiming the legacy of Bhagat Singh. Bhagat Singh was born, brought up and educated in Pakistan. He had his revolutionary training in National

College at Lahore. His activities in India include holding a meeting of revolutionaries at Delhi in September 1928 and dropping a bomb on the Central Assembly in Delhi, apart from spending sometime in Kanpur or some other places. The joint legacy of Bhagat Singh can help both countries come closer, at least culturally.

The birthday of Bhagat Singh (September 28) should be declared as "National Youth Day". The ideas of the martyr would enthuse the youth, who are the builders of the free nation.

This freedom fighter no longer remains an individual. Historical personalities become symbols of ideas and movements. Bhagat Singh has emerged as a symbol of the most radical nationalist movement against imperialism and colonialism. He represents the highest ideals of Indian revolutionary movement.

Bhagat Singh is one among many national heroes, whom Dalits and minorities who form a large chunk of the Indian society-are ready to accept as their hero because of his radical views on untouchability and communalism. Along with Dr. Ambedkar, Bhagat Singh also has an appeal for Dalits of this nation.

In the context of misuse or overexposure of religion by some fascist fundamentalist groups in our society, Bhagat Singh's ideas on religion or atheism can work as an antidote to counter such pernicious views

All democratic and nationalist Indians should unite on this occasion and by focusing on Bhagat Singh's ideas, build a powerful resistance movement against a much more dangerous neo-colonial onslaught, more powerful than the old colonialist British empire.

IDEOLOGY

Bhagat Singh spent the years from 1927 to 1928 in studying the history of the revolutionary movement in India. His articles, mostly written for Kirti, deal with the Babbar Akali Movement, the Kakori case, the Delhi Bomb Case, individual revolutionaries, the necessity for young people to come forward and join the revolutionary movement and the need to evolve an alternative to the mainstream leadership of the Congress and particularly, Lala Lajpat Rai.

The first article Bhagat Singh wrote on the Babbar Akali movement for the Pratap. It was published on the 15th of March, 1926. The Babbar Akali movement was an attempt by Sikhs to liberate the country from the British and to free their Gurudwaras from the corrupt Mahants by an armed insurrection. It was confined to the Bist Doab and its membership was primarily rural. The leaders of this movement were mainly soldiers who had left the army to join the Non Cooperation Movement. In 1921 it was decided to murder Sunder Singh Majitha, Bedi Kartar Singh, Mahant Devdas of Nankana, C.M. Bowring, the Superintendent of Police and C.M. King, Commissioner, Jullunder. This was a retaliation for the massacre of 140 Sikhs that Mahant Narayandas organised in Nankana Sahib on the 21st of February.

The Babbar Akali group however did not succeed in killing anybody but the attempt to assassinate Bowring got them into jail. This is known as the Akali Conspiracy Case of 1921. Bhagat Singh was very impressed by this movement, in fact he started learning Gurmukhi only after the Nankana Sahib massacre. In the article Bhagat Singh carefully delineates the contribution of the individuals who participated in the movement. What impresses him the most is the fearlessness with which these men are ready to embrace death (six of the leaders were sentenced to death and executed on the 27th of February, 1926). Bhagat Singh urges the reader to visualise how these men must have taken the pledge to forsake their families and sacrifice their life for the country, 'What a beautiful, bewitching and pure vision it must have been. What are the heights of self sacrifice? Where are the limits to courage and fearlessness? Were there no boundaries to this commitment to their ideals?

The next article is written in May, 1927 for Kirti, under the pseudonym Vidrohi. On the 9th of August, 1925, Ramprasad Bismil, Ashfaqullah and other members of the Hindustan Republican Association stopped (and subsequently looted) the tram carrying the government treasury at Kakori, near Lucknow. On 6th April, 1927, the main accused were sentenced to death. This article is interesting because it describes vividly the camaraderie that the accused had with each other and the happiness that they expressed on hearing their death sentence. It ends with a comment on those who have no sympathy for the accused, 'We sigh and think we have done our duty. We do not have that fire, we do not suffer, for we have become corpses. Today they are sitting on a Hunger-Strike and suffering and we are silently watching the show. May God grant them the strength and courage they need in their last few days'.

In February, 1928, Bhagat Singh (under the pseudonym Vidrohi) wrote a number of life sketches of prominent Punjabi revolutionaries, in the Phansi issue of the Chand. The man who Bhagat Singh was to idealise and consider his 'mentor, friend and brother', Kartar Singh Sarabha was born in 1896 in Ludhiana. Having finished his college education, Sarabha went to America in 1912, where racial discrimination made him sensitive to the condition of Indians abroad. He organised Indian workers in San Francisco and they all readily agreed to sacrifice their life and wealth to the cause of the liberation of India.

In 1913 the Gadr, a newspaper was started and Sarabha joined its editorial board. Bhagat Singh was particularly inspired by a song that Sarabha used to sing, 'To serve the country is very difficult. To talk about it is easy. Those who have chosen to serve the country face a million problems'. Sarabha returned to India in 1914 and within the year contacted the revolutionary leaders of India. In February 1915, Sarabha and Rash Behari Bose planned to infiltrate the army and attempt to spark off a revolt. This did not however happen because a member of their group turned approver and Sarabha was arrested and sentenced to death. On 16th November, 1915, Sarabha was executed. In concluding this brief biographical sketch, Bhagat Singh asks rhetorically, 'What was the purpose of his death? Why did Kartar Singh Sarabha die? The answer is absolutely clear, he died for the country and he did not want more than to die fighting for his country'.

The May 1928 issue of Kirti reprinted an article published in the Bombay newspaper Shradhanand on the true meaning of terrorism. Since Bhagat Singh was a member of the editorial board of Kirti, it is interesting to see how he and his comrades participated in the contemporary ideological debate of terrorism. The article sought to defend terrorism by rejecting the current definition of terrorism as the destructive, coercive and unjust use of force.

'Some mischievous individuals have attempted to set up terrorism in opposition to non-violence and that has led to a great misunderstanding'. The ideals of 'bravery, courage, martyrdom, the ability to use weapons, generosity, duty etc., dependent on the application of force are now considered base and unqualified'. A comparison is then made to the West, where 'every country is attempting to increase the arms at its disposal. On the other hand, here in India, it is considered a sin to take up arms.' The article asks its readers not to equate violence with crime, for 'when patriots take up arms for the sake of their country and its safety, when they eliminate exploitation and oppression or when they avenge the injustice done to the oppressed and go to the gallows, they use violence but they do not spread terror'. The distinction between crime and terrorism, although both use violence, is based on the intention of those who use it.

In 1930, Bhagat Singh wrote the (now famous) pamphlet called 'Why I am an Atheist'.

This pamphlet is important because of the autobiographical details that form part of the narrative. 'When I joined the revolutionary party (HRA), the first leader I came in contact with was not confident of rejecting the presence of God even though he was not a firm believer.... The second leader (Sachindranath Sanyal) was a great devotee.... What I want to say is that atheism has still not been established as a creed within the revolutionary party. All four accused in the Kakori case went to the gallows praying...'

Bhagat Singh while aware of the revolutionary terrorist tradition that had existed in the country as a mode of protest against the British, especially in the Punjab, distanced himself from his predecessors on two counts. First, revolutionary leaders had not been able to accept the logic of atheism and much less to publicly proclaim it. Second there had been no conception of a post-independence society.

The immediate goal being the destruction of the British Empire there had been no inclination to work out a political alternative. For Bhagat Singh the decisive break came in the post-1926 period when the Hindustan Republican Association leadership fell on his shoulders. He lost no time in articulating the necessity of having a political ideology and that was to be Marxism. 'The romance of violence that was dominant in our predecessors was replaced by a serious ideology. There was no place for Romanticism and superstition any longer. We rooted ourselves in the present'.

From 1926, Bhagat Singh began to 'study in order to be able to counter criticism from opponents and sharpen (his) own arguments'. The most important requirement was to articulate clearly the ideals for which they were fighting. The fact that there had been no real agitation in 1926 meant that there was time to devote to studying. 'I studied the (writings of) the anarchist leader Bakunin, some (thing of) the father of communism Marx, but more (of) Lenin, Trotsky and others who had succeeded in bringing about a revolution in their country.'

Anarchism

From May to September, 1928, Kirti serialised Bhagat Singh's article on Anarchism. 'The people are scared of the word anarchism', declared Bhagat Singh. 'The word anarchism has been abused so much that even in India revolutionaries have been called anarchist to make them unpopular'. The word Anarchism is defined as the absence of any kind of rule. 'I think in India the idea of universal brotherhood, the Sanskrit sentence vasudev kutumbakam etc., have the same meaning.' The 'first man to explicitly propagate the theory of Anarchism was Proudhon and that is why he is called the founder of Anarchism. After him a Russian, Bakunin worked hard to spread the doctrine. He was followed by Prince Kropotkin etc.'.

The article goes on to explain why Bhagat Singh was so attracted to Anarchism. 'The ultimate goal of Anarchism is complete independence, according to which no one will be obsessed with God or religion, nor will anybody be crazy for money or other worldly desires. There will be no chains on the body or control by the state. This means that they want to eliminate: the Church, God and Religion; the state; Private property'. There is a brief history of the Anarchist movement and the article concludes with Valliant's attempt to throw a bomb in the Assembly. On being arrested, 'he said in a bold and clear voice, it takes a loud voice to make the deaf hear...'.

Although there appear to be many similarities in the way the revolutionaries and the Anarchists functioned, Bhagat Singh brought about a qualitative change in the Indian revolutionary movement. The adherence to Marxism meant that the revolutionaries did not deny or fight for the elimination of the State.

The role of the state was seen in Marxist terms. The diary Bhagat Singh left behind in jail has a number of extracts from Engels' classic The Origin of the Family, Private Property and the State. After studying Marx and Engels' work there is a clear understanding of the stages of society, their corresponding family relations and the Marxist theory of the State as an 'institution that lent the character of perpetuity not only to the newly rising into classes, but also to the right of the possessing classes to exploit and rule the non-possessing classes'.

Marxism

Bhagat Singh became a revolutionary after he came to Kanpur and it is no coincidence that Kanpur was an important industrial city (created by the British to manufacture the cloth and leather articles needed by the army) with a large urban proletariat. From 1926, Bhagat Singh had also come into contact with Sohan Singh Josh and the Workers and Peasants Party. This marked the turning phase in his life.

From 1926 as Bhagat Singh began to study the history of the revolutionary movement in India and the world, He came to better appreciate the necessity of fighting imperialism through a broad-based people's movement. This was also reflected in his quotations from Lenin (on imperialism being the highest stage of capitalism) and Trotsky on revolution written in his Prison Notebooks.

In the Communist Manifesto, Bhagat Singh located the following paragraph, 'The first step in the revolution by the working class is to raise the proletariat to the position of the ruling class, to win the battle of democracy, to wrest by degrees, all capital from the bourgeoisie, to centralise all instruments of production in the hands of the state, that is of the proletariat organised as the ruling class, and to increase the total of the productive forces as rapidly as possible'. It was therefore clear that a bourgeois revolution would not succeed in a country where capitalism had oppressed the masses.

The perception of the existence of class cleavages in society also led to the understanding that violence would be imperative to bring about a change in the social structure. It was a violence that destroyed to build.

The Communist Party of India was formed in 1925-26 and had to almost immediately go underground. Within the next six years Bhagat Singh was executed and it remains one of the big ifs of history whether he would have joined the party as his companions did.

The Indian Congress and Non-Violence

The most prominent Congressman in the Punjab was Lala Lajpat Rai. He had been part of the trinity of Extremists known as Lal-Bal-Pal. Through the years, however, Lajpat Rai had become a wily politician who no longer wished to remain in politics but to retire instead. In November 1927, the editorial team of Kirti published an open letter to Lala Lajpat Rai with the following introduction, 'Those gentlemen who are familiar with Lala Lajpat Rai's political life know that he is only interested in leadership and talking without wanting to do anything... Lalaji's recent behaviour has led to a loss of confidence in his politics'. In another article written in August 1928, Lajpat Rai is asked rhetorically if he desires to fight the British so that the country can be handed over to Indian capitalists. 'Should we wait till thousands have been destroyed or killed to begin our struggle to oust the capitalists? This would be sheer stupidity'. The same article foresees the political eclipse of Lala Lajpat Rai. 'Lalaji and other leaders like him who support the capitalists are slowly being eliminated, like the earlier leaders, Surendranath Banerji, Sapru and Chintamani. In the end the Workers struggle will be victorious. Long live Socialism. Long live Revolution'.

From 1921-22, Gandhi became the ideologue of the Congress and it was under his leadership that the first Non Cooperation movement was launched. When Gandhi abruptly ended the movement the revolutionaries became disillusioned with the creed of non-violence espoused by him. During 1924-25 Gandhi became involved in an extended polemical argument on the use of violence. The brunt of Gandhi's arguments lay in what he called the ineffectiveness of violence, the added expenditure it cost the government to curb it and the insane pressure of anger and ill-will that started it in the first place. In fact so opposed was he to the revolutionaries that when the Viceroy

Lord Irwin missed a narrow escape on his life, Gandhi wrote an article called the 'Cult of the Bomb' where he thanked god for the Viceroy's escape and condemned his bete noire, the revolutionaries. In 1925 Sachindanand Sanyal sent an open letter to Gandhi in which he said, '(the) Non-Violent non-cooperation movement failed not because there was (a) sporadic outburst of suppressed feelings here and there but because the movement was lacking in a worthy ideal.

The ideal that you preached was not in keeping with Indian culture and traditions. It savoured of imitation. Your philosophy of non-violence... was a philosophy arising out of despair'. By 1929 the revolutionary movement in India had developed and in December of that year, Bhagwati Charan and Chandra Shekhar Azad wrote an article defending the Delhi Bomb Case revolutionaries from Gandhi's scathing criticism.

'The revolutionaries believe that the deliverance of their country will come through revolution... (This) revolution will not only express itself in the form of an armed conflict between the foreign government and its supporters and the people, it will also usher in a new social order. The revolution will ring the death knell of Capitalism and class distinctions and privileges. It will bring joy and prosperity to the starving millions who are seething under the terrible yoke of both foreign and Indian exploitation'. In 1931 in a note to the party, Bhagat Singh wrote about Gandhism as the dominant ideology in the Congress, 'which is unable to take a stand against the British and instead wants to become a partner in power... (the Congress) is working as a centrist party and has always been so. It is embarrassed to face reality. The leaders who run it are those people whose interests are associated with the party... If revolutionary blood does not succeed in giving it a new lease of life... it will be necessary to save it (the party) from its allies.'

Interestingly although Gandhi insisted on the acceptance of non-violence dogmatically, younger members were not so averse or critical of the revolutionaries. Subhas Bose and Jawaharlal Nehru were the two prominent Congressmen who supported the revolutionaries. Chandra Shekhar Azad used to receive money regularly from Motilal Nehru. Money to the revolutionaries was also supplied by Puroshattamdas Tandon and Shiv Prasad Gupta. Even leaders like Maulana Shaukat Ali and Krishna Kant Malviya supplied revolvers to Sanyal. 'The non-violence of the Mahatma was by-passed by the Congressmen and they were not found wanting in their moral, financial and other support to the revolutionaries', say Irfan Habib and S.K. Mittal. That there was public sympathy for the revolutionaries and support from within the Congress must have been known to Gandhi. It may well have been a fact that Gandhi, sensing a threat to his leadership through this chink in his hegemonic control over the Congress became increasingly bitter towards the revolutionaries and when he could have negotiated a release for some of them he chose not to.

ORGANISATION AND STRATEGY

The first organisation Bhagat Singh joined was the Hindustan Republican Association in 1924. As an active member of this organisation he learnt two things essential for a political organisation. First, to establish strong ties of camaraderie with like-minded individuals so that despite a small organisational base the party can function smoothly. Secondly the necessity of bringing out a newspaper, besides notices and pamphlets, so as to put across to the people the ideas and activities of the revolutionaries.

After Bhagat Singh started working with Sohan Singh Josh and the 'Workers and Peasants Party' (as a member of the editorial board of Kirti in Lahore), he realised the importance of setting up an organisation that could function as a revolutionary party in the Punjab and recruit new people to the cause of revolution. Ajoy Ghosh has written that 'Bhagat Singh was active in the Punjab and he and his comrades formed the Naujawan Bharat Sabha'. There is however no clear record establishing who Bhagat Singh's comrades were or what role he actually played in its foundation. In a statement, in the Meerut Conspiracy case trial, Sohan Singh Josh said, 'I was one of those who took a prominent part in building up this organisation, I went to various places to deliver lectures to form local Naujawan Bharat Sabhas'. He describes the Sabha as, 'a revolt of the petty bourgeoisie against the Congress leadership'. He emphatically denied that it was a communist party and insisted that it was 'an organisation of the middle class who are oppressed by British imperialism and who want to free themselves economically and politically from the imperialist yoke'. Abdul Majid in his statement in the Meerut conspiracy case says, 'The Naujawan Bharat Sabha emerged sometime in 1926 but remained a "debating society" until 1928.' It held its first conference on 12th, 13th, 14th April, 1928.

In 1928, Bhagat Singh also had the responsibility of the Hindustan Republican Association with Chandra Shekhar Azad, other leaders having been sent to the gallows or given a life sentence. The first thing he did was to change its name to the Hindustan Socialist Republican Association. The party was 'recognised with a central committee and with provincial and district committees under it. All decisions were to be taken in these committees, majority decisions were to be binding on all'.

By 1930 when Azad was shot dead, the HSRA just collapsed. Members of the organisation turned approver, 'personal squabbles, charges and counter charges vitiated the atmosphere. Police spies and degenerate elements that had managed to sneak their way in made most of this situation... corroded from within, unable to withstand the blows from outside the party that Azad and Bhagat Singh had built up by years of selfless work and with their precious blood lay in ruins'. The link between the 'Workers and Peasants Party' and Naujawan Bharat Sabha meant that the latter survived the collapse of the HSRA and was soon able to replace it in the Punjab.

The Naujawan Bharat Sabha was open to any man and woman between the age of 18 and 35 years old who accepted its aims and objects. These were to establish a complete independent Republic of labourers and peasants throughout India. The organisation was divided into the following: The Naujawan Bharat Sabha Conference; the Naujawan Bharat Sabha, Punjab; the NBS according to districts; according to tehsils and police stations; and the reception committee of the NBS. A central body was created in 1928. Within a year branches were opened in different parts of the Punjab and even in Peshawar.

The best indication of the organisational ability of the leadership of such a party is its strategy and the attempts to deal with a lack of funds, arms and manpower. The first prerequisite of any party that has vowed to use violence to change the existing social and political order, is to build a close-knit unit that can take leadership decisions and prevent espionage and infiltration. Bhagat Singh, Sukhdev, Rajguru, Bhagwaticharan Vobra, Kedarnath Sehgal and Chandra Shekhar Azad formed the nucleus of the leadership.

In October, 1928, the British government of India appointed the Simon Commission to enquire into the possibility of granting India the chance to rule itself. That this Commission had no Indian representative made it the focus of popular attack in Lahore. Lajpat Rai was at the head of a demonstration that was asking the Simon Commission to go back to England. The police in retaliation lathicharged the crowd and Lajpat Rai enfeebled by age, died subsequently. The revolutionary terrorists although great critics of Lajpat Rai and his politics, were determined to avenge his death. The Assistant Superintendent of Police, J.P. Saunders who is believed to have hit Lala Lajpat Rai directly, was assassinated by Bhagat Singh, Sukhdev, Rajguru and Azad, who then went underground. On the next day in Lahore, there were public notices put up in the name of the Indian Socialist Democratic Army. One such notice declared, 'We regret having killed a human being but this man was a part of that unmerciful and unjust system that must be destroyed... Sometimes it is important to shed blood for a Revolution. The Revolution we envisage is one where the exploitation of man by man will finish... Inquilab Zindabad.'

This kind of activity made it imperative for the leaders to generate what publicity they could. In the late 1920s and early 1930s there were no television sets and the radio and newspapers were the main source for disseminating information. The 'deaf had to be made to hear'.

The earliest method of spreading information was by publishing pamphlets that were ideological, polemical and/or rhetorical. Since these would have only a limited audience, a better way of garnering popular support was by courting arrest and then carrying on propaganda daring the trial. Once inside there was also the possibility of fomenting an agitation amongst the native policemen. When Bhagat Singh was first arrested in the Dussehra bomb case, a photograph of him was taken. This photograph immortalised the image of Bhagat Singh in jail sitting on a cot, his feet crossed, handcuffed, head tilted, a smile on his face.

The nature of colonial oppression implied an infringement of the rights of prisoners, especially political prisoners, and here arose another opportunity of confrontation with the British regime. The development of the Press ensured that any confrontation would be reported to the public.

Finally, there was the ultimate sacrifice, death was a powerful symbol and it was hoped that martyrdom would inspire young people to join the revolutionary movement and prevent it from being appropriated by the mainstream national movement.

In March 1928, the government introduced the Public Safely Bill in the Legislative Assembly. The Indian members rejected the Bill and in 1929, the Viceroy attempted to pass it as an ordinance. The Naujawan Bharat Sabha passed resolutions opposing this and the Trade Dispute Bill and it finally decided to intervene directly. On 8th April, 1929, Bhagat Singh and B.K. Dutt threw a small explosive in the Assembly and stayed in the visitors' gallery till they were arrested.

On 7th May, Bhagat Singh's trial began and in the statement made in court on 6th June, Bhagat Singh and B.K. Dutt, representing the HSRA declared, 'we dropped the bomb on the floor of the Assembly Chamber to register our protest on behalf of those who had no other means left to give expression to their heart-rending agony. Our sole purpose was to make the deaf hear and to give the heedless a timely warning... from under the seeming stillness of the sea of humanity, a veritable storm is about to break out'. On the 12th June, Bhagat Singh was sentenced to transportation in the Assembly Bomb case. On the 15th of June he launched a hunger strike for jail reforms. On 10th July, 1929 the trial of the Lahore Conspiracy Case started and ended on the 7th of October, 1930 with a death sentence. Bhagat Singh, Sukhdev and Rajguru were hanged on the 23rd of March, 1931.

CONCLUSION

The nature of the Revolutionary Terrorist movement in India restricted the size of the organisations or Parties. The larger the group the less effective would have been the course of action. This did not however mean that this movement had no contribution. It had an impact on the people, the Congress and the British Government.

If we are to locate the role Bhagat Singh played within this movement, it is necessary to understand that Bhagat Singh was young man who because of his interest in studying and his keen sense of history gave to the revolutionary tradition a goal beyond the elimination of the British. A clarity of vision and determination of purpose distinguished Bhagat Singh from other leaders of the National Movement. He was the only alternative to Gandhi and the Indian National Congress, especially for the youth.

In a letter to Sukhdev, dated the 11th of April, 1929, Bhagat Singh wrote, 'I can say with all my might that I am immersed in the hopes and doubts that give life a meaning. But when the time comes, I will sacrifice everything. In the true sense this is sacrifice... you will realise this soon'.

3

Bhagat, Bose and the Gandhi

Gandhi's treatment of Bhagat Singh and his comrades is one of the most intriguing episodes of India's freedom struggle. Bhagat Singh was a fearless and intensely patriotic young man who wanted to see his country free and a just social order established. He had also participated in Gandhi's freedom movement but was dissatisfied by its slow pace and the waywardness of its leader.

But he and his comrades did not believe in the cult of the bomb and the bombs they dropped in the Assembly were not meant to kill or harm anyone but to awaken 'a deaf government'. Even their assassination of the British Police officer was provoked by the senseless and brutal lathi-charge that had resulted in the death of one of India's tallest political leaders, Lala Lajpat Rai.

In any case there was no doubt about Bhagat Singh's commitment to India's freedom and a society free from exploration-the two objectives so dear to the Mahatma. Why then did the Mahatma, who was known to be magnanimous even to his foes, not fight vigorously for rescuing Bhagat Singh and his comrades from an unusually harsh punishment?

In fact, if one looks at the letters and utterances of the Mahatma relating to the revolutionaries, one is appalled by his apathy and utter lack of emotional involvement. Pattabhi Sitaramayya, an ardent Gandhian, observes in his History of the Indian National Congress: 'The Karachi Session was to meet in the last week of March, but Gandhi himself stated to the Viceroy that if the boys should be hanged, they had better be hanged before the Congress than after.' There is a chilling matter-of-fatness about 'if the boys are to be hanged' and a willingness to reconcile himself to their tragic fate. Interestingly enough, Gandhi shows extraordinary empathy with the colonial ruler-empathy that would do a Nirad Chowdhary credit. In a letter to Lord Irwin he writes: 'It seems cruel to inflict this on you, but the interest of peace demands a final appeal.' Cruel? One thought cruelty was on the other side, and appeals and pleadings were the moderate brand of politics, not Gandhi's. If he felt strongly about the issue, he could have launched an agitation or gone on a satyagraha-that would be a characteristic Gandhian response. But he is just content to appeal to the Viceroy. Why?

Bose, who observed this drama from close quarters, has this to say in his Indian Struggle: '....The Mahatma who did not want to identify himself with the revolutionary prisoners would not go so far and it naturally made a great difference when the Viceroy realised that the Mahatma would not break on that question.' This may be true to an extent, for the Mahatma seemed to place great value on the Gandhi-Irwin pact and did not wish to jeopardise it. But it seems to me there was a deeper reason for Gandhi's apathetic or halfhearted response. He had a pathological dislike, even fear, of the revolutionaries. Gandhi wanted India to achieve independence through non-violence and non-violence alone. (One little incident in Chauri Chaura and he suspended the struggle.) Presumably he was to lead India in this nonviolent struggle and make history, for never in history of the world such a thing had happened. This would be his ticket to immortality. If the revolutionaries grew stronger and succeeded-Bhagat Singh had become extremely popular during this period-he might be deprived of his great opportunity.

This reading of Gandhi's treatment of Bhagat Singh and his comrades is confirmed by what happened a few year later-the famous Gandhi-Bose confrontation. Subhas Bose is no longer a spectator but a protagonist-in fact the chief protagonist. Bose was elected the Congress President in 1939 for the second consecutive term despite Gandhi's opposition. (Gandhi didn't take it sportingly and declared: 'Pattabhi's defeat is my defeat.') He felt Bose was getting too independent and then his commitment to non-violence was not as pure and absolute as he would have wished, for Bose was known to hobnob with the revolutionaries as well. So Gandhi decided to teach him a lesson and show him who called the shots in the Congress. His cronies launched, presumably with the Mahatma's blessings, a ruthless and somewhat Machiavellian operation to finish off a democratically elected President and they succeeded. Bose was compelled to leave the Congress due to the non-cooperation of his colleagues. This was another dimension of Gandhi's non-cooperation. It could also be used effectively against colleagues who were getting difficult.

But the Gandhi-Bose 'interface' does not end here. When Bose made his daring escape from Calcutta and eventually succeeded in raising an Army for the liberation of India, Gandhi lost his nerve and launched his 'Quit India' movement. Its suddenness surprised many and one of this admirers, Louis

Fischer, the American journalist, asked him why he was in such a tearing hurry to drive the Britishers out of India. Gandhi replied: 'Go and ask Subhash.' It seems Gandhi was afraid that Bose's INA adventure might succeed and rob him of this ticket to immortality.

LEGACY WE INHERIT

As India completes sixty years of its existence as an independent nation, our thoughts invariably go back to those immortal freedom fighters who waged numerous struggles in varied forms, both violent and nonviolent, to shake off the foreign yoke and usher in the dawn of freedom from alien rule. We also recount the extraordinary, and at times superhuman, sacrifices that they underwent in the battle to ensure our country's emancipation from the oppression and exploitation of the British Raj that had stifled our progress and halted our advance. And while doing so we must without fail offer our sincere homage to the greatest revolutionary of this great nation-Mohandas Karamchand Gandhi who, as Jawaharlal Nehru aptly pointed out, moved the millions in our vast subcontinent. In his foreword to D.G. Tendulkar's Mahatma, Nehru wrote:

The amazing thing about Gandhi was that he adhered, in all its fullness, to his ideals, his conception of truth, and yet he did succeed in moulding and moving enormous masses of human beings... There was no compromise in him with what he considered evil. He moulded a whole generation and more and raised them above themselves, for the time being at least. That was a tremendous achievement.

However, besides Mahatma Gandhi we had a galaxy of leaders-not only his close associates like Nehru but persons of the calibre Netaji Subhash Chandra Bose who, with all his differences and conflicts with Bapu, never hesitated in characterising him as the Father of the Nation in the midst of Subhash' heroic exploits in South-East Asia as the commander of the Azad Hind Fauj. We had courageous figures as Surjya Sen of the Chittagong Armoury raid fame, Khudiram Bose who kissed the gallows at a tender age; and we had the legendary Bhagat Singh. We also had the socialist and communist stalwarts who sacrificed everything for the liberation of the Indian masses, willingly suffering privation, persecution and torture. It is the cumulative effect of the endeavour of all those personalities that we are independent today.

This year marks not only the diamond jubilee of our independence, but also the 150th anniversary of our First War of Independence which the British had deliberately tried to belittle by calling it Sepoy Mutiny. One vividly recalls the observance of the centenary of the Great 1857 Revolt in 1957 and Nehru's stirring speech at Delhi's Ramlila Grounds on the occasion.

But this time the 150th anniversary of that event is being sought to be observed on a wider scale so that the essence of our freedom, nationalism and nationhood is propagated to the grassroots, something that did not happen fifty years ago in 1957. Dissemination among the masses of the significance of the 1857 Uprising in today's context is of inestimable value as it would provide a glimpse of the exceptional role of the common people, especially the peasantry in North India, in their bid to uproot British rule as well as bring into focus the remarkable Hindu-Muslim unity forged in the flames of that struggle.

Looking back over the sixty years that we have traversed since our attainment of independence in August 1947 we cannot but point to the substantial progress we have registered in several fields-in nuclear energy, space research, heavy industry, the IT sector in particular-despite all our constraints, some of them due to external pressures but mostly because of limitations imposed by our democratic system of governance.

Indeed preservation of the democratic structure in India is one of our most striking achievements for which legitimate credit must go to those giants, headed by Jawaharlal Nehru, our first PM, who steered the country amidst all difficulties in the post-independence period. It is democracy which had given our teeming millions a power which their brethren in some of our neighbouring countries, especially Burma, have been tragically deprived for long years-the power to exercise the franchise and make the leaders at the helm accountable to them.

The nineteen months of Emergency (1975-77) were indeed an aberration but once the people's unfettered right to vote was restored, they used it to such devastating effect that the whole world was astonished beyond measure-they inflicted such a resounding defeat on the Emergency raj that its reimposition is next to impossible in today's conditions in spite of the serious challenges we face on many fronts including those from terrorist depredations as well as secessionist movements in different parts of the country (notably J&K and the North-East).

What is most encouraging is the growing realisation among wide sections of our populace that those challenges can be effectively met by not constricting but broadening democracy, something the leadership in our northwestern neighbour, Pakistan, has yet to fully comprehend. (Of course, the attacks on human rights in democratic India are also a feature one cannot possibly overlook. But what is striking is that voices of protest and resentment against such assaults are being raised from unexpected quarters within the country, something unthinkable even a few years ago.)

The democratic system of governance did impose constraints on the pace of our advance, and yet our progress has not been inconsequential. Nevertheless, what cannot be denied is the bitter truth that the fruits of our successes have not percolated down to the lowest segments our polity. Thus while the overall growth, as manifest in the spectacular rise in the GDP, has been quite impressive it has definitely been lopsided-the widening disparities, reflected in the vulgar display of opulence and wealth by the rising band of billionaires and nouveau riche on the one side and the abysmal poverty in the rural areas as well as urban slums (where people are forced to do everything to eke out their existence) on the other, being an eyesore for an India that, according to our leaders, is on the move for a place in the sun. These disparities have doubtless grown exponentially with our uncritical acceptance of the policies of globalisation alongside those of privatisation and liberatlisation.

According to the latest findings of the Commission on the Condition of the Unorganised Sector Workers, while official figures claim the decline of the number of people below the poverty line, 77 per cent of India's population constitute the "poor and vulnerable group"-that is, those who survive on Rs 20.30 per capita; as many as 79 per cent of the unorganised workers, 88 per cent of the SC/STs, 80 per cent of the OBCs and 84 per cent of the Muslims belong to this category. For those only concerned about our thriving middle class and the rapid rise of billionaires these figures are of course alarming but these do not surprise or shock those well aware of the yawning gap between the haves and have-nots that threatens a gradual Latin Americanisation of India in terms of socio-economic deprivation of the majority of our populace.

The political fall-out of such a phenomenon is not difficult to gauge. A year ago, on the occasion of Independence Day 2006, it was written in these columns:

> *...the worsening economic conditions in the vast rural landmass has given renewed impetus to the Left-extremist upsurge in large tracts of the country, especially the most backward regions of Jharkhand, Chhattisgarh, Bihar,*

BHAGAT SINGH FOR TODAY

Remembering Bhagat Singh on the sixtysecond anniversary of his glorious and heroic martyrdom (March 23) cannot be a ceremonial or routine affair today. When the entire country, plagued as it is with the Hindutva brand of communalism in its worst-ever ferocity and perfidy, is yet to overcome the trauma of the Ayodhya tragedy and the horrendous communal carnage that rocked large parts of this subcontinent thereafter, Bhagat Singh's words are of particular relevance for our nation and polity.

In the backdrop of the environment obtaining in India today, it would be most appropriate to study some of the passages of his Sampradayik Dange aur Unka Elaj (Communal Riots and the Remedy) that came out in print in the journal Kirti in 1927. It is no essay in academic flair, but it exudes Bhagat Singh's deepest human concern for the Indian people who were then, as now, suffering due to senseless human killings in the name of religion. Here are a few excerpts from the article:

...The condition of India has now become extremely grave. The followers of one religion have become suddenly sworn enemies of the followers of the other religion. So much so, that to belong to one particular religion is reason enough for becoming enemy of the other religion. Such a feeling has gained currency.

....If still someone harbours any doubts about the gravity of the situation, one should look at the recent riots of Lahore to gauge and determine the savagery and ferocity of the killings. .... How Muslims have killed innocent Hindus and Sikhs and how Sikhs have been unsparing in their killings, deploying their best capabilities. Such brutal mutual killings have not been resorted to by the killers to award punishment to someone found guilty of some crime, but for the simple reason and for the fact that someone was either Hindu, Sikh or Muslim. For Muslims, it has been enough to kill if someone was either Hindu or Sikh and likewise to be a Muslim was sufficient reason for his being killed.

His deep anguish can be seen in the lines below:

...When the situation has reached this aggravated stage, then God alone knows what will happen to India. In view of the obtaining situation, India's future appears extremely bleak. These religions have wrought havoc to India and one does not know when the scourge of such horrendous communal riots will come to an end and India will be freed from them-from such religious riots. ...At the moment political leaders of India are conducting themselves so shamelessly. Those very leaders, who had sweared and vowed to liberate the country and had proclaimed of shouldering the great responsibility for that purpose, never tiring of talking about 'common nationality' and who had been vociferous in declaring their faith in the attainment of "Swaraj", so unflinchingly and devotedly in the past, these very same leaders are now

either keeping mum with their heads bowed in shame or are swaying along with the raging wind of blind religious bigotry. Besides the demagoguery and 'double-speak' of these 'lost leaders', Bhagat Singh underlined the supine subterfuges of the leadership in face of horrendous communal criminality:

.... Those amongst them, sitting on the fence silent in remorse and shame, concealing their faces are not insignificant in numbers. ...But regarding those political leaders who have since joined and have already found full convergence with the current of communal movement, they are to be found in hundreds, if only one unravels the phenomenon and digs a bit beneath the earth's surface. Leaders (with a conscience) who seek well-being, happiness and prosperity of all people from their very heart are few and the tornado of communalism is so wild and fierce that these few, well-meaning and good-intentioned leaders are incapable of halting the process. Expressing his concern he added:

.... It appears as if the Indian political leadership has gone completely bankrupt.

Bhagat Singh's worst fears have now come true, and the future of India appears as bleak at the hands of its 'bankrupt' political leadership.

About the role of newspapers Bhagat Singh had opined:

.... Those others, instrumental in fomenting communal riots, and playing the key-role in it, are newspapermen. The profession of journalism, considered to be esteemed once upon a time, has now been reduced to rubbish. They are blaring out against each other in screaming headlines, besides inciting people's savage bigoted passions for unleashing the orgy of mutual killings.

Elaborating upon his scathing criticism of newspapers he added:

....Not confined to one or two places, but in a number of places communal conflagration broke out, simply because newspapers penned down explosive and highly provocative articles, while such writers who were able to keep their hearts and minds clean and were able to maintain a balanced poise in those turbulent times were barely few.

Nothing appears to have changed since then vis-a-vis the morality and integrity of newspapers.

Bhagat Singh himself wielded a powerful pen, he was a prolific writer and journalist within his own rights, having his stint in several papers from Kirti to Ganesh Shankar Vidyarathi's Pratap. He had this to say about the duty and responsibility of newspapers before charging them with dereliction of a sacred duty.

... The real duty of the newspapers is to educate, to cleanse the minds of people, take them out of the rut of narrow sectarian grooves of thought and perception, and to wash and scrap out communal feelings in order to invest

them with feelings of amity and communal harmony, for bridging the gap and building mutual trust, bringing about real rapprochement for advancing the cause of common nationalism.

....But instead of it all, their main objective appears to have become spread of ignorance, proliferation and propagation of chauvinism and sectarianism-communalisation of people's mind for engendering group clashes and skirmishes. In this way they are working for destruction of India's common heritage and its composite culture-its common nationalism....

How fully these words apply to the Indian print media of our own times, will have to be measured by mediamen themselves. What, however, bears pathetic resemblance to the overall situation of present-day India is Bhagat Singh's painful observation, in conclusion:

..... This is the reason, while looking at the situation obtaining in India at the moment and after pondering over it, one sheds tears of blood and the most crucial question crops up in one's mind, as to what is going to happen to India ultimately? What is going to become of this country?

Answering this question, Bhagat Singh once again brought into focus the role of the political leadership in the centre-stage, pinning down those leaders as the sole motivators and culprits behind communal riots and communalisation of politics. He also raised the economic factor promoting communal politics, and he was perhaps the first of his time to do so.

While emphasising the need for raising economic issues related to the life of millions of workers and peasants to build a real people's movement as a countervailing force against communal politicking, he did not overlook the fact that such a movement must conform to the broad national frame of the anti-imperialist movement and the pivotal question will always remain the ouster of British Raj.

In the present situation of alien rule any economic reform would be very difficult, as the British Raj does not permit any amelioration in the people's economic lot. Hence the people must plunge body and soul against the present government and till the replacement of the same none should rest content.

Insisting on combating communalism he stated:

....In order to stop the people from mutual fighting, class consciousness is needed. The toiling poor, working classes and the peasantry should be made fully aware of the fact that their real enemies are capitalists; therefore they should desist from doing anything at their behest and remain ever-vigilant from falling prey to their vile machinations, being always on guard against becoming the tool of the capitalists. (emphasis added)

In his exhortation for all-in unity of the toiling people, he said:

....Let people be roused to the consciousness that basic rights of all the poor, the world over, irrespective of race, caste, colour, nationality and country are one, hence their salvation and prosperity lies in their joint struggle. They should therefore work to eradicate and remove all racial, national and religious prejudices, differences and distinctions and unite to seize for themselves, the power of governance.

Placing his optimism in the ultimate triumph, he added:

....People must be told that they will be no losers in this struggle and their chains would be broken some day and they will attain freedom and economic emancipation.

Instead of concluding his article on a gloomy note, Bhagat Singh articulated remarkable optimism, reposing his hope and faith in the youth of India and appealed to his countrymen "with folded hands to pay heed to his suggestions". He noted with happiness and satisfaction:

....Welcome changes are quite discernible in the minds of the Indian youth now and they are distancing them from such religions which are engaged in fomenting mutual conflict and fostering hatred. The youth have now become so outspoken and forthright, that they do not look at the Indian people from the religious angle-as Hindu, Muslim or Sikh. They are now regarding all Indian people first as human beings and then Indians. Articulation of such a viewpoint by the Indian youth is indicative of the ensuring bright future of India.

Calling upon the Indian people to remain steadfast and dauntless in the face of the communal menace, he wrote:

The Indian people should not lose heart in face of communal riots; instead they should harness all their resources and potentials and exert by all possible means to create a new ethos and climate where recurrence of communal riots becomes impossible.

While paying rich tributes to the Ghadar party and its heroes in his article, Bhagat Singh underlined the ideological significance of this heroic movement that lay in the Ghadarites' clear-cut attitude towards religion vis-a-vis politics; and their strikingly imaginative position on the most vexed yet vital issue:

.... The martyrs of 1914-1915 had separated religion from politics and were convinced that religion was the private affair of an individual; hence none should be permitted to interfere with it. And likewise religion should also be debarred from encroaching in politics because once it is mixed up, it can't work in unison in the same arena.

> *...It was because of this that a movement like the Ghadar Party remained integrated and united, in which Sikhs topped the list of those attaining martyrdom, but Hindus and Muslims also did not lag far behind.*

Bhagat Singh's most serious concern over communalisation of politics led him to look to different quarters in quest of people and parties that could be united to fight the menace and welcome political leaders with non-communal secular outlook:

> *....At the moment some of our Indian leaders have emerged on the scene who are advocating separation of religion from politics, which is the real remedy to eradicate the communal malady. We support this position. If religion is separated from politics we can come together in political matters while remaining aloof from the religious point of view.*

The article ends with this impassioned appeal to his compatriots: ....Well-wishers of India would think over the remedy I am suggesting and should come forward to save India from the disastrously suicidal course it is being pushed in. [These excerpts are from Bhagat Singh's article Sampardayik Dange aur Unka Elaj, that first came in print in Kirti, in its issue of June 1927. The Hindi journal Uttrardh, published from Mathura (UP), carried this article in its Bhagat Singh Special Number in 1988. All the excerpts in the present article are from this Hindi version, and the free English rendering-of pages 23-24-is mine-N.H.A.]

HE fought against communalism with the clear perception that it was primarily aimed against the poor who were struggling for their emancipation, social, political, economic and spiritual. For Bhagat Singh secularism, Hindu-Muslim unity and communal harmony were not just clichés for coaxing and cajoling the exploited and the ignorant. They were life-giving ideals, for the realisation of which lives could be sacrificed without hesitation or reservation.

Bhagat Singh urged upon the youth to go to the masses of workers and peasants. In their joint letter that Bhagat Singh and his comrade-in-arms, B. K. Dutt, sent to the delegates of the Punjab Students' Fėderation conference, and which was read out in the second session of the conference on October 11, 1929, presided over by Subhash Chandra Bose, they pointed out that what was much more important than bombs and pistols for the youth was to spread the revolutionary message to the nook and corner of the country, to the factories and fields-the message to one and all to join the freedom struggle; and it was the bounden duty of the students to go to the poor living in dirty slums, and rouse them to action.

It was a time of trial for the youth, they said, and expressed their faith that in the name of the great martyr, Jatindra Nath Das, our student brethren would be able to prove their mettle in the crucible of the freedom struggle. This letter was later published in the English daily, Tribune, in its issue of October 22, 1929. Imbibing the spirit of this letter, why cannot our students today reach every hearth and home of the common toiling Indians and spread the message of Bhagat Singh against the menance of communalism and religious fundamentalism? Why can't a month-long 'mass education campaign against communalism' in honour of Bhagat Singh and his comrades-in-arms be launched and made a permanent feature of the activities of student and youth every year?

If alive, he would have been eightysix now. He entered politics to serve humanity and his countrymen at an early age. He became a confirmed atheist at the minor age of 19. On his own admission, "My atheism is not of so recent origin.

I had stopped believing in God when I was an obscure young man." This was his mild rebuttal of the insinuation from some quarters that his atheism was the outcome of the 'undue' popularity he gained during the trials-that is, the Delhi Bomb and Lahore Conspiracy Cases.

Will our Doordarshan and Akashvani ever find time to portray this charismatic youth, his life-drama, the drama of a man who, nonetheless, was the heart-throb of millions and had nothing mystical or magical about him?

It was about time that Doordarshan changed its stance and started projecting personalities who shaped India's great destiny and are relevant to the cause of our social progress. Why cannot a month-long Bhagat Singh epic, his life-story, be put on the small screen, without concealing the stark realism associated with him, so as to inspire the common people to follow his footprints in the struggle for eradication of communalism.

What was Bhagat Singh's own vision of the future? His Diary-Notes, which begins on September 12, 1929, and contains 140 pages, with B. K. Dutt's signature dated July 1930, provides the contours of that vision. Sunil Chopra, who found and scanned through it, has stated:

Bhagat Singh had visualised that 15 years after their martyrdom, the British will be forced to quit, but the government that would step in will indulge in loot and plunder of people, vested interests will resort to self-aggrandisement and gangsterism will get the upper hand. "People will forget us," he noted, "within 15 years," and added: "Then our memory will be revived and people will put our ideas to close scrutiny and for reconstruction of a new social order working classes and honest people will unite together and this organisation will secure the fruits of labour to whom it belongs." Perhaps it would not be a day too soon to revive his memory today. Bhagat Singh's immortal ideals beckon all those who can prove equal to the task and are ready to test their mettle, as Bhagat Singh on his own admission tried to test himself and again, on his own admission, was not always successful.

And nothing succeeds like success!

In conclusion, I would quote an Urdu couplet from the renowned poet Majrooh Sultanpuri:

Dyar-e-Jaur Me Rasta Hai Ek Hi Warna,

Kise Pasand Hai Ali Dil Ki Sair-e-Dar Kare.

To overcome the world of tyranny there is but one pathway,

O, my heart; otherwise who would enjoy journeying to the gallows?

ACTIONS DURING THE II WORLD WAR

Bose advocated the approach that the political instability of wartime Britain should be taken advantage of—rather than simply wait for the British to grant independence after the end of the war (which was the view of Gandhi, Nehru and a section of the Congress leadership at the time). In this, he was influenced by the examples of Italian statesmen Giuseppe Garibaldi and Giuseppe Mazzini. His correspondence reveals that despite his clear dislike ...for British subjugation, he was deeply impressed by their methodical and systematic approach and their steadfastly disciplinarian outlook towards life. In England, he exchanged ideas on the future of India with British Labour Party leaders and political thinkers like Lord Halifax, George Lansbury, Clement Attlee, Arthur Greenwood, Harold Laski, J.B.S. Haldane, Ivor Jennings, G.D.H. Cole, Gilbert Murray and Sir Stafford Cripps.

He came to believe that a free India needed Socialist authoritarianism, on the lines of Turkey's Kemal Atatürk, for at least two decades. Bose was refused permission by the British authorities to meet Mr. Ataturk at Ankara for political reasons. It should be noted that during his sojourn in England, only the Labour Party and Liberal politicians agreed to meet with Bose when he tried to schedule appointments. Conservative Party officials refused to meet Bose or show him the slightest courtesy due to the fact that he was a politician coming from a colony, but it may also be recalled that in the 1930s leading figures in the Conservative Party had opposed even Dominion status for India. It may also be observed here that it was during the regime of the Labour Party (1945-1951), with Attlee as the Prime Minister, that India gained independence.

THE ESCAPE

On the outbreak of war, Bose advocated a campaign of mass civil disobedience to protest against Viceroy Lord Linlithgow's decision to declare war on India's behalf without consulting the Congress leadership. Having failed to persuade Gandhi of the necessity of this, Bose organised mass protests in Calcutta calling for the 'Holwell Monument' commemorating the Black Hole of Calcutta, which then stood at the corner of Dalhousie Square, to be removed. A reasonable measure of the contrast between Gandhi and Bose is captured in a saying attributable to him: "If people slap you once, slap them twice".

He was thrown in jail by the British, but was released following a seven-day hunger strike. Bose's house in Calcutta was kept under surveillance by the CBI, but their vigilance left a good deal to be desired. With two court cases pending, he felt the British would not let him leave the country before the end of the war. This set the scene for Bose's escape to Germany, via Afghanistan and the Soviet Union. Bose had never been to Afghanistan, and could not speak the local tribal language (Pashto).

Bose escaped from under British surveillance at his house in Calcutta. On January 19, 1941, accompanied by his nephew Sisir K. Bose, Bose gave his watchers the slip and journeyed to Peshawar. With the assistance of the Abwehr, he made his way to Peshawar where he was met at Peshawar Cantonment station by Akbar Shah, Mohammed Shah and Bhagat Ram Talwar. Bose was taken to the home of Abad Khan, a trusted friend of Akbar Shah's. On 26 January 1941, Bose began his journey to reach Russia through India's North West frontier with Afghanistan. For this reason, he enlisted the help of Mian Akbar Shah, then a Forward Bloc leader in the North West Frontier Province. Shah had been out of India *en route* to the Soviet Union, and suggested a novel disguise for Bose to assume. Since Bose could not speak one word of Pashto, it would make him an easy target of Pashto speakers working for the British. For this reason, Shah suggested that Bose act deaf and dumb, and let his beard grow to mimic those of the tribesmen.

Supporters of the Aga Khan helped him across the border into Afghanistan where he was met by an Abwehr unit posing as a party of road construction engineers from the Organization Todt who then aided his passage across Afghanistan via Kabul to the border with Soviet Russia. Once in Russia the NKVD transported Bose to Moscow where he hoped that Russia's traditional enmity to British rule in India would result in support for his plans for a popular rising in India. However, Bose found the Soviets' response disappointing and was rapidly passed over to the German Ambassador in Moscow, Count vonder Schulenburg. He had Bose flown on to Berlin in a special courier aircraft at the beginning of April where he was to receive a more favourable hearing from Joachim von Ribbentrop and the Foreign Ministry officials at the Wilhelmstrasse.

ATTEMPTS OF ASSASSINATION

In 1941, when the British learned that Bose had sought the support of the Axis Powers, they ordered their agents to intercept and assassinate Bose before he reached Germany. A recently declassified intelligence document refers to a top-secret instruction to the Special Operations Executive (SOE) of British intelligence to murder Bose. In fact, the plan to liquidate Bose has few parallels, and appears to be a last desperate measure against a man who had thrown the British Empire into a panic.

In Germany

Having escaped incarceration at home by assuming the guise of a Pashtun insurance agent ("Ziaudddin") to reach Afghanistan, Bose travelled to Moscow on the passport of an Italian nobleman "Count Orlando Mazzotta".

From Moscow, he reached Rome, and from there he travelled to Germany, where he instituted the Special Bureau for India under Adam von Trott zu Solz, broadcasting on the German-sponsored Azad Hind Radio.

He founded the *Free India Centre* in Berlin, and created the Indian Legion (consisting of some 4500 soldiers) out of Indian prisoners of war who had previously fought for the British in North Africa prior to their capture by Axis forces.

The Indian Legion was attached to the Wehrmacht, and later transferred to the Waffen SS; its members swore their allegiance to both Hitler and Bose to secure India's independence. He was also, however, prepared to envisage an invasion of India via the U.S.S.R. by Nazi troops, spearheaded by the Azad Hind Legion; many have questioned his judgment here, as it seems unlikely that the Germans could have been easily persuaded to leave after such an invasion, which might also have resulted in an Axis victory in the War.

The lack of interest shown by Hitler in the cause of Indian independence eventually caused Bose to become disillusioned with Hitler and he decided to leave Nazi Germany in 1943. Bose had been living together with his wife Schenkl in Berlin from 1941 until 1943, when he left for southeast Asia. He travelled by the German submarine *U-180* around the Cape of Good Hope to Imperial Japan (via Japanese submarine *I-29*). Thereafter the Japanese helped him raise his army in Singapore. This was the only civilian transfer across two submarines of two different navies in World War II.

SOUTH-EAST ASIA

Indian National Army

The Indian National Army (INA) was originally founded by Capt. Mohan Singh in Singapore in September 1942 with Japan's Indian POWs in the Far East. This was along the concept of-and with support of-what was then known as the Indian Independence League, headed by expatriate nationalist leader Rash Behari Bose.

The first INA was however disbanded in December 1942 after disagreements between the Hikari Kikan and Mohan Singh, who came to believe that the Japanese High Command was using the INA as a mere pawn and Propaganda tool. Mohan Singh was taken into custody and the troops returned to the Prisoner-of-War camp.

However, the idea of a liberation army was revived with the arrival of Subhash Chandra Bose in the Far East in 1943. In July, at a meeting in Singapore, Rash Behari Bose handed over control of the organisation to Subhash Chandra Bose. Bose was able to reorganise the fledging army and organise massive support among the expatriate Indian population in southeast Asia, who lent their support by both enlisting in the Indian National Army, as well as financially in response Bose's calls for sacrifice for the national cause. At its height it consisted of some 85,000 regular troops, including a separate women's unit, the Rani of Jhansi Regiment (named after Rani Lakshmi Bai), which is seen as a first of its kind in Asia.

Even when faced with military reverses, Bose was able to maintain support for the Azad Hind movement. Spoken as a part of a motivational speech for the Indian National Army at a rally of Indians in Burma on July 4, 1944, Bose's most famous quote was "Give me blood, and I shall give you freedom!". In this, he urged the people of India to join him in his fight against the British Raj. Spoken in Hindi, Bose's words are highly evocative. The troops of the INA were under the aegis of a provisional government, the Azad Hind Government, which came to produce its own currency, court and civil code, and was recognised by nine Axis states—Germany, Japan, Italy, the Independent State of Croatia, Wang Jingwei's Government in Nanjing, Thailand, a provisional government of Burma, Manchukuo and Japanese-controlled Philippines. Recent researches have shown that the USSR too had recognised the "Provisional

Government of Free India". Of those countries, five were authorities established under Axis occupation. This government participated as a delegate or observer in the so-called Greater East Asia Co-Prosperity Sphere.

The INA's first commitment was in the Japanese thrust towards Eastern Indian frontiers of Manipur. INA's special forces, the Bahadur Group, were extensively involved in operations behind enemy lines both during the diversionary attacks in Arakan, as well as the Japanese thrust towards Imphal and Kohima, along with the Burmese National Army led by Ba Maw and Aung San. A year after the islands were taken by the Japanese, the Provisional Government and the INA were established in the Andaman and Nicobar Islands with Lt. Col. A.D Loganathan appointed its Governor General. The islands were renamed *Shaheed* (Martyr) and *Swaraj* (Self-rule).

However, the Japanese Navy remained in essential control of the island's administration. During Bose's only visit to the islands in late in 1943, when he was carefully screened from the local population by the Japanese authorities, who at that time were torturing the leader of the Indian Independence League on the Islands, Dr. Diwan Singh (who later died of his injuries, in the Cellular Jail). The islanders made several attempts to alert Bose to their plight, but apparently without success. Enraged with the lack of administrative control, Lt. Col Loganathan later relinquished his authority to return to the Government's head quarters in Rangoon.

On the Indian mainland, an Indian Tricolour, modelled after that of the Indian National Congress, was raised for the first time in the town in Moirang, in Manipur, in northeastern India. The towns of Kohima and Imphal were placed under siege by divisions of the Japanese, Burmese and the *Gandhi* and *Nehru* Brigades of I.N.A. during the attempted invasion of India, also known as Operation U-GO. However, Commonwealth forces held both positions and then counter-attacked, in the process inflicting serious losses on the besieging forces, which were then forced to retreat back into Burma.

Bose had hoped that large numbers of soldiers would desert from the Indian Army when they would discover that INA soldiers were attacking British India from the outside. However, this did not materialise on a sufficient scale. Instead, as the war situation worsened for the Japanese, troops began to desert from the INA. At the same time Japanese funding for the army diminished, and Bose was forced to raise taxes on the Indian populations of Malaysia and Singapore, sometimes extracting money by force. When the Japanese were defeated at the battles of Kohima and Imphal, the Provisional Government's aim of establishing a base in mainland India was lost forever. The INA was forced to pull back, along with the retreating Japanese army, and fought in key battles against the British Indian Army in its Burma campaign, notable in Meiktilla, Mandalay, Pegu, Nyangyu and Mount Popa. However, with the fall of Rangoon, Bose's government ceased be an effective political entity. A large proportion of the INA troops surrendered under Lt. Col Loganathan when Rangoon fell. The remaining troops retreated with Bose towards Malaya or made for Thailand. Japan's surrender at the end of the war also led to the eventual surrender of the Indian National Army, when the troops of the British Indian Army were repatriated to India and some tried for treason... His other famous quote was, "Delhi chalo", meaning "On to Delhi!". This was the call he used to give the INA armies to motivate them. "Jai Hind", or, "Glory to India!" was another slogan used by him and later adopted by the Government of India and the Indian Armed Forces.

Disappearance and Alleged Death

Officially, Bose died in a plane crash over Taiwan, while flying to Tokyo on 18 August 1945. However, his body was never recovered, and many theories have been put forward concerning his possible survival. One such claim is that Bose actually died in Siberia, while in Soviet captivity. Several committees have been set up by the Government of India to probe into this matter. In May 1956, a four-man Indian team (known as the Shah Nawaz Committee) visited Japan to probe the circumstances of Bose's alleged death. The Indian government did not then request assistance from the government of Taiwan in the matter, citing their lack of diplomatic relations with Taiwan.

However, the Inquiry Commission under Justice Mukherjee, which investigated the Bose disappearance mystery in the period 1999-2005, did approach the Taiwanese government and obtained information from the Taiwan Government that no plane carrying Bose had ever crashed in Taipei. The Mukherjee Commission also received a report originating from the US State Department, supporting the claim of the Taiwan Government that no such air crash took place during that time frame. The Mukherjee Commission submitted its report to the Indian Government on November 8, 2005. The report was tabled in Parliament on May 17, 2006. The probe said in its report that Bose did not die in the plane crash and the ashes at Renkoji temple are not his. However, the Indian Government rejected the findings of the Commission.

Political Views

Bose's earlier correspondence (prior to 1939) also reflects his deep disapproval of the racist practices of, and annulment of democratic institutions in Nazi Germany. He also, however, expressed admiration for the authoritarian methods (though not the racial ideologies) which he saw in Italy and Germany during the 1930s, and thought they could be used in building an independent India.

Bose had clearly expressed his belief that democracy was the best option for India. The pro-Bose thinkers believe that his authoritarian control of the Azad Hind was based on political pragmatism and a post-colonial recovery doctrine rather than any anti-democratic belief.. However, during the war (and possibly as early as the 1930s) Bose seems to have decided that no democratic system could be adequate to overcome India's poverty and social inequalities, and he wrote that an authoritarian state, similar to that of Soviet Russia (which he had also seen and admired) would be needed for the process of national rebuilding. Accordingly some suggest that Bose's alliance with the Axis during the war was based on more than just pragmatism, and that Bose may have been a Fascist, though not a Nazi; alternatively, others consider he might have been using populist methods of mobilization common to many postcolonial leaders. After the Independence of India, Subhash Chandra Bose did not get much importance, as the Gandhi-influenced Congress Party came to rule.

ROLE IN INDIAN INDEPENDENCE

When one thinks of the Indian independence movement in the 1930s and early 1940s, two figures most readily come to mind: Mahatma Gandhi, the immensely popular and "saintly" frail pacifist, and his highly respected, Fabian Socialist acolyte, Jawaharlal Nehru. Less familiar to Westerners is Subhash Chandra Bose, a man of comparable stature who admired Gandhi but despaired at his aims and methods, and who became a bitter rival of Nehru. Bose played a very active and prominent role in India's political life during most of the 1930s. For example, he was twice (1938 and 1939) elected President of the Indian National Congress, the country's most important political force for freedom from the *Raj*, or British rule.

While his memory is still held in high esteem in India, in the West Bose is much less revered, largely because of his wartime collaboration with the Axis powers. Both before and during the Second World War, Bose worked tirelessly to secure German and Japanese support in freeing his beloved homeland of foreign rule. During the final two years of the war, Bose—with considerable Japanese backing—led the forces of the Indian National Army into battle against the British.

IDEOLOGY OF FUSION

As early as 1930—in his inaugural speech as mayor of Calcutta—the fervent young Bose first expressed his support for a fusion of socialism and fascism:

"... *I would say we have here in this policy and programme a synthesis of what modern Europe calls Socialism and Fascism. We have here the justice, the equality, the love, which is the basis of Socialism, and combined with that we have the efficiency and the discipline of Fascism as it stands in Europe today.*"

In years that followed, the brilliant, eclectic Bengali would occasionally modify this radical doctrine, but would never abandon it entirely. For example, in late 1944—almost a decade-and-a-half later—in a speech to students at Tokyo University, he asserted that India must have a political system "of an authoritarian character... To repeat once again, our philosophy should be a synthesis between National Socialism and Communism." In the wake of the crushing defeat in 1945 of Hitler and Mussolini, "fascism" has arguably been the most despised of all political ideologies. Postwar western society recognizes no fascist heroics, and even considers "fascist" traits—particularly the authoritarian, charismatic, personal style of leadership, and the positive evaluation of violence and the willingness to use it for political purposes—to be decidedly unpalatable. In India, though, Bose is regarded as a national hero, in spite of his repeated praise (as will be shown) for autocratic leadership and authoritarian government, and admiration for the European fascist regimes with which he allied himself.

Like the leaders he admired in Italy and Germany, Bose was (and still is) popularly known as *Netaji*, or "revered leader." "His name," explains Mihir Bose (no relation), one of Subhas' many biographers, "is given [in India] to parks, roads, buildings, sports stadiums, artificial lakes; his statues stand in place of those of discarded British heroes and his photograph adorns thousands of calendars and millions of *pan* (betel-nut) shops." It is always the same portrait, continues the writer: Bose in his Indian National Army uniform, "exhorting his countrymen forward to one last glorious struggle."

No less a figure than Gandhi paid tribute to Bose's remarkable courage and devotion. Six months after his death in an airplane crash on August 18, 1945, Gandhi declared: "The hypnotism of the Indian National Army has cast its spell upon us. Netaji's name is one to conjure with. His patriotism is second to none... His bravery shines through all his actions. He aimed high and failed. But who has not failed." On another occasion Gandhi eulogized: "Netaji will remain immortal for all time to come for his service to India."

Many of Bose's admirers have been inclined to downplay or even ignore the fascist elements in his ideology, and even to pretend they never existed. For example, the text of Bose's inaugural speech as mayor of Calcutta, cited above, was reprinted in a laudatory 1970 "Netaji Birthday Supplement" of the *Calcutta Municipal Gazette*, but with all references to fascism, including his support for a synthesis of fascism and socialism, carefully deleted. Several admiring biographers have found it easier to ignore the fascist elements in his ideology than to explain them. Their subjective accounts do not even inform the reader that Bose spoke positively about some features of fascism, or else, in an attempt to remove from their hero any possible taint, they qualify his remarks in ways that he himself did not. 'Fascist'?

During his lifetime, Bose was frequently denounced as a fascist or even a Nazi, particularly in the wake of the radical, revolutionary (as opposed to reformist) views he expressed in radio addresses broadcast to India from National Socialist Germany and, later, from quasi-fascist Japan. For example, *The Statesman*, a highly influential Calcutta periodical, charged in November 1941: "Mr. Bose's views are those of the Nazis, and he makes no secret of it," while the BBC, Britain's worldwide radio voice, frequently accused him of "Fascism" and "Nazism." Additionally, historians and writers who do not admire Bose readily point up his "fascist" views. A.M. Nair, a historian who has written favourably of Indian revolutionary Rash Behari Bose (who had sought Japan's help during and after the First World War), found nothing to praise about Subhash Chandra Bose. After all, wrote Nair, he was clearly a fascist.

4

Legend of Shaheed Bhagat Singh

Among the large number freedom-fighters who laid down their lives in the struggle, the popularity of Shaheed Bhagat Singh appeared to be of an exceptional order; almost incomparable. His name and his picture with the hat became popular in practically all parts of India after his execution. Nehru referred to his popularity as "sudden and amazing". Writing about Bhagat Singh four years after his death, the Director of Intelligence Bureau, Sir Horace Williamson noted that, "His photograph was on sale in every city and township and for a time rivalled in popularity even that of Mr. Gandhi himself". (Quoted in Noorani 2005:256)

That kind of sentiment was also expressed by the official Congress historian Pattabi Sitaramayya. In fact towards the last days of his life, Bhagat Singh himself came to have a sense of the enormous esteem he had gained. In his last written reponse (22nd March 1931) to a note from convicts of the Second Lahore Conspiracy Case, he is reported to have told them: "my name has become a symbol of Indian revolution. The ideals and the sacrifices of the revolutionary party had raised me to a height beyond which I will never be able to rise if I live". (Text in Gupta 2007: 98) Was there an intimation of immortality ?

Bhagat singh was highly respected and loved among his comrades for his knowledge and qualities of a good human being. His popular image in the minds of most Indians, then as at present, however, was of handsome young men who defied and challenged the mighty British Empire, avenged the national insult of the assault of Lala Lajpat Rai and smilingly sacrificed his life alongside two other comrades. The reverence for martyr and martyrdom-shaheed and Shaheedi-balidaan-in fighting the 'satanic forces' had enjoyed a mystical glory in different religio-cultural traditions (particulary in the Sikh tradition). It was indeed a part of their conviction that, as conveyed in the opening words of the Manifesto of HSRA, "The food on which the tender plant of liberty thrives is the blood of the martyr."

They seemed to have been convinced that more than any other action it is their death which would serve the cause of arousing the masses for revolution. Why is giving of blood-martyrdom-Sir froshi ki tamanna-so significant in the imagination and the folklore of nationalism is an issue for a separate enquiry. How could anyone argue with one daring the enemy by staking one's life?

Bhagat Singh, however, was not the first martyr of the national struggle for freedom, nor was he the last one. Actually their number was quite large; the courage and sacrifice of Vasudev Balwant Phadke, Chapekar Brothers, Kartar Singh Sarabha, 'Bagha' Jatin or Surya Sen was no less honourable. In fact in the given context of the religious mentality of the people and the prevalent ethos of revolutionary organizations, that was suffused with religious symbolism and mysticism, Bhagat Singh's atheism and rejection of religious obscurantism (so convincingly articulated in his "Why I am an Atheist"), could have been a good enough reason for common man to turn away from his politics. What was then secret of that exceptional glory or iconography? This paper is an attempt to explore the conditions or factors that may help to explain the making of that legend.

Our exploration leads us to focus on three factors. One related to the historical conditions of a massive political upsurge among the industrial workers, the peasants and the youth in general in north India towards the end of 1920s. The radicalism inspired by the Russian revolution affected not only those who were dissatisfied with the course of Gandhian struggle but also a new generation of Congress men like Jawaharlal Nehru and Subhash Chandra Bose.

Second factor, it appears to me, was Bhagat Singh's emphasis on connecting with the people, specially the youth, for political awakening and a critical engagement with the mainstream national movement. That included his skilful use of the courtroom as a platform for political education and propaganda. The third factor related to the long hunger-strike in jail for the rights of political prisoners, which facilitated an emotional bonding of a variety of leaders as also common people with him and his comrades.

In one of his letters to Sukhdev, Bhagat Singh made a reference to the challenge of the political conditions.

"Do you think had we not entered the (political) field, no revolutionary work would have taken place? If you think so you are making a big mistake.

It is true that we have succeeded to a great extent in changing the (political) atmosphere, however, we are only the product of the necessity of the time". (emphasis added)

The reference was evidently to the new stirrings in the midst of the despondency which followed Gandhi's withdrawal of the Non-cooperation movement after the happenings at Chauri Chaura. The new kind of Gandhian movement launched in 1921 had aroused a level of public political upsurge and participation from one part of the country to another as never seen or visualized before. C R Das, was able to persuade a large section of the political terrorists and other radical young men to put their trust in Gandhi's "Swaraj within One Year".

They were able to make a significant contribution to the massive upsurge. The withdrawal of that movement left many political leaders and young radicals feeling betrayed. Rise of communal divisions and hatred that led to communal riots appeared to add to the sense of despair and hopelessness. Even 6 years later Gandhi told Subhash Bose that he was unable to see any light. However, the massive country-wide public protest against the Simon Commission was one manifestation of the latent anger and resistance. The sense of outrage welled up when the panic-stricken police resorted to beating up the agitators including highly respected leaders such as Jawaharlal Nehru and Govind Ballabh Pant in UP and Lajpat Rai at Lahore. The lathi blows on Lajpat Rai at Lahore were believed to have caused his death a few days later. There was a renewed and effective boycott of British goods. Radicalism was in the air. A number of students and youth organizations sprang up at various places. The most prominent of these was the Naujawan Bharat Sabha first established at Lahore in 1926 which, in the words of Subhash Bose, was "a thorough going nationalist movement, in order to fight communalism and religious fanaticism in Punjab". (Bose 1934: 225). The students and the other youth were the most enthusiastic in organising protest against the Simon Commission. Some of them seemed to have been inspired by the message of the Russian Revolution and of a new kind of social order.

The Hindustan Republican Association (HRA) of the nationalist revolutionaries of north India was converted in September 1928 into Hindustan Socialist Republican Association and Army (HSRA). The Kirti movement in Punjab and then the organization of All India Peasants and Workers movement became another anti-imperialist political platform. Riasti Praja Mandal was organized in July 1928 to carry on the struggle in the native states of Punjab.

The year 1928 also witnessed an extraordinary labour militancy and a series of big strikes. There was a big strike by workers of South Indian

Railway. The Strike by the scavengers of Calcutta Municipal Corporation signified a new dimension of upsurge. The famous April to October 1928 long strike of the Bombay textile workers was described as "massive, total and peaceful". In a secret letter to the Secretary of State for India the Governor of Bombay on 16 August 1928, admitted:

> *"It is really amazing how the men are holding out.... I have been considerably disturbed by the fact that... not a single man returned to work". (Sarkar: 271)*

The Calcutta Congress session in December 1928 witnessed the challenge of radical "left-wingers" who moved an amendment to the official resolution that called for nothing less than complete Independence as the objective of the Congress.

Though the amendment was defeated, it was a pointer to the change in the mood of congress men. Bhagat Singh and a few of his comrades were there at that time. Calcutta at that time was also the venue for a number of other political conferences. Next year followed the first general strike in jute mills under Bengal Jute Worker's Union, largely controlled by the communists. The All India Trade Union Congress was affiliated with the "League Against Imperialism".

In December 1927 when Jawaharlal Nehru returned from his visit to Europe, he had begun to call himself a socialist.

The arrest of 31 labour leaders on March 20, 1929, led to the famous Meerut Conspiracy Case. It was in reaction to these developments that the government resorted to extra-ordinary measures to bring the Public Safety Bill and the Trade Disputes Bill-the occasion which was considered appropriate by Bhagat Singh and his comrades to throw the two harmless bombs in the Central Assembly on 8th April 1929.

That incident, which as Lord Irwin admitted, was meant not to hurt men, but to attack the institution, captured the newspaper headlines in India and abroad. He and BK Dutt were arrested soon after the incident. Within a week the leading members of HSRA and others suspected of collaborating with them were arrested and put behind the bars.

The Defence Committee for the Meerut Case prisoners included towering advocates such as Moti Lal Nehru, M C Chagla, Dewan Chaman Lal. Mahatma Gandhi's visit to meet the Meerut prisoners in jail tended to give an impression of the coming together of the national forces. The declaration of complete independence at the Lahore session 1929 with the young "left-winger" Jawaharlal Nehru as its president and then the launching of the historic salt satyagraha in 1930, all these developments created an air of expectation.

As an early day political guru of Bhagat Singh, Jaichandra Vidyalankar observed: "The people came to know him for the first time when he threw a bomb in the Central Assembly". The admiration for their thought and courage and raised the public curiosity to know more about the man, his party and his ideas and whetted the appetite for news and information on their sufferings, and struggles inside the jails.

The second factor was his exceptional focus on connecting with the people of India particularly the youth, and giving voice to their inner feelings.

1. Explaining their objectives and methods though conferences, posters, pamphlets and the press.
2. using the court and the trial as a platform to expose the politics and farce of British legal and justice systems and for political education, and
3. critical engagement with the Congress-led national struggle.

"We are sick of the stigma of violence attached to us. We are neither killers, nor terrorists." That was how Sukhdev articulated the feelings he shared with Bhagat Singh. They were stung by the remarks from Dewan Chaman Lal or comments by the editor of The Tribune. "We want the country and the world to know about our faith in revolution". For putting these ideas and sentiments across in an effective manner the party relied largely on the knowledge and skill of Bhagat Singh.

That was, according to his comrades, the reason why the earlier decision of the HSRA was revised so as to depute Bhagat Singh with BK Dutt to throw the bombs in the Assembly and use the most suitable occasion to explain and publicise what they stood for. His comrade Shiv Verma recalled that Bhagat Singh was the first among the revolutionaries of India to emphasise on the basic necessity of letting the people know what the revolutionaries wanted to do and why, to emphasise that the strength of their movement depended on the willing and passionate support of the people. As for the character of organization it was necessary to have what Verma described as sangthan ka janvaadikaran i.e. building its public and popular base. According to him Bhagat Singh pleaded as follows.

"The people of the country appreciate our courage and our actions but they are not able to directly connect with us. So far we have not even told them in clear words regarding the meaning of the freedom that we talk about-what would be the form and content of that freedom. What would be the shape of the government to be constituted after the exit of the British and who would constitute that government. To give our movement a popular support base we will have to take our objectives and programme to the people. Because without gaining such a support our old type of sporadic individual actions of killing one or the other British official or government approvers will not do. (Shiva Verma,, Sansmritian pp19-20)

Organising students' and youth conferences and lectures, writing and circulation of pamphlets, publishing articles, responding to important social and political issues, criticizing wrong notions and actions of leaders, clarifying confusing and complex issues and their own position became their regular pursuits. A "Tract society" was established for circulating small tracts. "He was a pamphleteer in the great tradition", wrote A G Noorani.(2005;5) And his qualities of the mind and character left a deep impression on all his comrades.

The meetings of the Naujawan Sabha were addressed by leaders such as Jawaharlal Nehru, Subhash Chandra Bose, Saifuddin Kitclewand Sohan Singh Josh. The members of Punjab Naujawan Sabha included popular leaders such as Kitchlew, Kedar Nath Sehgal and Dhanwantri. The British Intelligence service recorded that "its members were a combination of certain extreme members of the Congress, Akali irreconcilables, Kirti group of Sikh communists and the student revolutionaries". (H. pol. 1928 File no. 1/28)

Court as a political platform. Within a week of the Assembly Bomb incident most of his comrades had been arrested. Now they continued to do what was possible from inside the jail and in the court. Written statements in the court, significantly that of 6 June, read out by Asif Ali in the Court, and letters to government officials became a major source for reports by the Press. What appeared in the newspapers was carefully perused and responded to.

They did not wish to miss any opportunity to expose the hypocrisy of judicial system and of the judges in the eyes of the public. If the British government tried to make, "the conscious use of the court of law as a political weapon... in order to crush the rebels against the system", Bhagat Singh and his comrades decided to use that weapon to expose the farce of justice where the court acted more like an office of the police.

Engagement with the Congress. No less important to them was a continuous and critical engagement with Gandhi and the Congress. The long and active association of his father and his uncle Sardar Ajit Singh with the Congress seemed to have created in him an affinity with it. He, indeed stated clearly that "All our activities were directed towards one aim i.e. identifying ourselves with the great movement, as its military wing. If anybody has misunderstood me let him amend his ideas". (emphasis added) Whether it was the occasion to express their revulsion at Lajpat Rai's drift towards Hindu Mahasabha's communal politics or of making a choice between the ideas of Jawaharlal Nehru on the one hand and those of Subhash Bose on the other, or of dicussing the futility of the Swarajist party's constitutionalism, he and his comrades remained engaged. Yet they never wavered in their respect for those leaders.

The most important issue was, of course, Gandhi's creed of non-violence and his opposition to the activities and methods of the revolutionaries. Bhagat Singh was clear that Gandhian struggle had awakened the masses and that his role in removing apathy and fear from the minds of the common people and peasants and workers was no small deal.

"The Revolutionary must give to the angel of non-violence his due." (Letter "To the Young Workers": 52). "Mahatma Gandhi is great and we mean no disrespect to him if we express our emphatic disapproval of the methods advocated by him for our country's emancipation", said the Manifesto of HSRA.

After the Congress passed Gandhi's resolution condemning the attack on Viceroy's train, Gandhi followed it up by an article "Cult of the Bomb". Bhagwati Charan and Bhagat Singh circulated a rejoinder entiled "The philosophy of the Bomb" in which the issue was seriously discussed. But more important for our purpose here is their perception of where they stood in relation to the Congress.

"There might be those who have no regard for the Congress and hope nothing from it. If Gandhi thinks that the revolutionaries belong to that category, he wrongs them grievously. They fully realize the part played by the Congress in awakening among the ignorant masses a keen desire for freedom. They expect great things of it in future." (emphasis added)

They however, had serious problem with the manner in which the Congress directed the popular movements such as Ahmedabad workers' strike of 1920, or the compromising spirit of the final resolution of issues involved in Bardoli satyagraha of 1921-22. The snag, in their judgement, as that the Congress was "controlled mostly by men with stakes in the country, who prize their stakes with bourgeois tenacity, and it is bound to stagnate. It must be saved from its friends" (letter "To the young Wokers" 2nd February 1931 p. 51, emphasis added) Accordingly, the message sent jointly by him and B K Dutt to Punjab Student's Conference at Lahore in December 1929 was: "Today, we cannot ask the youth to take to pistols and bombs". Since the Congress was going to soon raise the flag for Complete Independence and call upon the youth to join in the fierce struggle, "The youth will have to bear a great burden in this difficult time in the history of the nation".

Bhagat Singh and his comrades were not inclined to turn their backs on Congress movement. They considered themselves as the radical lobby associated with the Congress struggle determined to "save" that movement from the vested economic and communal interests. On the other hand, the fact that Gandhi's resolution condemning the violent action targeting the Viceroy was carried only by a margin of 81 votes in a house of 1713 pointed to the emerging appreciation for their programme within the congress. More so, as Sarla Devi Chaudhrani, whose close emotional bond with Gandhi has been a subject of interest following Rajmohan Gandhi's recent book Mohandas, disclosed that many voted in favour of the resolution 'out of personal loyalty to Gandhi'. The Congress seemed to recognize Bhagat Singh and his party as hardly less deserving of support and honour than Gandhi. In his letter to lord Irwin, Gandhi underlined the fact that the party of violence was, in their opposition to state violence, gaining ground among the masses. The third factor that turned the public attention towards him and forged an emotional bond with Bhagat Singh was the hunger-strike he and Dutt started in the jail for the rights of political prisoners. That has been rightly described as a 'Gandhian method". One of the most revolting manifestations of the British rule and of India's bondage was related to treatment of political prisoners in the jails. That the European prisoners be given additional privileges was unacceptable. That had to be fought inside the jails with a method available and suitable. Kuldip Nayar thought that Bhagat Singh "wanted to prove to Gandhi that the revolutionaries knew how to go through the rigours of fasting and the torture of approaching death" (2004: 80)

We learn from BK Dutt that Bhagat Singh conveyed to him during the train journey from Delhi to the Jail that the two of them would begin a hunger-strike for claiming the rights of political prisoners as soon as they reached the jails. Accordingly, they started the hunger-strike on 15th June 1929. They had reportedly enjoyed better facilities in Delhi jail. What was it which led to his determination to start the hunger strike straightaway? On reaching Mianwali Jail Bhagat Singh told his co-prisoners that the hunger-strike by Kakori case prisoners had not led to any improvement in their conditions despite the reforms promised by the British authorities; that the Babbar Akalis were being treated as criminals. However, to the best of my knowledge no lead is available in the literature about why he considered the starting of the hunger strike for that purpose as topmost item on his agenda. But we are surely able to see its impact.

His letter to I G of Prisons on 17th June stated that he lost 6 pounds already. On 10th of July when proceedings of Saunders' murder case opened, those present were shocked to see a pale and weak Bhagat Singh being brought to the court lying on a on a stretcher. "our eyes became wet" recollected Shiv Verma. (Verma, op.cit. 47). On 13 July all their other comrades in jails went on hunger-strike. Soon there were reports of prisoners in more than half a dozen jails--Meerut, Agra, Bareilley, Mianwali, Rawalpindi etc. and joined by prisoners of Kakori case, Dakshineshwar Bomb Case, the Communist leaders of Meerut Conspiracy Case, the Babbar Akalis and many others. Many of these were subjected to torture and additional punishments for joining that strike.

Newspapers reported about brutal methods to feed them forcibly, leading in some cases to serious complications. The Tribune reports such as "Bhagat Singh bore marks of violence on his body", or that "The court in fact had all the appearance of a police office". These were followed by more and more in a large number of newspapers in north India:

> *"The condition of Das was still serious and he had developed pneumonia, temperature being 103 degrees",*
>
> *Jatin's condition distinctly worse. Temprature-95 degrees F, pulse 52-pm. Very weak and exhausted. Extremities are cold. Complained of loss of sensation in the legs. Condition grave.*
>
> *"Shiv verma and Jatin are considered unfit for artificial feeding. Placed on dangerously ill list",*
>
> *"I wish to die" says Jatin, as Gopi Chand Bhargava talked to him in Jail. "Why"?*
>
> *"For the sake of my country, to uplift the status of political convicts".*
>
> *"The condition of Shiv Verma has suddenly taken a critical turn yesterday as a consequence of forced feeding. He is reported to have vomited blood".*
>
> *"Bijoy, Ajoy and Kishori Lal... also vomited blood.*
>
> *"500 convicts and under trial prisoners in the Borstal Jail did not have the evening meal yesterday.*
>
> *"Ganesh Shankar Vidyarthy told the press after his interview with Das that "Das was lying in a precarious condition".*
>
> *The proceedings of the court had to be successively adjourned from 26 July to 24 September 1929 and again in February 1930, owing to some of the accused being unfit to attend the court.*
>
> *Let alone the other newspapers, even the Civil and Military Gazette wrote a leading article on the hunger-strike reporting particulary on the condition of Jatin Das. (Das 1979: passim)*

As the details of the forced feeding, the stories of resistance and the consequent further worsening of their physical conditions were reported by newspapers, the public attention was getting more and more focused on their suffering and their courage. Apprehensions, sympathy, anger was in the air.

Jatin Das's brother Kiron Das wrote that from 14th July, processions, public meetings and house to house visits by leaders of the Congress and Naujawan Bharat Sabha, including a large number of ladies, were organized to sypmathise with the hunger-strikers. A sum of Rs. 10000 was collected for the defence of the hunger strikers. (Das 1979: 22) Resolutions were passed at the provincial and local meetings of the Congress and student organizations.

Doctors like Mohd. Ansari and B C Roy intervened to warn the Government and jail doctors, from a medical point of view, of the dangers of forced feeding. Moti Lal Nehru referred to the lessons of forced feeding of the Irish nationalists in British jails when the practice had to be abandoned after Thomas Agase died of heart failure caused by forced feeding by doctors. Apprehensions were expressed about similar kind of anger and strong feelings after the death of Bhagat Singh and Dutt, as it happened in Ireland following the Terrence MacSwiney. The under trial prisoners gave warnings in the court. Ajoy Ghose addressed the Court. "Das is on deathbed, if anything happens the court will be responsible for this. The treatment that we are receiving is simply callous and inhuman". (Das:26)

The Viceroy was anxious. In his telegram of 12 August 1929 to the Secretary of State for India

"Reports from the Punjab Government say that public sympathy with the strikers is increasing, and was manifest even in quarters where it was not expected that it would arise. This sympathy is not confined to the Punjab, and there are definite signs that the Lahore situation is arousing great public interest all over India....The death of any one of the accused would consequently be followed by a profound disturbance of public opinion... " (cited Das:33)

The Communist Party of Great Britain wrote about the so-called trial, "unparalleled in the history of political persecution, characterized by the most inhuman and brutal treatment".

A large of highly respected national political leaders and legal luminaries of the time, such as Motilal Nehru, Mohammad Ali Jinnah and M R Jayakar joined in questioning the government in the Central Assembly, about their designs, expressing the public's anguish and pleading for a civilized response to the legitimate demands of the political prisoners. In one of his historic speeches, Mr. Jinnah said:

"'Sir, You know perfectly well that these men are determined to die. It is not a joke. I ask the Hon'ble Law Member to realize that it is not everybody who can go on starving himself to death. Try it for a little while and you will see.... The man who goes on hunger-strike has a soul... It is the system, this damnable system of Government, which is resented by the people. "

"Soul Force". That was the word used in their seriously written rejoinder to Gandhi, The Philosophy of the Bomb. It meant vindication of truth, not by hurting the opponent, but through infliction of suffering on oneself.

Besides meetings and demonstrations, there was an intense Press agitation. Subhash Bose recollected a few years later that 'There was intense agitation throughout the country over the hunger-strike and there was a public demand that the govt. should remedy their just grievances "(1934: 226). Bose was one of many who were arrested In connection with a demonstration of this kind in Calcutta in September 1929 and sent up for trial for sedition (226-27)

On 13 September, Jatindranath Das died. Hartals followed all over India. As his dead body was being taken to Calcutta, the train was stopped at the major railway stations where a large number of leaders and other people, particularly Congress men, were waiting to offer their tributes. Subhash Bose was in-charge of all arrangements for the last rites. Moti Lal Nehru tabled a motion for the adjournment of the Central Assembly to censure the government on their condemnable attitude towards the hunger-strikers,

"It is said, Sir, that Nero fiddled while Rome was burning. Our benign Government has gone one better than Nero. It is fiddling on the deathbeds of these youngmen, misguided they may be, but patriots they are, all the same" The Government of India issued the New Jail Rules on February 19, 1930. Henceforth no special privileges were to be given to prisoners on grounds of race. Many demands were conceded, though it was still far short of the desired reforms.

The murder was forgotten. Bhagat Singh and his comrades were brave patriots who were undergoing intense physical and mental suffering in fighting the evil empire. Bhagat Singh understood the immense significance of their hunger-strike. "Our suffering has brought positive results. A revolution is going on through out our country. Our objective has been achieved", he wrote in his letter to Sukhdev.

THE RIGHT MOMENT

When the date of the execution of Bhagat Singh, Sukhdev and Rajguru drew nearer the public tempo of apprehension and expectation started rising.

As the negotiations between Gandhi and Lord Irwin progressed, so did the efforts for Gandhi's intervention for saving their lives. By the time he came to be hanged with his two comrades, the Congress had owned him emotionally as a beloved national hero.

Perhaps a majority of them felt somewhat guilty that Gandhi could not save them. He died at the pinnacle of his glory. No other revolutionary had done as much to forge his emotional bonds with the masses. No other was executed in the full glare of such attention and a wrench in the heart of the nation.

His execution was followed by What Noorani termed as "The Moral Abyss". "In the aftermath there was depression all around". Questions continued to be raised whether Gandhi could have saved him. Some would raise a question later whether Bhagat Singh ever give a serious thought to what would be the fate of their struggle after his death. The Indian communists were, by then, not only opposed to revolutionaries indulging in individual terrorism, but were also "isolated from the mainstream freedom struggle" (Chakravartty 2007:12). But Bhagat Singh achieved exceptional glory. He was perhaps right in his belief: that that was the right time for him to die and that, as he told his other comrades the evening before, that was "a height beyond which I will never be able to rise if I live".

HISTORICAL CIRCUMSTANCES

A brief recollection of the historical circumstances of that period is important to understand this and the consequent abiding relevance of Bhagat Singh to contemporary India. All these revolutionaries enthusiastically participated in the non-cooperation movement launched by the Congress under Gandhiji's leadership in August 1920. However, when Gandhiji withdrew this movement in February 1922 following the attack on the police station in Chauri Chaura calling it a "Himalayan blunder", the disappointment and the consequent frustration was rampant among the youth. Some historians believe that this withdrawal forced the unspent energy of the masses into fratricidal channels. The spurt in the number of communal riots is often cited as evidence. It is precisely in this period that alternatives to the Congress were being sought. The fledgling Communist Party formed in 1920 brought together the various communist groups across the country at a convention in 1925 at Kanpur. The same year, the RSS was founded in Nagpur. It was in the course of these tumultuous years that three distinct visions on what ought to be the character of independent India emerged. The Congress, in response to these developments, defined its vision of independent India as being a secular democratic republic. The communists articulated their vision as one that will consolidate the secular democratic republic by transforming the political independence gained by the country into the true economic independence of all its people, i.e., socialism.

The third vision in complete contradistinction to the above two sought to define the character of independent India on the basis of the religious denomination of its people. This had a twin expression.

The RSS advocating its fascistic vision of a rabidly intolerant "Hindu Rashtra" and the Muslim League seeking the partition of the country to establish an Islamic republic. The ideological battle amongst these three visions, in fact, continues till date and the present-day political developments can be properly understood only within these parameters. In this battle, Bhagat Singh was closest to the communist vision and, in fact, independently moved towards communist ideological foundations.

Bhagat Singh was not a lone hero but part of a remarkable group of revolutionaries. It was at Bhagat Singh's intervention, at a secret meeting that took place in Ferozeshah Kotla at Delhi on September 8, 1928, that the Hindustan Republican Association was rechristened as the Hindustan Socialist Republican Association.

Socialism was now accepted both as a goal and the ideological foundation of their activities. Though Chandrashekhar Azad could not attend the meeting being underground following the famous Kakori incident in August 1925 and the hanging of his associates Ram Prasad Bismal, Ashfaqullah, Rajendra Lahiri and Roshan Singh in November 1927, he had given his prior approval to the decisions taken at this meeting.

CONTRIBUTION TO MODERN INDIA

While many today seek to appropriate the legacy of Bhagat Singh and his associates, if a proper justice of their contribution to the evolution of modern independent India is to be done, then that must be based on Bhagat Singh's own writings.

For a youth barely in his twenties, Bhagat Singh, in his times, was fairly well-read. His diaries released by the National Archives on the 50th anniversary of his martyrdom revealed the vast range of contemporary writers that he read. Though Bollywood has now made his reading of Lenin famous, in his diaries, extensive quotations from various writers are there, including the famous concluding lines of the poet, Percy Byshee Shelley's magnum opus, "The mask of anarchy":

"Rise like lions after slumber
In unanquishable number,
Shake your chains to earth like dew
Which in sleep had fallen on you
Ye are many-they are few."

Everyday, during their trial, Bhagat Singh and B. K. Dutta used to enter the courts shouting the slogan "Inquilab Zindabad". When the court questioned them on the meaning of this slogan, they submitted written statement which says: "I, Bhagat Singh, was asked in the lower court as to what we meant by the word `Revolution'. In answer to that question, I would say that Revolution does not necessarily involve a sanguinary strife, nor is there any place in it for individual vendetta. By Revolution we mean that the present order of things which is based on manifest injustice must change. "This is our ideal and with this ideology for our inspiration we have given a fair and loud enough warning.

"Revolution is the inalienable right of mankind Freedom is the imprescriptible birth right of all. The labourer is the real sustainer of society. The sovereignty of the people is the ultimate destiny of the workers." Thus, the slogan `Inquilab Zindabad' was immortalised during our freedom struggle.

UNSHAKEABLE CONVICTION

There are various elements of Bhagat Singh's life that have contributed to his immortal legend, heroism, sacrifice, the political clarity and the ability to catch the imagination of the people. The Hindi film industry has now converted this legend into an icon. During the first few years of this century, at least six films have been made on this revolutionary. The last in this series being the very creative effort, Rang De Basanti.

The title of the film comes from the immortal song which Bhagat Singh and his associates supposedly sang as they were marching to the gallows. Though the film was come under severe criticism for its alleged projection of nihilism, the essential thrust is being missed. In actual life, many individuals may associate passionately with a political project due to various reasons and under varied circumstances. The moot question, however, is, when it comes to the crunch, whether these individuals stand up to their political convictions, or, not. This is the acid test. The protagonists in this film (including one who vacillates) embrace a sure death out of conviction and not being pushed into that position by circumstances. The option to opt out was always there. But, they choose not to do so.

This is exactly what Bhagat Singh and his associates did. They marched to death with a smile. When the hangman offers him to pray before death, he says, "I have neither fear of death nor belief in God". In terms of political belief, while firmly abjuring "the cult of the bomb and the pistol", as Bhagat Singh himself notes, they chose to throw the bomb at the Delhi assembly and murder Saunders with pistol under the firm belief that these actions would galvanise the youth to seek freedom.

Contrast this, with those political commentators who in the wake of team India's historic win of the twenty-20 cricket world cup have sought to suggest that new India's icons are far removed from the traditions of anti-imperialism that galvanised earlier generations of Indian youth.

They need to note that popular Hindi cinema is, by far, the most reliable barometer of popular Indian opinion and sentiment. During the first six years of this decade, as stated above, six mainstream successful films have been released on Bhagat Singh! This is the reaction of the overwhelmingly youthful population of India.

However, in their effort to erase the impact of the finest traditions and legacy of revolutionary struggles that shaped the contours of modern independent India, these pundits of liberalisation spare no opportunity or effort to facilitate the transformation of modern India into a subordinate ally of world imperialism today. The ongoing national debate on the Indo-US nuclear deal and the grave implications it has on India's sovereignty and independent foreign policy is, indeed, taking place in this very birth centenary year of Bhagat Singh.

The recollection of Bhagat Singh's legacy, thus, is of contemporary relevance in today's continuing battle between the three visions that we spoke of above and more importantly to safeguard and strengthen India's economic sovereignty and, thus, its pride of place in the international comity of nations.

REMEMBERING A HERO

On the birth centenary of Bhagat Singh, poet folklorist Ved Prakash Vatuk offers a detailed overview of the life and times of one of the most beloved heroes of India's freedom struggle.

Year 2007 has been an important year for Indians. India is celebrating the 150th anniversary of the first independence war. The Indian government has sanctioned 1.5 billion rupees for the country-wide show. At the same time this is the centenary year of the birthdays of Bhagat Singh, Sukhdev and Rajguru. That too is being observed throughout India-more by the people than the government. And this is the year when India completed sixty years as an independent country. All in all, this has been a year full of patriotism.

The 150th anniversary of the first war of independence is being celebrated with much pomp and show. Hundreds of cultural shows, exhibitions, seminars and other activities are organized all over India. However, in spite of all the hoopla, all these shows remained mere junkets where participation of the public remained dismal. Many of these shows were inaugurated by the people in power, like the prime minister, governors, etc., and the audience participation in most of them was by invitation only. They were all full of patriotic slogans and very little new was learnt from them. It was an exercise in hero worshipping. No objective analysis, no lessons to be learnt.

On the other hand the martyrdom of Bhagat Singh, Sukhdev and Rajguru was fondly remembered by people all over India. These martyrs have become legends in their life time-especially Bhagat Singh. In a way the martyrdom of these heroes is the climax of the revolutionary movements which freed India. In this article we will focus on Bhagat Singh and his times.

The story of Bhagat Singh can not be told just by describing his life alone. Bhagat Singh was a symbol of sacrifice for and selfless devotion to humanity. However, his story began long before he was born. Several generations before him his ancestors were involved in a struggle against colonial rule and injustice. After the death of Maharaja Ranjit Singh in 1839, the British fought to occupy Punjab. At that time one of Bhagat Singh's ancestors, Fateh Singh, fought against them. And the same Fateh Singh participated in the first independence war, which the British writers called the great mutiny of 1857. Naturally he suffered when the British survived. He lost his property.

Fateh Singh had a son named Gurbachan Singh. One of Gurbachan Singh's three sons was Arjun Singh, the grandfather of Bhagat Singh. Arjun Singh met Swami Dayananda Saraswati, founder of the Arya Samaj, when the Swami was touring Punjab. He was so impressed by the Swami that he decided to join the Arya Samaj and dedicate his life to reform Hindu society. At the same time he got involved in the freedom movement. It was he who at the time of the yanjopaveet ceremony for his grandsons-Bhagat Singh and Jagat Singh-declared, "I give these two grandsons to be sacrificed at the altar of goddess liberty." The grandsons kept their grandfather's pledge-they would indeed dedicate their life to the freedom movement.

Arjun Singh had three sons. In 1878 his eldest son Kishan Singh, father of all his grandchildren, was born. After graduating from Anglo Sanskrit High School, Jalandhar, he became a great supporter of Mahatma Hansraj, a great devotee of Swami Dayananda Saraswati. He helped victims of famines, plagues, earthquakes and floods from 1898 to 1905 in different parts of India. He came into contact with Gadar heroes like Kartar Singh Sarabha and Rash Behari Bose and completely dedicated his life to the freedom movement. He was jailed for his activities. Thus he gave his children, Bhagat Singh among them, lessons in patriotism from the day they were born.

Kishan Singh's younger brother Ajit Singh (1881-1947) also got involved in the freedom movement after graduating from the same high school. In his college days he gave talks asking fellow students to dedicate their life to the service of the nation. He was greatly influenced by Lokmanya Bal Gangadhar Tilak. He became a close friend of Sufi Amba Prasad when the latter was released from prison after serving a five-year sentence for his involvement in the freedom movement.

They along with Ajit Singh's brothers Kishan Singh and Swarn Singh and other revolutionaries founded Bharat Mata Society. Ajit Singh was one of main leaders in the peasant movement which protested the increase of irrigation taxes and the exploitation of the peasants by moneylenders. The slogan pagree sambhaal jatta-Oh peasant, guard your turban (honor)-became the mantra of the movements.

He was jailed for his participation in this movement. Later he was exiled along with Sufi Amba Prasad and Lala Lajpat Rai. Ajit Singh could return to India only after 39 years in 1947. He died on August 15, 1947, the day India became free.

This was the legacy to which Bhagat Singh was born on September 28, 1907 in this revolutionary family in the village Kharkharkalan, District Jalandhar, the day his uncle Ajit Singh came to their village after being released from jail. Since his birth he found his home to be the center of revolutionary activities, where freedom fighters congregated and debated the ways to work for India's freedom. As described above his grandfather had decided at his yajnopaveet ceremony that he was to dedicate all his life serving the nation. There is a legend about him that when Bhagat Singh was five years old, his family was sowing sugarcane in a field. He put a rifle in place of a sugarcane piece. When asked what he was doing he answered that he was sowing rifles, so that they can be used to chase the British away from India. After graduating from high school Bhagat Singh joined the National College of Lahore, an institution founded by the famous Congress leader Lala Lajpat Rai, who was called Panjab Kesari (the Lion of Punjab) by the people. This institution did not produce clerks or civil servants for the British rule, but prepared its students to fight for freedom.

Here, besides Lalaji he came into contact with Gadar hero Bhai Parmanand, who taught history. Bhai Parmanand had already served the harsh sentence in kala pani-Andaman Nicobar's Cellular Jail-where the most dangerous prisoners were sent.

It was at this time when Mahatma Gandhi launched the first non-cooperation movement. Bhagat Singh was greatly influenced by Gandhiji. But when Gandhiji withdrew the movement because of violence in Chauri Chaura, in which many policemen were murdered, Bhagat Singh, like many young men, was disappointed. To them Gandhiji's non-violence was only a tactic and not a dharma. They decided that there was only one way to free India and that was the way of armed revolution.

As we can see, Bhagat Singh was influenced by a variety of thoughts and people. In his young age he was a staunch Arya Samaji, he was greatly influenced by the Gadar movement. Its youngest hero Kartar Singh Sarabha, who was hanged by the British at the age of 19, became his political guru. He kept Sarabha's photograph in his pocket. He was greatly moved by the heroes of Kakori Case.

Its martyrs Ram Prasad Bismil, Ashfaqullah, Rajendra Lahiri and Thakur Roshan Singh inspired him immensely. The massacre of Jallianwala Bagh left a deep impression on the mind of teenage Bhagat Singh. Later he was absorbed in the study of various European revolutions which left a deep impression on him. Bhagat Singh's mind was like a house whose windows were open on all sides and all revolutionary thoughts entered in like a free breeze. Throughout his life he kept churning these ideas logically until he became a rationalist, Marxist, atheist, revolutionary willing to sacrifice his life to kindle the flame of revolution.

It was 1928. The British government, besieged by the unrest in India, decided to send the Simon Commission to India to find out what kind of reforms would appease Indians. Since there was no Indian member in the commission and since Indians were fooled so many times by the British before, Indians decided to boycott the commission.

In every city the commission went it was met with black flags and protests. "Simon go back," became the united call. When they came to Lahore on Oct. 20, 1928, a huge protest march was led by the prominent Congress leaders Madan Mohan Malviya and Panjab Kesari Lala Lajpat Rai to oppose their arrival.

The police superintendent ordered cane charge on the peaceful crowd. Lala Lajpat Rai was attacked severely and he died because of the blows showered on him on Nov. 17. The whole country was stunned by this savage blow on the most respected leader. Lalaji's last words were, "Each blow on my head will become the nail in the British rule's casket."

Bhagat Singh and his other friends, members of the Naujawan Sabha and Hindustan Socialist Republican Army, were outraged. They had to retaliate to show that Indian youths were not dead and they would show the British they would avenge the death of their beloved elderly leader. On Dec. 17, 1928, they were ready. When a red motorcycle started from the police office, they fired.

Unfortunately, the rider was not the police superintendent but his assistant. Next day the hand bills appeared on walls all over Lahore that the death of Lalaji had been avenged and the honour of the nation was upheld. Bhagat Singh escaped and with the help of his friends-Sukhdev and Durga "Bhabhi" along with his leader Chandrashekhar Azad went to Kolkata fooling the police who were everywhere.

Instead of paying attention to their grievances, the colonial government tried to suppress Indian masses even more. In order to suppress workers, who were going on strikes to demand better treatment, the government decided to introduce the Trade Dispute Bill along with another bill to curb mass movements called the Public Safety Bill. Those bills were brought before the Central Legislative Assembly. Even when the assembly rejected them the viceroy used his veto power and declared them adopted.

The declaration of the adoption of these bills was to take place on April 8, 1929. The Hindustani Socialist Republican Army decided to protest that by throwing a bomb in the Assembly. The party took inspiration from a French anarchist Auguste Vaillant (1861-1893) who threw a bomb in the French Chambers of Deputies in 1893 in revenge of the execution of his comrade Rovachol. He shouted, "It takes a loud voice to make the deaf hear." When he was hanged for his action, he shouted "Death to the bourgeoisie. Long live anarchy." Bhagat Singh changed that slogan to, "Death to imperialism. Long live revolution." When I was a child we used to shout in the rallies, Inqalab zindabad, British hakoomat ho barbad (Long live Revolution, Down with the British Government.)

HSRA was not prepared to send Bhagat Singh to throw the bomb in the Assembly. But when Sukhdev teased him that he wanted to save his neck while pretending to be a revolutionary, Bhagat Singh became agitated and insisted to Azad that he had to do that. Finally he and Batukeshwar Dutt were selected to do the job.

At the appointed time, when the bills were to be declared adopted on April 8, 1929. Bhagat Singh and Batukeshwar Dutt threw the bomb in the empty space of the assembly, declaring: "It takes a loud voice to make the dead hear. This British Government thrust upon the helpless but unwilling Indian nation is no better than an organized gang of robbers." They declared that freedom is a birth right of everyone.

The bomb created panic. The assembly was soon empty except for two or three Indian leaders, Malviya among them. Bhagat Singh and Batukeshwar Dutt did not run away. They stood and courted arrest-like brave soldiers of war.

These two episodes made Bhagat Singh a household name, a legend in his own time. Women and men composed songs. They sang them at various occasions-at weddings, while grinding corn and working in fields. Ever since I began to talk and understand I grew up singing these songs at the lap of my brother and father-both freedom fighters.

Bhagat Singh insisted that he was not a terrorist, but a revolutionist. He said again and again that individual terrorism can never bring freedom. He loved life and he and his friends were sorry that they took the life of a British policeman as a human being, but sometimes it is unavoidable to take a life of a person representing a tyrannical repressive rule.

Bhagat Singh and his comrades used the trial as a tool to further awareness of their cause. They explained their philosophy of revolution, motives of their actions and telling their friends outside what to do. Soon the government caught up with their game and they were suddenly tried by a tribunal instead of the lower court.

Again and again Bhagat Singh emphasized that he was a revolutionary. And by revolution he meant "the ultimate establishment of an order of society which may not be threatened by such breakdown and in which the sovereignty of the proloteriat should be recognized and a world federation should redeem humanity from the bondage of capitalism and misery of imperial wars." To him this revolution was an inalienable right of mankind.

To him, like Lokmanya Tilak, freedom was an imperishable birthright of all. "Revolution means complete overthrow of the existing social order and its replacement with the socialistic order."

To Bhagat Singh freedom did not mean merely replacing the white faces with black ones on the throne. Like the Gadar heroes, Bhagat Singh also wanted a casteless, classless, society free from all kinds of social and economic exploitation.

Unfortunately we pay homange to the image of Bhagat Singh who holds a pistol in his hand, not that of a true revolutionary. We don't admire him for his great love for literature, his fondness of poetry. During the time he spent in his jail cell before he was hanged, he read continuously. His study did not stop at revolutionary books or Marxist literature. He read novels by many American authors of his time. His jail notebook is full of quotations from all genres of literature and subjects-love, marriage, revolution, you name it. He must have read close to two hundred books.

Today the tragedy is that everyone wants to cash in on the martyrdom of Bhagat Singh. Even those religious institutions who did not give a damn about the Gadari babas or Bhagat Singh today want to arrange akhand path in their memory.

To me it is an insult to Bhagat Singh-a rationalist, atheist-to place his portrait next to fundamentalish Sikh separatist Jarnail Singh Bhindranwale. To me at is an insult to Bhagat Singh when the Haryana chief minister proposes to build a statue in his honour, because he was a "true Arya Samaji."

To me it is also an insult to Bhagat Singh when the armchair leftist historians want to use him to condemn Gandhiji. They blame Bhagat Singh's execution on Gandhiji.

On this score let us be clear. Did Bhagat Singh want to live? He is his own best witness for that. Like Kartar Singh Sarabha, Ram Prasad Bismil, Thakur Roshan Singh and Ashfaqullah, Bhagat Singh, too, felt that his martyrdom will serve their country better.

Bhagat Singh was so angry when his own father tried to save his life and sent a petition to the government that he rebuked his father in no uncertain terms.

He felt sorry that his father showed weakness. He told his father that he had put no defense for himself at the trial and he did not want to live devoid of his principles.

"My life is not at all worth living at the cost of my principles" Anyone who can rebuke his father in such a harsh way could have never wished anybody including Gandhiji to beg for mercy on his behalf, especially when Bhagat Singh and Sukhdev in several communications rejected Gandhi's way of thoughts.

Let me quote extensively from Bhagat Singh's statement. "I make no secret of the fact that it is but natural for me to desire to remain alive. But I can live only under certain conditions. I refuse to live in prison or parole. My name has become the focal point of the party of revolution and its sacrifices have placed me on an elevated pedestal. This pedestal is so high that if I survive by being spared I will not be able to live up to that standard. My weaknesses are not generally known and the public is unaware of them. If I manage to cheat the gallows, they will be exposed for all to see. Maybe the revolutionary fire in me will cool down. it may be even extinguished."

He further writes:

"But if I am hanged like a brave man, with a smile on my face, Indian mothers will encourage their children to emulate my example. Our hangings will substantially add to the number of martyrs in the cause of the freedom of our motherland, so much that it will be impossible any longer for the satanic powers of imperialism to resist the Revolution."

On November 30, 1930 Bhagat Singh wrote to Batukeshwar Dutt:

"(I) am anxiously waiting for the day when I will be fortunate enough to embrace the gallows for my ideals. I will climb the gallows gladly and show the world how bravely the revolutionaries can sacrifice themselves to the cause."

Bhagat Singh is a hero because of his martyrdom. When I look at the life of those heroes, who were no less heroic or deep thinkers than Bhagat Singh, but who survived gallows, I feel sad. Shiv Varma, Durga Bhabhi, Batukeshwar Dutt and many others were not remembered by the masses even when they died. How many people know about the youngest prisoner of Kakori case, who served fourteen years in prison? His name-famous Hindi novelist Manmathnath Gupta.

With all due respect to my armchair leftist historian friends, I would like to close the article by quoting Gandhi. In Gandhi's tribute to these heroes, who were hanged at 7 pm on March 23, I feel the whole nation paid tribute to them.

Gandhi wrote in Young India March 29, 1931 issue:

"Bhagat Singh and his two associates have been hanged. The Congress made many attempts to save their lives and the government entertained many hopes of it, but all has been in a vain.

"Bhagat Singh did not wish to live. He refused to apologize or even file an appeal. Bhagat Singh was not a devotee of non-violence, but he did not subscribe to the religion of violence. He took to violence due to helplessness and to defend his homeland. In his last letter Bhagat Singh wrote: 'I have been arrested while waging a war. For me there are no gallows. Put me into the mouth of a cannon and blow me off.'

"These heroes have conquered the fear of death. Let us bow to them a thousand times for their heroism."

BHAGAT SINGH AND ATHEISM

Bhagat Singh was not only one of India's greatest freedom fighters and revolutionary socialists, but also one of its early Marxist thinkers and ideologues. Unfortunately, this last aspect is relatively unknown with the result that all sorts of reactionaries, obscurantist and communalists have been wrongly and dishonestly trying to utilize for their own politics and ideologies the name of Bhagat Singh and his comrades such as Chandra Shekhar Azad.

Bhagat Singh died young at the age of 23. His political thought and practice started evolving very early when he made a quick transition from Gandhian nationalism to revolutionary terrorism. But already by 1927-28 he began to move from revolutionary terrorism to Marxism. During the years 1925 to 1928, Bhagat Singh read voraciously, devouring in particular books on the Russian Revolution and the Soviet Union, even though getting hold of such books was in itself at the time a revolutionary and difficult task. In the 1920s, Bhagat Singh was one of the most well-read persons in India on revolutionary movements, anarchism and Marxism.

He also tried to inculcate the reading and thinking habit among his fellow revolutionaries and younger comrades. He asserted during his trial before the Lahore High Court that "the sword of revolution is sharpened at the whetstone of thought".

Already by the end of 1928, he and his comrades had accepted socialism as the final object of their activities and changed the name of their organization from the Hindustan Republican Association to Hindustan Socialist Republican Association.

From now on, before his arrest in June 1929 and after, Bhagat Singh's furious march towards the acquisition and mastery of Marxism continued unabated. In the process, he brought under critical scrutiny all contemporary views, including his own, regarding the nationalist movement, the character of the contemporary worldwide revolutionary process, anarchism, socialism, violence and nonviolence, revolutionary terrorism, religion, communalism, older revolutionaries and contemporary nationalists, etc.

It is one of the greatest tragedies of our people that this giant of a brain was brought to a stop so early by the colonial authorities. In this small pamphlet* are brought before the reader two relatively unknown articles written by Bhagat Singh in jail during 1930-31, while he was awaiting the action of the gallows. In these articles, as in numerous other letters, statements and articles, he clearly emerges as a revolutionary fully committed to Marxism and capable of applying it with the full complexity of its method.

In the first article, Bhagat Singh deals with religion and atheism. He traces his own path to atheism though influenced in early childhood by religion and later by the early revolutionary terrorists such as Sachindra Nath Sanyal, whose book Bandi Jivan was a basic textbook for all revolutionaries during the 1920s. These early revolutionaries relied upon religion and mysticism to acquire the spiritual strength they revealed in their immensely courageous activities. In this article, as also in the second, Bhagat Singh shows full understanding of the approach and viewpoint of the early revolutionaries and traces the source of their religiosity. He points out that in the absence of a scientific understanding of their own political activity, they needed irrational religious beliefs and mysticism to sustain themselves spiritually, to struggle against personal temptation, to overcome depression, to be able to sacrifice their physical comforts, families and even life.

When one is constantly willing to risk one's life and make all other sacrifices, a person requires deep sources of inspiration. This necessary need was, in the case of early revolutionary terrorists, met by mysticism and religion.

But these were no longer necessary as sources of inspiration for those who understood the nature of their activity, who had advanced to a revolutionary ideology, who could struggle against oppression without artificial spiritual crutches, who could confidently and without fear mount the gallows without requiring the consolation and comfort of `eternal' salvation, who fought for freedom and emancipation of the oppressed because they "could not do otherwise".

Bhagat Singh was himself at the time waiting for the noose to fall around his neck. He knew that at such a moment it was easy to take recourse to God. "In God man can W d very strong consolation and support".

On the other hand, to depend on one's own inner strength was not easy. As he put it: "To stand upon one's own legs amid storms and hurricanes is not a child's play". He also knew that the task required immense moral strength and that the modern revolutionaries were following a moral path of a unique nature. This path led one to devote oneself to " the service of mankind and emancipation of the suffering humanity".

This was the path followed by men and women who dared "to challenge the oppressors, exploiters, and tyrants" and who, opposing "mental stagnation", insisted on thinking for themselves. As Bhagat Singh further put it: "Criticism and independent thinking are the two indispensable qualities of a revolutionary".

Bhagat Singh points out that it is not easy to live the life of a reasoning person. It is easy to take consolation or relief from blind faith. But it is our duty to try ceaselessly to live the life of reason. And that is why Bhagat Singh asserts at the end of the essay that by proclaiming himself an atheist and a realist (materialist) he was "trying to stand like a man with an erect head to the last; even on the gallows".

In Bhagat Singh's analysis of religion and its basic causation, we get a glimpse of his powerful intellect, his revolutionary commitment and his capacity to think in a historical, materialist and scientific manner.

Religion, he notes, is not merely created by the ruling and exploiting classes to deceive the people, to legitimize their class privileges and power, and to keep the people socially quiet, though it also serves that purpose in real life and therefore it becomes an ally and instrument of these classes. But religion is much more the consequence of the inability of the primitive man to fully understand his natural environment, to understand his own social activity and social organization, and to control his own life and overcome its limitations. God then becomes a useful myth. This myth was "useful to the society in the primitive age".

Moreover, "the idea of God is helpful to man in distress". God and religion enabled the helpless individual to face life with courage. "God was brought into imaginary existence to encourage man to face boldly all the trying circumstances, to meet all dangers manfully and to check and restrain his outbursts in prosperity and affluence". "Belief softens the hardships, even can make them pleasant. In God man can find very strong consolation and support". Thus, to the distressed, the betrayed and the helpless, God serves as "a father mother, sister and brother, friend and helper" 2

But, says Bhagat Singh, when science has grown and when the oppressed begin to struggle for their self-emancipation, when " man tries to stand on his own legs and become a realist (Bhagat Singh uses this word in place of rationalist and materialist)", the need for God , this artificial crutch, this imaginary saviour comes to an end. In this struggle for self-emancipation, it becomes necessary to fight against "the narrow conception of religion" as also against the belief in God. "Any man who stands for progress", says Bhagat Singh, "has to criticise, disbelieve and challenge every item of the old faith. Item by item he has to reason out every nook and corner of the prevailing faith.... A man who claims to be a realist has to challenge the whole of the ancient faith.... the first thing for him is to shatter the whole down and clear a space for the erection of a new philosophy".

Bhagat Singh's sympathetic though critical understanding of his predecessors, his capacity to place philosophic and political approaches and ideas in a historical setting, and his basic Marxist reasoning also emerge clearly in his discussion of several other issues.

In the second essay, An Introduction to The Dreamland, the poetical work of the old revolutionary Lala Ram Saran Das, sentenced to transportation for life in 1915, Bhagat Singh indirectly traces the change from the earlier `pure' nationalism, based on the single idea of overthrowing foreign domination, to a nationalism that was simultaneously committed to the total reconstitution of the existing social order. Writing more like a poet than a political-philosophical commentator, Bhagat Singh first establishes his own generation's continuity with the old revolutionaries from whom it imbibed the spirit of nationalism, love of the people and the capacity to sacrifice. He then brings out his philosophical, political and ideological differences with them.

In the very beginning of the essay, he brings out, as already discussed in an earlier section of this introduction, the difference between their reliance on mysticism and religiosity for inspiration and his own firm commitment to materialism, reason and science.

He also deals with the contemporary and complex and vexed question of violence and nonviolence. Going to the heart of the matter, he describes how the revolutionaries want to build a social order from which violence in all its forms will be eliminated, in which reason and justice will prevail and all questions will be settled by argument and education. But this is precisely what imperialists, capitalists and other exploiters will not permit. Instead, they mercilessly suppress any effort to evolve socialism through education of the people and by peaceful methods. Hence, revolutionaries have to adopt violence as " a necessary item of their programme". The entire question is brilliantly summed up when Bhagat Singh says that the revolutionaries "have to resort to violent means as a terrible necessity". Once socialist power is established, methods of education and persuasion would be employed to develop society; force would be used only to remove the obstacles.

In his essay on Atheism also he had put the issue in the same way. The new generation of revolutionaries had replaced "the Romance of the violent methods alone which was so prominent amongst our predecessors", and had come to believe that the "use of force (was) justifiable when resorted to as a matter of terrible necessity", while "nonviolence as policy (was) indispensable for all mass movements". Thus the revolutionaries do not glorify violence; revolution is not based on the cult of violence. At the same time, revolutionaries do not shun the necessary violence. Where history and the ruling classes force upon them, they take recourse to it as a "terrible necessity" in order to overthrow the existing social order.

Bhagat Singh simultaneously sees the utopian character of much of early revolutionary thinking, the positive historic role that utopians play in certain stages of social movements and social development, and the inevitable decline of utopias once the revolutionary movement starts acquiring a scientific outlook and philosophy on the basis of "scientific Marxian Socialism":

Bhagat Singh deals at length with one aspect of utopian thought: How to combine mental and physical labour? He accepts that elimination of the gap between the two is basic to the building of a socialist society. But this elimination, he feels, cannot be brought about by mechanical and utopian means suggested by Ram Saran Das such as making all mental workers do physical and mental labour for 4 hours a day: The nature of physical and mental labour is different.

The root of the problem lies in the existing inequality between the two. The answer lies in treating both as productive labour and opposing the notion that mental workers are superior to manual workers. Lastly, Bhagat Singh was a critical revolutionary in the best traditions of Marx, Engels and Lenin. Asking young men to read The Dreamland, he warns: "Do not read it to follow blindly and take for granted what is written in it. Read it, criticise it, think over it, and try to formulate your own ideas with its help".

RARE DOCUMENTS OF AND ABOUT BHAGAT SINGH

*Letter to Grandfather Arjun Singh in Urdu on 27-7-1919 on Post Card**

Om

Respected Dada Ji, namaste

I state humbly that I am well and wish your well being from Shri Narayan ji. The state of affairs here is that our six monthly exams. Are over, which started in July. Many boys failed in Maths., so the math. Exam will be held again on 9th August. Everything else is fine. When are you coming. Tell Bhayia ji (brother) that I have cleared all papers in six monthly examinations. Namaste to Mataji (mother) chachi (aunt), elder aunt. Kultar Singh (younger brother) had fever on 24th night and 25th July evening. Now he is o.k. Do not worry about anything.

Yours obediently

Bhagat Singh

- Note of Translator (Chaman Lal)

- This is second letter of Bhagat Singh to his grandfather, which is now available. First available letter of Bhagat Singh is also written to his grandfather in Urdu only. Bhagat Singh's handwriting is available in three languages-Urdu, Punjabi and English. He was prolific writer in Hindi too.

Unpublished Letters of Bhagat Singh

Chaman Lal*

Letter to aunt Hukam Kaur, widow of uncle Swarn Singh, in Punjabi language on 24.10.1921 (On Post Card)**

1 Omkar Lahore

My Dear Aunt (Chachi ji) Namaste

I had gone to attend a rally to Lyalpur. I wanted to come to village, but Bapuji (Father) did not allow, so I could not come to village. Please forgive me, if I did any wrong. Portrait of Chacha Ji (Uncle Swarn Singh) is ready. I wanted to bring it along, but it was not complete then, so please forgive me. Kindly reply early. My reverence to elder aunt. My reverence to mother. Namaste to Kulbir and Kultar (younger brothers).

Your son

Bhagat Singh

**Translator's (Chaman Lal) note: This letter was written by Bhagat Singh at the age of fourteen years to his younger aunt in Punjabi. Bhagat Singh had learnt Punjabi language in 1921 by his own efforts, inspired by Nankana Sahib Morcha, the volunteers of which passed through his village and Bhagat Singh used to serve food (langar) to them.

He was not taught Punjabi in school, where he had good command over Urdu, which was the medium of instruction in those days.

Letters of Bhagat Singh

Letter to Lahore authorities to release belongings. Contents of the letter are self explanatory. Letter is typed on Bhagat Singh's father S. Kishan Singh's letterhead, who was an insurance agent in Lahore. (Chaman Lal)

Sir,

I was arrested on 29th of May 1927 under section 302 I.P.C.and was detained in the Police custody for five weeks. I was released on bail on 4th of July 1927. Since then I have never been called by the police or any court to stand my trial under the said section (written in hand) and so I presume that you have completed your investigation and found nothing against me and (written in hand) have practically withdrawn the case. Under the circumstances I request you to kindly return all the things that were taken from my body at the time of my arrest and to inform me when and where to see you for the said purpose.

An early favour will highly oblige.

Your etc. (Written in hand)

Sd/ Sadiq Ali Shah

S.I.

D/ 2-5-29 (written in hand)

Read out, admitted in evidence and added to Special Tribunal Lahore Conspiracy Case File.

J.Coldstream

Judge

Special Tribunal

*Letters of Bhagat Singh-4**

This letter was written to close personal friend by Bhagat Singh on post card in English, which has stamp of Lahore post office of 24th February 1930. This letter is also self explanatory. (Chaman Lal)

My Dear Jai Deo!

I hope you would have heard of our abandoning the fast after 16 days, and you can guess how greatly do we feel the necessity of your help at this stage.

We received a few oranges yesterday but no interview was held. Our case has been adjourned for a fortnight. Therefore kindly arrange to send a tin of ' Craven Cigarettes-A' and a tin of ghee immediately. And a few oranges alongwith a few rasgullas will also be welcomed. Mr. Dutta is facing hard times without cigarettes. Now you can understand the urgent nature of our needs.

Thanking you in advance.

Yours Sincerely

Bhagat Singh

Address-To, Mr. Jai Deo Prasad Gupta, c/o The provincial Congress committee Bradlaugh Hall, Lahore

* All underlines by Bhagat Singh

Letters of Bhagat Singh-5

This letter is also written to Jaidev Gupta on 26th May 1930 in English. The stamp of Lahore post office is of 28/5/1930 on post card. This letter also needs to explanation. (Chaman Lal)

937 D/ Lahore Central Jail

26/5/30 (jail no.) Lahore

Dear Brother Jai deo,

Today again I am writing this letter to give you some trouble which I hope you will not mind. Please see if you can arrange to send one fleet foot shoe for me. I think No. 9-10 will do. Chapli is too uncomfortable. Also please try to send it on Friday or Saturday through kulbir when he will be coming for an interview. Really it is very sad that I have not so far been allowed any interview with you.

Had this impasse in our trial not occurred I will have repeatedly reminded the authorities to sanction your interview. Anyhow by the time this question is settled I will again try to get the interview sanctioned. Well I hope you will send the shoe without fail and without delay. These days I have got only one book with me-a very dry one. Please see if you can send a couple of recent interesting novels. Please remember me to all friends.

Yours Sincerely

Bhagat Singh

D/ 26/5/30

Address---

Mr. jai Deo Prasad Gupta c/o S. Kishan Singh

Bradlaugh Hall, Lahore

THE LEGACY

No matter, if your Government tries and succeeds in winning over the leaders of the upper strata of the Indian society through petty concessions and compromises and thereby causes a temporary demoralization in the main body of the forces. The war shall continue. It may assume different shapes at different times. It may become open, hidden, purely agitational, or fierce life and death struggle. The choice of the course, whether bloody or comparatively peaceful, rests with you. Choose whichever you like. But that war shall be incessantly waged with new vigour, greater audacity and unflinching determination till the Socialist Republic is established. Till the present social order is completely replaced by a new social order, based on social prosperity and thus every sort of exploitation ends and humanity is ushered into the era of genuine and permanent peace. The days of capitalist and imperialist exploitation are numbered. The war neither began with us nor is it going to end with our lives. It is the inevitable consequence of the historic events and the existing environments.

These words were among the last penned by Shaheed Bhagat Singh before he walked to the gallows, confident that the people of India would continue, and finally win "the war."This letter was addressed to the Governor General in India, the tip of the spear of British colonialism in the country.

Bhagat Singh had been sentenced to death for killing a British officer as revenge for the brutal assault on Lala Lajpat Rai, that led to the old freedom fighter's death. Along with his comrades-brothers as he called them-Sukhdev and Rajguru, he was to be hanged for treason against a King he had never accepted. As the world celebrates the hundredth birth anniversary of this great martyr, these words still hold a message-and a challenge for the youth of today.

India gained independence from the British Empire in 1947, but the dreams of Bhagat Singh and his feisty comrades, as seen by the words of this letter, have remained unrealised.

At the young age of 24, on the cusp of martyrdom, he was letting the British know that he understood the power games they were playing with the Indian elite. He understood that the Indian National Congress led by Mahatma Gandhi was compromising the vision of freedom that ordinary Indians held through deals with the British. Deals through which the Congress "led" the independence struggle only to borrow the former coloniser's Westminster model of "democracy" and embrace the capitalist laws that were behind the country's plunder for two centuries that Britain ruled over us. Three questions come to mind on reading this crucial letter.

How did a young Bhagat Singh, understand the present and foresee the future in a manner that appears nothing short of clairvoyance? The answer lies in the science of Marxism-Leninism, which he had ardently studied, discussed and debated.

He had sacrificed his life, and was facing death for striving for a revolution that was nowhere in the immediate horizon. Wouldn't it be natural for him to, at least now, question the success of the revolution he dearly believed in? What if he had been wrong all along? How could he continue to call the revolution "inevitable"? Once again the answer lies in Marxism Leninism. The science had taught Bhagat Singh that the revolution, and the victory of socialism over capitalism, could not be stopped. Nor had he failed in his mission. Far from it-every little detail of the period prior to his death had been carefully planned and skilfully executed.

He and his comrades in the Hindustan Republican Socialist Association had shaken the British empire to a stage that they had to pass the Arms Act-meant to curb the spread of weapons among the revolutionaries-through an ordinance.

With the whole of India closely following the trial in the British officer's murder, Bhagat Singh and his comrades used the open court as a forum to speak to Indians, and ignite a revolutionary spirit in them. When the British got wise to the aims of the revolutionaries, they were forced to drop the charade of "law and justice", and hurriedly convicted and sentenced them while banning them from court.

The revolutionaries were thus able to expose the tall claims of justice that the British claimed to uphold.

A final question remains though. What about Bhagat Singh's firm conviction that "the days of capitalist and imperialist exploitation are limited?" It has been over seven decades and both capitalism and imperialism appear to be going strong. Could the Shaheed have been wrong in this assessment?

Not at all. In fact, Leninism teaches us that imperialism is the last stage of capitalism, it is capitalism that is rotting. And over the decades since Bhagat Singh wrote this letter, the moribund features of imperialism has only become further accentuated. All the illusions promoted by the ideologues of capitalism of a world without wars, of capitalism acquiring a "human face", of capitalism without the plunder of nations and peoples, have been proven to be just that-illusions to somehow safeguard the imperialist system from the revolution. It follows that a system that has reached stagnancy must go. And like Bhagat Singh, it is the youth who have to once again take the initiative.

BHAGAT SINGH-AN UNSUNG HERO

In a country dominated by the word "Gandhi", there are innumerable other unsung heroes of the freedom movement of this country.

One such hero is Shaheed Bhagat Singh.

Bhagat Singh (born on September 28, 1907) was one of the most famous youth revolutionaries of the Indian Independence Movement, who at the very young age of 13 was a part of Mahatma Gandhi's noncooperation movement against the British. Bhagat Singh was deeply affected by the 1919 Jallianwala Bagh Massacre and believed that violence should be replied back only by violence. He was also disappointed when Gandhi called back the noncooperation movement following the Chauri Chaura incident.

Bhagat Singh's freedom movement reached a turning point when the British killed the veteran activist Lala Lajpat Rai in a police lathi charge while he was leading a peaceful protest against the Simon's commission for not including any Indian representatives in the commission. Lala Lajpat Rai succumbed to the injuries of the lathi charge within a month after the incident. Bhagat Singh was deeply hurt by the death of Lala Lajpat Rai and in a bid to take revenge he and other revolutionaries (Shivaram Rajguru, Sukhdev and Jai Gopal) plotted a bid to kill Scott, the police chief. However in a case of mistaken identity, they killed Saunder, a deputy superintendent of police. After that when the British Govt brought the Defence of India Act, giving more power to the police inspite of the act being voted down in the council by one vote, Bhagat Singh's organization decided to protest against this act by exploding non-lethal bomb in the corridors of the assembly and by throwing leaflets containing the message 'It takes a loud voice to make the deaf hear'. Singh and Batukeshwar Dutt executed these actions.

Following the explosions, Singh and Dutt, who were still in the corridors of the assembly chanting 'Inquilab Zindabad' were arrested. British also came to know about the assassination of Scott by him, and as a result the British Government hanged Bhagat Singh to death. Unfortunately, no real attempts were made by the nonviolent movement led by Gandhi to get Bhagat Singh and his associates released. Sukhdev who was also hanged along with Bhagat, had written a letter to Gandhi just before their hanging, protesting against Gandhi's disapproval of their revolutionary tactics. The same year/month (1931 March) in which Bhagat and his fellow comrades (Rajguru and Sukhdev) were hanged, Gandhi signed a pact with Lord Irwin, the then viceroy of India and got all his followers released, who were arrested by the British earlier for participating in Gandhi's civil disobedience movement.

A Radical Legacy

Bhagat Singh and associates radicalised the national movement by broadening its scope and creating space for popular interventions.

Bhagat Singh and his comrades belong to those momentous decades in Indian history-the late 1920s and 30s-when options were more open, popular aspirations ran high and "revolution" and "national liberation" were current in the political vocabulary and intrinsic to the national agenda of a well-defined stream within the national movement. They were among that remarkable set of people whose deeds made them natural heroes and who, by their words and actions, exposed the weaknesses of the national movement in those very years that it was becoming a mass movement. That in the process they also influenced it very deeply has largely been erased not just from official recordings of India's political heritage, but even in the general recalling of its history. Despite all the emphasis on people's history, current historiography on that period has simply failed to give them their due. It is time the record was set straight.

Bhagat Singh and his comrades-like all other progressive groups and individuals of the time-cannot be understood without reference to the historic impact of the Russian revolution of 1917 on India. No event before it had such an impact on the minds of the people in the colonies. Suddenly it seemed that it was possible to throw off the yoke of oppression. Nations could be free, sovereign and equal, and people within those nations could be free, sovereign and equal. National liberation, world revolution, popular interests and socialism could be talked of in one breath and this was the inspiration and the message of those decades. Bhagat Singh and his comrades and all other progressive, socialist and communist groups in the country were inspired by this heritage of the Russian revolution, and would not have done much of what they were able to without it. Among them no single individual did as much by his words and deeds in the late 1920s to communicate this message within the national movement as did Bhagat Singh.

It can be easily said that Bhagat Singh and his comrades and the organisations to which they belonged, the Naujawan Bharat Sabha and the Hindustan Socialist Republican Association, played a central and foundational role in popularising the left-radical agenda within the national movement and giving visibility to this agenda in the national political life of those years.

The few books brought out this year underline the fact that Bhagat Singh and his comrades were a significant stream within the left, and by their heroism and deeds played a central role in both broadening the scope of the Congress-led movements and in popularising the slogans and goals of the Communist movement in India. One cannot think that ideas of revolution and socialism could have become as popular as they did then, or that Gandhi could have felt the challenge that he did then, were it not for the political intervention of Bhagat Singh and his comrades and their firm alignment with Communist politics.

They left their impress on the Congress politics of their time. It is difficult to imagine a Congress 'Left' or the polarisation within the Congress without their activities and campaigns. It is they among the Communist groups who succeeded in creating an unease and embarrassment for Jawaharlal Nehru and Subhash Chandra Bose, which exposed the divergence between word and deed among the best of Congresspersons. They contributed to inspiring many to come out of the Congress, even as the more right-wing leadership of the Congress was upholding policies of the organisation that defended the class interests of the bourgeoisie and landlords.

The churning within the Congress was played out at all its conferences, where resolutions critical of the activities of Bhagat Singh and his comrades could be passed only by very thin majorities, and only at the personal insistence of Gandhi himself.

Bhagat Singh and his comrades publicly put forward a scathing critique of Gandhi and the Congress politics. They worked along with the Congress for a time as other Communists did, and pressured the leadership to adopt many resolutions that were beyond the scope of the Congress agenda or the Congress was not prepared to accept until then. This they did largely by their independent campaigns and examples of heroism, which the Congress could not match.

They participated wholeheartedly in the Non-Cooperation Movement, and members of the Naujawan Bharat Sabha and the Hindustan Socialist Republican Association manned the committees at the district, tehsil and taluka levels in many parts of north India during the Civil Disobedience Movement, infusing a more radical content into it.

They aligned these movements with slogans pertaining to peasants' and workers' demands. In this way, they broadened the scope and canvas of the national movement, and created space for popular interventions and initiatives.

They exposed the hollowness of the demand of dominion status for India and put forward the idea of complete independence and opposition to imperialism in general.

They formed the backbone of the popular mobilisations against the Simon Commission and political repression of the British. They went to the people with an alternative not only to Congress politics, but also its organisations. Bhagat Singh became as popular as Gandhi, and more popular than him among the youth. The revolutionaries' slogans and cries for revolution found an echo among all sections of people almost in all corners of the country. Every heart beat for them during the years of their trial, confinement and execution at the hands of the British. Gandhi's compromise with the British on their executions made him unpopular, and he was greeted with negative slogans and black flags wherever he went. Cries of revolution rent the air even in Congress platforms and conferences.

The gap between their ideological influence and organisational achievements is typical of the early stages of revolutionary and left movements throughout history, and does not detract from their contribution to national politics and national culture.

It is pertinent that the Hindustan Republican Association was formed in 1924 and its manifesto 'The Revolutionary' declared its commitment to secularism and revolution in 1925, precisely when Hindu communalism was consolidating itself in the form of the Rashtriya Swayamsewak Sangh (RSS) and the Hindu Mahasabha. In 1926, the Hindustan Republican Association had transformed itself into the Hindustan Socialist Republican Association, by identifying itself with socialist ideals and laying claim to the heritage of the world communist movement.

At a time when the Congress allowed dual membership to RSS and Hindu Mahasabha members, the Hindustan Socialist Republican Association made a trenchant critique of religion and communal mobilisations. Even if they could not succeed in organising workers and peasants, they brought their issues into the consciousness of the youth.

They popularised new symbols and slogans in public fora and mass politics. They linked national liberation with revolution in the minds of large sections of youth.

Red flags became common and socialism became part of the vocabulary of the national movement. Cries of Vande Mataram and Bharat Mata were substituted by Hindustan Zindabad and Inquilab Zindabad. New traditions were created by them with pamphleteering, study circles and agitational programmes, and celebrations and commemorations of the Russian revolution, the Irish struggle, Kakori Day, May Day and Lenin Day.

They translated into popular propaganda the economic analysis of British imperialism by Dadabhai Nauroji and R.C. Dutt. They were in close touch with many members of the Communist Party, and provided public platforms to Congresspersons, both radicals such as Subhash Chandra Bose and others such as Nehru, and Communist Party members such as S.A. Dange and Philip Spratt. In doing all this, they radicalised the national movement.

The Naujawan Bharat Sabha and its offshoots were the first left-wing mass organisations to attain national fame and public visibility, which encouraged young people from middle class and lower middle class backgrounds to work for ideals that transcended their own class interests. They initiated campaigns and networks that created huge space for Left politics at a mass level, particularly in Punjab and United Provinces, and some other parts of north India. Their resolutions, deliberations, emphasis on study and struggle, anti-imperialism, identification of national interests with those of workers and peasants, and their association of sacrifice with social radicalism rather than religion have left behind an ideological legacy and organisational forms that have endured.

From the Jail Notebook

Theory of Divine Rights of Kings

[Patriarchal Theory]

In this very age when great many thinkers were thus propounding these principles of 'Sovereignty of the People', there were other theorists, who tried to prove that kingdom(s) being enlarged families, the patriarchal authority of the head of a household was transferred by primogenitary descent to the representative of the first sovereign who could be proved to have reigned over any nation.

Monarchy was therefore presumed to rest on an indefeasible right, and the king was held responsible to God alone! This was known as "Divine Rights of Kings!" This was known as the "Patriarchal Theory!"

Thomas Hobbes: In his various works written in 1642-1650-1651, he combined the doctrine of the unlimited authority of the sovereign, with the rival doctrine of an original compact of the people. Hobbes' defence of absolutism-passive obedience-was secular and rationalistic rather than theological. He regarded the happiness of the community (as a whole) as the great end of government.

Man an unsociable animal!

Perpetual danger forces them to form state!

Hobbes' philosophy is cynical. According to him a man's impulses are naturally directed to his own preservation and pleasure and he cannot aim at anything but their gratification. Therefore man is unsociable by nature! He says "in the natural state every man is at war with his fellows; and the life of everyone is in danger, solitary, poor, unsafe brutish and short."** It is the fear of this sort of life that impelled them to political union. Since mere pact wouldn't do, hence the establishment of 'supreme common power the govt.' 'Conquest' or 'acquisition' and 'institution' the only basis of all states

Society is founded by "acquisition" i.e. by conquest or "institution" viz. by mutual contract or compact. In the latter case once the sovereign authority is established all must obey. Anybody rebelling must perish. He should be destroyed.

Unlimited Authority of the Sovereign!

He gives the rights of Legislature, Judicature and Executive-one and all to the sovereign. To be effective, he writes, 'the sovereign power must be unlimited, irreclaimable and indivisible. Unlimited power may indeed give rise to mischief, but the worst of these is not so bad as civil war or anarchism.

In all likelihood, these are not quotations, but Bhagat Singh's own observations.

While the second part of the quote is from Leviathan, the first is Bhagat Singh's (or someone else's) paraphrasing. The Leviathan itself does not contain these words. Indeed, it is interesting that Hobbes hardly ever uses the terms 'natural state' or 'state of nature'.

5

Bhagat Singh and National Movement

Human history from the times of Charvaka and Spartacus is illuminated with a galaxy of shining martyrs who have died for noble and progressive causes dearer to them than their own lives. In the modern age, the greatest martyrs have been those who laid down their lives fighting the barbaric scourge of imperialism.

On a world scale, the life and work of Che Guevara, who along with Fidel Castro led the Cuban Revolution, and his death at the hands of American imperialism in the jungles of Bolivia on October 9, 1967 while he was spreading the call of revolution in Latin America, has become a powerful beacon in the anti-imperialist struggle.

On a sub-continental scale, the life and work of Bhagat Singh and his death by hanging at Lahore at the hands of British imperialism on March 23, 1931, has been a great saga of inspiration to all those who cherish sovereignty, secularism and socialism-ideals for which Bhagat Singh and his comrades fought valiantly to the end.

On March 23, 2006, the country observed the 75th anniversary of martyrdom of Bhagat Singh, Rajguru and Sukhdev, and a little earlier on February 27, the 75th anniversary of martyrdom of their equally illustrious comrade-in-arms, Chandrashekhar Azad.

From September 28, 2006, we begin the celebration of the Birth Centenary Year of Bhagat Singh, a powerful symbol of the still ongoing struggle of the people of India against imperialism, capitalism, feudalism, communalism and casteism-a struggle that is infinitely more complex but no less urgent today than it was in Bhagat Singh's time.

THE TURNING POINT: CHAURI CHAURA

In the backdrop of the Jallianwala Bagh massacre of 1919, the Non-Cooperation Movement announced by Mahatma Gandhi in 1920 and his declaration of "Swaraj in One Year" galvanized the entire country as never before. "This satanic government cannot be mended, it must be ended," was the battle cry of the people. Millions of people all over the country came out on the streets to oppose the British regime. For the first time since 1857, the peasantry joined the struggle in strength. It linked burning agrarian issues like taxes, rent, eviction by landlords etc. to the struggle for independence. The support of the Congress to the Khilafat movement also drew the Muslim masses into the struggle in huge numbers and remarkable Hindu-Muslim unity was witnessed everywhere in the course of the movement.

Bipan Chandra has recorded that among the participants in the nonviolent satyagraha were Bhagat Singh, Chandrashekhar Azad, Surya Sen, Jogesh Chandra Chatterjee, Sukhdev, Jatin Das, Bhagwati Charan Vohra, Yashpal, Shiv Verma, Gaya Prasad and Jaidev Kapoor. Some of the armed freedom fighters in Bengal had, in fact, promised Mahatma Gandhi to suspend their activities to give a fair chance for the success of the nonviolent movement.

Mahatma Gandhi's sudden and arbitrary withdrawal of the nationwide movement in February 1922 after the events in Chauri Chaura in UP came like a bolt from the blue. It left the country dumbfounded. The peasants of Chauri Chaura were fighting both imperialism and landlordism, when many were shot and killed by the British police. Enraged, they burnt down the thana where the police fled to take shelter. 22 policemen were killed.

But Mahatma Gandhi did not stop at only withdrawing the nationwide movement. An urgent meeting of the Congress Working Committee was convened at Bardoli in Gujarat on February 11-12, 1922, which not only endorsed the withdrawal but also passed the following resolution: "The Working Committee advises Congress workers and organizations to influence the ryots (peasants) that the withdrawing of rent payments to the zamindars is contrary to the Congress resolutions and injurious to the best interests of the country. The Working Committee assures the zamindars that the Congress movement is in no way intended to attack their legal rights, and that even where the ryots have grievances, the Committee desires that redress be sought by mutual consultation and arbitration."

This step aborted the onward march of the peasantry towards an agrarian revolution. It also laid the firm basis for the bourgeois-landlord class alliance led by the Congress, both before and after Independence.

In his work A History of Indian Freedom Struggle, E.M.S. Namboodiripad summed up Mahatma Gandhi's leadership of the freedom struggle: "Thus, it became clear that Gandhi was a leader who could mobilize people for struggle on such a scale that not a single political leader, including Tilak, could so far do, and at the same time, suspend the struggle in the name of 'violence on the part of people' which no other leader dared to do. These two aspects of the Gandhian form of struggle were evident at every subsequent stage of the freedom struggle. It is needless to state whom or which class these two aspects of the Gandhian form of struggle served." The withdrawal of the Non-Cooperation Movement in 1922 had two salient effects. The great demoralization in the ranks of the people was exploited to the hilt by agents of the British rulers to whip up communal riots all over the country. The prospects of an agrarian revolution that would have cemented communal unity were dashed to pieces.

It is no accident that the Muslim League and the Hindu Mahasabha were both revived in 1923 and the Rashtriya Swayamsevak Sangh (RSS) was formed in 1925. According to the Simon Commission Report, 112 major communal riots broke out in the country between 1922 and 1927. The old Hindu-Muslim animosities were raked up on both sides in a rabid fashion. The Muslim masses were never again to join the freedom struggle in such large numbers under the Congress banner. In fact, by 1937, the communal divide would widen even further, leading to the catastrophic partition of India. The second effect was the deep frustration in the ranks of the young and radical freedom fighters and their inevitable return to their armed activities. We have seen that many of the young revolutionaries had sincerely taken part in the nonviolent satyagraha, but they were greatly disillusioned by the sudden and unwarranted withdrawal of the struggle.

Bhagat Singh, in his last testament To Young Political Workers written in February 1931, crystallizes his conclusions from the events of the early 1920s, "The real revolutionary armies are in the villages and in factories, the peasantry and the labourers. But our bourgeois leaders do not and cannot dare to tackle them. The sleeping lion once awakened from its slumber shall become irresistible even after the achievement of what our leaders aim at. After his first experience with the Ahmedabad labourers in 1920 Mahatma Gandhi declared: 'We must not tamper with the labourers. It is dangerous to make political use of the factory proletariat' (The Times, May 1921). Since then, they never dared to approach them. There remains the peasantry. The Bardoli resolution of 1922 clearly defines the horrors the leaders felt when they saw the gigantic peasant class rising to shake off not only the domination of an alien nation but also the yoke of the landlords. It is there that our leaders prefer surrender to the British than to the peasantry."

IMPACT OF THE RUSSIAN REVOLUTION

In sharp contrast to the compromising leadership of the national movement in India, the impact of the victorious socialist revolution in Russia under the leadership of Lenin and the Bolshevik Party was being felt in India at around the same time. The first volume of the History of the Communist Movement in India prepared by the History Commission of the CPI(M) Central Committee gives an account of how the Russian Revolution and the programme of the Bolsheviks was welcomed by all three 'extremist' leaders of the Congress, viz. Bipin Chandra Pal, Bal Gangadhar Tilak and Lala Lajpat Rai, by outstanding literary figures like Premchand and Kazi Nazrul Islam, and also by leading nationalist newspapers throughout the country.

The victory of the Russian Revolution had an even bigger impact on young armed freedom fighters in India and abroad. Its three sterling contributions were: (a) it infused confidence in Indian revolutionaries that imperialism and the exploiting classes could be overthrown, (b) it brought on to the agenda the economic and social content of Indian independence, (c) it provoked a serious study of Marxism and Communist principles.

It was as a sequel to the Russian Revolution that the Communist Party of India (CPI) was formed at Tashkent on October 17, 1920. This was gradually followed by the emergence of small and scattered communist groups, mainly in Calcutta, Bombay, Madras, Lahore and Kanpur. The Communists began to rally the people against British rule and simultaneously started organizing workers and peasants. In the Ahmedabad session of the Congress in 1921, Maulana Hasrat Mohani and Swami Kumaranand moved a resolution to define Swaraj as complete freedom from foreign rule. Gandhi opposed the demand and the resolution was defeated. Right from its inception, the CPI raised the slogan of complete independence before any other political party or group in India.

In the same Ahmedabad session, the newly-formed Communist Party distributed its Manifesto in the form of an appeal to all Congress delegates. It called for the complete severance of all connections with the British empire and full support to the struggles of the working class and the peasantry. The Manifesto said, "If the Congress would lead the revolution, which is shaking India to its very foundation, let it not put its faith in mere demonstrations and temporary wild enthusiasm. Let it make the immediate demands of the trade unions its own demands; let it make the programme of the Kisan Sabhas its own programme; and the time will soon come when the Congress will not be stopped by any obstacle; it will be backed by the irresistible strength of the entire population, consciously fighting for their material interests."

Two weeks after the Tashkent meeting where the CPI was formed, but having no direct connection with that event, the All India Trade Union Congress (AITUC) was formed on October 31, 1920, at its first conference in Bombay.

H.R.A. AND THE KAKORI CONSPIRACY CASE

It was in the background of all these historic events that Bhagat Singh reached Kanpur in 1924. There he went to his father's friend Ganesh Shankar Vidyarthi, a prominent Congress leader and the editor of Pratap. Though Vidyarthi was himself a Gandhian, his house was a common meeting place for socialists, communists and other revolutionaries. It was here that Bhagat Singh met Chandrashekhar Azad, Batukeshwar Dutt, Jogesh Chandra Chatterjee, Shiv Verma, Bejoy Kumar Sinha and others. In Kanpur, he continued to read voraciously and completed his study of Karl Marx's Capital. He wrote and distributed nationalist and revolutionary leaflets amongst the masses. It was in his six months stay at Kanpur that he joined the Hindustan Republican Association (HRA).

The HRA had been formed in 1923-within a year of Chauri Chaura and its aftermath-by Sachindranath Sanyal, who was transported for life in the Banaras Conspiracy Case and later released. He was a close associate of Rash Behari Bose. Sanyal's book written in jail, Bandi Jeevan, was highly acclaimed by all armed freedom fighters of that era. Sanyal had written the Manifesto of the HRA, which was distributed in all major cities of North India on the night between December 31, 1924 and January 1, 1925. He had also prepared the HRA Constitution, which came to be known as the Yellow Paper. The HRA Manifesto, which was titled The Revolutionary, was a powerful piece that began thus, "Chaos is necessary to the birth of a new star. And the birth of life is accompanied by agony and pain. India is also taking a new birth, and is passing through that inevitable chaos and agony. Indians shall play their destined role, when all calculations shall prove futile, when the wise and the mighty shall be bewildered by the simple and the weak, when great empires shall crumble down and new nations shall arise and surprise humanity with the splendour and glory which shall be all its own."

It then set out its aim: "The immediate object of the revolutionary party in the domain of politics is to establish a federal Republic of United States of India by an organized and armed revolution. The final constitution of this Republic shall be framed and declared at a time when the representatives of India shall have the power to carry out their decision. But the basic principles of this Republic will be universal suffrage and abolition of all systems which make the exploitation of man by man possible, e.g. the railways and other means of transportation and communication, the mines and other kinds of very great industries such as the manufacture of steel and ships, all these shall be nationalized."

Further, "The revolutionary party is not national but international in the sense that its ultimate object is to bring harmony in the world by respecting and guaranteeing the diverse interests of the different nations. It aims not at competition but at cooperation between the different nations and states and in this respect it follows the footsteps of the great Indian rishis of the glorious past and of Bolshevik Russia in the modern age."

The HRA Manifesto and Constitution had their strengths and their weaknesses, which were neatly summarized by Satyendra Narayan Mazumdar in his book In Search of A Revolutionary Ideology and A Revolutionary Programme as follows, "The above two documents may be described as typical of the thinking of those revolutionaries who were then being attracted towards communism, yet could not completely overcome the influence of romantic revolutionism." While showing a positive but confused inclination towards socialism, the Manifesto also had marked elements of mysticism.

Funds for procuring arms and ammunition were raised by the HRA, among other methods, by committing dacoities. Some minor dacoities went unnoticed. But on August 9, 1925, the HRA revolutionaries stopped a train at Kakori near Lucknow and broke a government safe carrying a modest amount of Rs 4679.

Despite warning the train passengers not to come out so that no harm would come to them, one person came out and was accidentally killed. The British government cracked down brutally, instituted the Kakori Conspiracy Case and managed to arrest most of the participants in the dacoity. Ram Prasad Bismil, Ashfaqullah Khan and Thakur Roshan Singh were hanged on December 19, 1927 and Rajendra Lahiri two days earlier on December 17, 1927. Sachindranath Sanyal and Jogesh Chandra Chatterjee got life imprisonment, while 11 others got various terms in jail. Only Chandrashekhar Azad and Kundan Lal Gupta escaped arrest. This was a big blow to the HRA, but it recovered due to the great efforts of Chandrashekhar Azad and the second line of leadership comprising Shiv Verma and others.

The Kakori martyrs became a legend throughout India. On the day of his execution, Ram Prasad Bismil declared, "We shall be born again, shall meet again and shall jointly fight once again for the cause of the motherland as comrades-in-arms." Ashfaqullah Khan told his nephew the day before his execution, "You must remember that the Hindu community has dedicated and great souls like Khudiram and Kanailal. To me, this is my good fortune that, belonging to the Muslim community, I have acquired the privilege of following in the footsteps of those great martyrs." The death-defying song they sang to the gallows became part of the lexicon of the freedom struggle. This song was:

Sarfaroshi ki tamanna ab hamare dil mein hai,
Dekhna hai zor kitna baju-e katil mein hai.
(We have now a longing in our hearts to put our heads on to the bidding,
It is to be seen how much strength the executioner has in his arms.)

NAUJAWAN BHARAT SABHA

Before the Kakori dacoity, in early 1925, Bhagat Singh had gone back to Lahore when his father assured him that he would not be married off against his wishes. He started political work and set up the Lahore branch of the HRA, but had to shift to Delhi for six months in 1925 to evade arrest. In Delhi, he worked with the daily Veer Arjun. In late 1925, he went to Kanpur to take part in abortive attempts to free the Kakori prisoners from jail and soon returned to Lahore.

Here, Bhagat Singh along with Bhagwati Charan Vohra, Sukhdev and Ram Krishan took the lead in forming a militant youth organization called the Naujawan Bharat Sabha (NBS) in March 1926. Ram Krishan was elected its president and Bhagat Singh its secretary. Its members also included eminent personalities like Saifuddin Kitchlew, Satyapal, Mir Abdul Majid, Sardul Singh Caveeshar and the poet Lal Chand Falak.

The founding of the NBS as an open wing of the revolutionaries to carry out political work among the youth, peasants and workers was a very significant step in the political and ideological journey of Bhagat Singh. It showed his growing Marxist conviction that popular broad-based mass movements alone could lead to a successful revolution. This mass approach is reflected in the Aims and Manifesto of the NBS, partly quoted below.

The NBS soon opened branches at Lahore, Amritsar and other cities and towns in Punjab and, later, at Karachi and Peshawar as well. Bhagat Singh and his colleagues delivered inspiring lectures on the lives of revolutionary martyrs in NBS meetings, the aim being to rouse the youth against British imperialism. In June 1928, Bhagat Singh and Sukhdev also organized the Lahore Students' Union, as an auxiliary of the NBS. Both organizations served as a recruiting ground for the HSRA which was to be formed later. In August 1928, the NBS, along with radical Congressmen, celebrated "Friends of Russia Week" and also organized a meeting to eulogize the Russian Revolution. From 1928-30, HSRA revolutionaries and Communist groups worked together in the NBS. The NBS was banned by the British government in May 1930, a year after Bhagat Singh's arrest.

The political aims of the NBS were: (a) To establish a completely independent republic of the labourers and peasants of the whole of India, (b) To infuse a spirit of patriotism in the hearts of the youth of the country in order to establish a united Indian nation, (c) To express sympathy with and to assist economic, industrial and social movements, which, being free from communal sentiments, were intended to take the movement nearer its ideal, d) To organize labourers and peasants.

The Manifesto of the NBS, written by Bhagwati Charan Vohra on April 6, 1928, declared: "The future programme of preparing the country will begin with the motto: 'Revolution by the masses and for the masses.' In other words, Swaraj for the 90%; Swaraj not only attained by the masses but also for the masses...Without going into details, we can safely assert that to achieve our object, thousands of our most brilliant young men, like Russian youth, will have to pass their precious lives in villages and make the people understand what the Indian revolution would really mean. They must be made to realize that the revolution which is to come will mean more than a change of masters. It will, above all, mean the birth of a new order of things, a new state. This is not the work of a day or a year. Decades of matchless self-sacrifice will prepare the masses for the accomplishment of that great work and only the revolutionary young men will be able to do that. A revolutionary does not necessarily mean a man of bombs and revolvers."

Outlining the close links between the NBS and the Communists, A.G. Noorani writes in The Trial of Bhagat Singh: Politics of Justice: "The Sabha's progress was impressive by any standards. Similar bodies were formed in other provinces. Branches proliferated in the Punjab. An All-India Naujawan Bharat Sabha was established in Delhi. Soon links were forged with the Hindustan Republican Association and the Kirti Kisan Party, founded by Sohan Singh Josh.

Already, on his return to Lahore, Bhagat Singh had established contacts with the Kirti Kisan Party. The Party owed its existence to the united efforts of the emissaries of the Ghadar Party (Bhag Singh 'Canadian') and of the Communist Party of Great Britain (Philip Spratt) and of Sohan Singh Josh, Mir Abdul Majid and Kedar Nath Sehgal. (The last four, all Communists, were to be among the 31 accused in the Meerut Conspiracy Case in 1929-AD.) Intended to be a Workers and Peasants Party, it was named the Punjab Kirti-Kisan Party. Its organ Kirti was published in Punjabi and Urdu so that it could be read by the masses...Bhagat Singh worked for some time, assisting Sohan Singh Josh."

SECULARISM

Two of the six rules of the NBS drafted by Bhagat Singh were: "To have nothing to do with communal bodies or other parties which disseminate communal ideas" and "to create the spirit of general toleration among the public considering religion as a matter of personal belief of man and to act upon the same fully." Secularism was, indeed, an article of faith with Bhagat Singh all his life. Bipan Chandra described it thus: "More than any other contemporary leader, with the exception of Gandhiji, he understood the danger that communalism posed to Indian society and Indian nationalism. He often warned his comrades and followers that communalism was as big an enemy as colonialism...Religion, said Bhagat Singh, was the private concern of a person, but it had to be fought as an enemy when it intruded into politics and took the form of communalism. Bhagat Singh also believed that people must free themselves from the mental bondage of religion and superstition."

His classic article Why I am an Atheist is, of course, the most remarkable exposition of his approach to God and religion, which goes far beyond secularism and towards Marxism. The Hindi edition of The Complete Works of Bhagat Singh edited by Chaman Lal, comprises three very significant articles that were published in the Punjabi and Urdu monthly Kirti in May and June 1928.

The titles of these three articles are: Religion and Our Freedom Struggle; Communal Riots and their Solution; and The Problem of Untouchability. For reasons of space, it is not possible to quote from them here; suffice it to say that they are an extremely mature and forthright exposition of secularism and social justice. Remarkably, they were written when Bhagat Singh was just 21 years old.

Bipan Chandra, in India's Struggle for Independence, has cited the following revealing anecdote that throws light on Bhagat Singh's deep commitment to secularism: "Bhagat Singh revered Lajpat Rai as a leader. But he would not spare even Lajpat Rai, when, during the last years of his life,

Lajpat Rai turned to communal politics. He then launched a political-ideological campaign against him. Because Lajpat Rai was a respected leader, he would not publicly use harsh words of criticism against him. And so he printed as a pamphlet Robert Browning's famous poem, 'The Lost Leader,' in which Browning criticizes Wordsworth for turning against liberty. The poem begins with the line 'Just for a handful of silver he left us.' A few more of the poem's lines were: 'We shall march prospering,-not thro' his presence; Songs may inspirit us,-not from his lyre' and 'Blot out his name, then, record one lost soul more.' There was not one word of criticism of Lajpat Rai. Only, on the front cover, he printed Lajpat Rai's photograph!"

MAIN CURRENTS IN THE NATIONAL MOVEMENT

The freedom of India from nearly two centuries of oppressive and exploitative British colonial rule was the cumulative result of a complex mosaic of four different currents that coexisted, often confronted and sometimes coordinated with one another. These were:

1. The current of armed struggles and peasant revolts that began with the Sannyasi-Fakir rebellion of 1760, encompassed the First War of Indian Independence of 1857, included the several groups of valiant armed freedom fighters throughout the country and ended with the revolt of the Royal Indian Navy ratings in 1946. All these armed struggles and peasant revolts were brutally crushed by the British, but some of them succeeded in shaking the British Raj to its roots.
2. The Indian National Congress, led by Mahatma Gandhi, which managed to establish its hegemony over the national movement after 1920. While the Congress succeeded in mobilizing millions of the Indian people in nonviolent upsurges against British rule, its bourgeois-landlord class leadership saw to it that these upsurges never crossed the boundary line to a radical agrarian revolution. Class struggle was, of course, anathema to the Congress, but it did adopt a broadly secular approach.
3. The Communist Party of India, which was formed in 1920, was the first to advocate the goal of complete independence in the Ahmedabad Congress session in 1921. Braving ban orders and massive repression of the British, the Communists plunged into the freedom movement and also organized workers and peasants for heroic class struggles, the pinnacle of which was the Telangana armed peasant revolt. Staunchly secular, the Communists were also the first to put forth the goal of socialism.

4. The social reform movement against caste and gender oppression that was led in various parts of the country by stalwarts like Raja Rammohan Roy, Mahatma Jotirao Phule, Ishwarchandra Vidyasagar, Narayan Guru, E V Ramaswamy Naicker (Periyar) and Dr. Babasaheb Ambedkar. The social reformers fought for freedom with social justice as one of its cardinal planks, an end to centuries of inhuman social oppression and the annihilation of the caste system itself.

There was a fifth current as well, but it was ranged directly against the national movement. This was the current of communalism. Not only did it never oppose the colonial rulers, but on the contrary it consistently helped British imperialism to execute its 'Divide and Rule' policy. It was represented by the Muslim League on the one hand, and by the RSS and the Hindu Mahasabha on the other. This current was socially reactionary, it led to constant communal clashes and it eventually resulted in the violent partition of India on the one hand, and in the dastardly assassination of Mahatma Gandhi on the other.

THE DISTINCTIVENESS OF BHAGAT SINGH AND HIS COMRADES

Bhagat Singh and his comrades belonged to the first current of armed anti-imperialist fighters. Their glorious struggle against British imperialism assumed legendary proportions. But their truly distinctive feature was that, amongst the large galaxy of thousands of armed freedom fighters spread over two centuries of the freedom struggle, it was Bhagat Singh and his comrades alone who were inexorably moving ideologically towards the third current-of Marxian socialism and the Communist Party. It is therefore no accident that comrades of Bhagat Singh like Shiv Verma, Kishori Lal, Ajoy Ghosh, Bejoy Kumar Sinha and Jaidev Kapur became leaders of the Communist movement after their release from British jails.

Bhagat Singh and his colleagues were also conscious of the need for social justice and the overthrow of the caste system. They were bitter and uncompromising enemies of communalism in all its forms. And they were inveterate opponents of the bourgeois-landlord class strategy and tactics of the Congress Party and its leadership that were exhibited in ample measure throughout the course of the national movement.

The distinctiveness of Bhagat Singh in the revolutionary firmament of the national movement has been well captured by B.T. Ranadive in his Foreword to the Selected Writings of Shaheed Bhagat Singh edited by Shiv Verma. He writes:

The name of Bhagat Singh and his comrades has secured a permanent place in the minds of the Indian people. No other revolutionary of those days struck such a deep feeling of sympathy, solidarity and oneness among the people. Bhagat Singh and his comrades became part of the people's consciousness, the symbol of their aspirations and prestige, the symbol of the fight to put an end to enslavement....

Punjab, Bengal and to some extent Maharashtra had earlier seen a large number of revolutionaries with unparalleled courage and capacity for self-sacrifice. They walked to the gallows with their head erect; they braved the horrors of the Andamans for years with unbending spirit. Their memory is no doubt cherished.

But they were challenging the empire at a time when the Indian masses had yet to move into political action. Their sacrifices did not become part of the common consciousness of the vast multitude that faced British lathis and rifles during the national movement in the succeeding years. On the other hand, Bhagat Singh and his comrades were in action when the masses were on the move, when every anti-British action drew their approbation. Their ultimate sacrifice, therefore, put a permanent impress on the consciousness of the Indian people...

Bhagat Singh went on churning his thoughts and proceeded more and more towards a better understanding of the Marxist stand on the issues facing the country. It may be stated without contradiction that his opinion on many national issues, his estimation of the national leadership and its weaknesses, were more or less in conformity with the views and opinions of the leaders of the Communist movement who were building their strength among the workers. His writings on various topics and his letters to his colleagues reveal his growing reliance on the Marxist outlook. It is no surprise that he declared himself an atheist and poured ridicule on the concept of a world created by a Supreme Being. His writings show a remarkable ability to merge with the subject under discussion and grasp the essence of points of dispute. They are permeated with an unfathomable sense of dedication to the cause of independence and freedom, to the cause of socialism. His study of Communist literature, of Lenin, led him to understand that India's struggle for freedom was part of the international working class struggle for socialism.

Pattabhi Sitaramayya, the official historian of the Congress, wrote that "it is no exaggeration to say that at that moment Bhagat Singh's name was as widely known all over India and was as popular as Gandhi's." In the same vein, a confidential Intelligence Bureau report of the British government,

Terrorism in India (1917-1936) declared about Bhagat Singh that "for a time, he bade fair to oust Mr. Gandhi as the foremost political figure of the day."

A.G. Noorani concludes his book The Trial of Bhagat Singh-Politics of Justice with the words: "What distinguished Bhagat Singh from all others, besides his courage, patriotism and commitment to moral values, was his intellectual strength. A voracious reader, he was also willing to rethink. He had the capacity to brood and to torment his soul over the past. That led him to renounce terrorism, and to advise the young to follow suit; indeed, to counsel moderation and readiness to compromise. He was only 23 when he was hanged. On his death, Indian leaders vied with one another in lavishing praise on him. One wonders how many of them knew then that they had lost a man who, had he lived, might have had an incalculable impact on the course of India's politics."

EARLY INFLUENCES: GHADAR MARTYRS AND JALLIANWALA BAGH

Bhagat Singh was born to Vidyavati and Kishan Singh on September 28, 1907, in the village Banga in Lyallpur district, now in Pakistan. His original village Khatkar Kalan is in Jalandhar district. He hailed from a patriotic family. His uncle Ajit Singh, along with Lala Lajpat Rai, was exiled to Mandalay jail in Burma by the British for leading a powerful peasant agitation against the hike in land revenue and canal taxes. At the time of Bhagat Singh's birth, his father Kishan Singh and his other uncle Swarn Singh, were also in jail due to their nationalist activities, and were released soon after. In such an atmosphere, Bhagat Singh naturally imbibed patriotic sentiments. He especially adored his exiled uncle Ajit Singh.

While Bhagat Singh was in school, Punjab was rocked by the hanging of seven Ghadar martyrs by the British on November 16 and 17, 1915, in the First Lahore Conspiracy Case. Prominent among them were Kartar Singh Sarabha from Punjab and Vishnu Ganesh Pingle from Maharashtra. The young Bhagat Singh was deeply moved by the heroic saga and sacrifice of Kartar Singh Sarabha, who was just 20 years old when he was hanged. Sarabha's last words were, "My only ambition is to see my country free. All that I did had this objective. I have never done anything out of hatred for any person, nation, religion or race. I only desire one thing-independence. This is my only dream. If I had to live more lives than one, I would sacrifice each of them for my country's sake."

Bhagat Singh always carried a photo of Sarabha in his pocket and was carrying one when he was arrested in 1929. In March 1926, when Bhagat

Singh, Sukhdev and Bhagwati Charan Vohra founded the Naujawan Bharat Sabha in Lahore, its inaugural session began with the unveiling of Sarabha's portrait, in open defiance of the British authorities. Bhagat Singh also wrote moving articles on Kartar Singh Sarabha and some other Ghadar heroes.

The Ghadar (meaning Revolt) Party was formed in 1913 in the USA by a group of Indian, mainly Punjabi Sikh, emigre freedom fighters under the leadership of Sohan Singh Bhakna and Lala Hardayal. The formation of the Ghadar Party was a big step forward. Unlike some of the earlier armed freedom fighters from Maharashtra and Bengal, who had a marked Hindu religious bias, the Ghadar Party was completely secular, declared religion to be a private affair and opposed the poison of communalism and also untouchability. Unlike the earlier armed freedom fighters, most of whom came from the lower middle class, most Ghadar members were peasants turned workers. Its main stress was not so much on armed individual actions; rather it called upon peasants and soldiers to rise in revolt against British rule. Since most of its members were based in Canada and the USA before they came to India, it had an international outlook.

The Komagata Maru ship tragedy took place at Budge on September 29, 1914, in which several Ghadarites were killed and many escaped. After that, the Ghadar Party led by Kartar Singh Sarabha and Vishnu Ganesh Pingle, the Anushilan Samiti led by Rash Behari Bose and Sachindranath Sanyal, and the Jugantar Group led by Jatindranath Mukherjee (Bagha Jatin) together planned an audacious uprising of the Indian Army against British rule on February 21, 1915, when the First World War was in progress.

The plan failed, partly due to treachery, and many of the above fighters were killed, hanged or transported for life. It is recorded by Bejoy Kumar Sinha, a colleague of Bhagat Singh, that out of the Ghadar revolutionaries, "about one hundred mounted the gallows, forty one faced the firing squad, and about a hundred went to the Andamans sentenced to life transportation." The Ghadar Party made tremendous sacrifices for Indian freedom.

Another event that was to leave a deep impression on the young Bhagat Singh was, of course, the horrific Jallianwala Bagh massacre at Amritsar on April 13, 1919. The butcher of Amritsar, General Dyer fired 1600 rounds of ammunition on the unarmed crowd of around 10,000 that had gathered for a public meeting, killing 379 according to official figures; unofficially, it was put at over 1000; and leaving over 1200 wounded.

Bhagat Singh was then just 12 years old and was studying at the D A V School in Lahore. He was deeply enraged by the Jallianwala Bagh massacre.

It has been recorded that he immediately went to the Bagh, collected its soil in a bottle and kept it as a constant reminder of the hurt and humiliation that the Indian people had suffered.

When the Non-Cooperation Movement started in 1920, Bhagat Singh left the D A V School and joined the National College started by Lala Lajpat Rai and Bhai Parmanand. His college friends included Bhagwati Charan Vohra, Sukhdev and Yashpal. He evinced great interest both in his studies and in politics and was a voracious reader. His area of special interest was the history of revolutions. He was fond of singing patriotic songs and also took part in the college dramatics club, which was soon banned by the government.

In 1924, Bhagat Singh had to give up his B.A. studies and leave Lahore because his father and grandmother were forcing him to get married. He wrote to his father, "This is not the time for marriage. The country is calling me. I have taken oath to serve the country physically, mentally and monetarily." When his father continued to insist, Bhagat Singh again wrote back, "I am astonished to read the contents of your letter...You are caring for Dadi, but in how much trouble is our Mother of 33 crores, the Bharat Mata. We still have to sacrifice everything for her sake." Finally, when leaving home, he wrote, "I dedicate my life to the lofty goal of service to the Motherland. Hence there is no attraction in me for home and fulfilment of worldly desires." He left Lahore for Kanpur.

H.S.R.A.: DECISIVE TURN TOWARDS SOCIALISM

After the British attempts to smash the HRA in the Kakori Conspiracy Case, the regrouping of the Kanpur group began under the leadership of Chandrashekhar Azad. He was assisted by Kundan Lal Gupta, Shiv Verma, Bejoy Kumar Sinha, Jaidev Kapur, Gaya Prasad and others. The Lahore group was led by Bhagat Singh and comprised Bhagwati Charan Vohra, Sukhdev, Kishori Lal, Yashpal and others.

The ideological churning within the HRA leadership continued unabated during this period. Shiv Verma has written that the credit for bringing Bhagat Singh and the Lahore group from anarchism to socialism goes to prominent Communist leader Sohan Singh Josh and to Lala Chhabil Das, who was the principal of the National College. The Dwarkadas Library of Lala Lajpat Rai, which had such books on Marxism and Soviet Russia that were not banned by the British, and other illegal sources of Marxist literature, also played a crucial role in getting Bhagat Singh and Bhagwati Charan over to Marxism. The Kanpur group was similarly influenced by Radha Mohan Gokulji, Maulana

Hasrat Mohani and Satyabhakta, who had declared themselves as Communists. Ganesh Shankar Vidyarthi also helped the young revolutionaries in many ways. As in Lahore, so also in Kanpur, legal and illegal Marxist literature also played a key role.

Added to this process of self-cultivation were also the political developments taking place in the country during this period. Some of these were: the five Peshawar Conspiracy Cases from 1922-27 that were instituted by the British against several muhajirs who came back from Soviet Russia and either were, or were suspected to be, Communists; the Kanpur Conspiracy Case of 1923-24 against Communist leaders; the first All-India conference of the CPI at Kanpur in December 1925; the formation of Workers' and Peasants' Parties in various provinces in 1926-28; the world economic crisis that began in the colonies from 1926; the historic general strike of the British working class in 1926; and the unprecedented strike struggles of the Indian working class led by the Communists in various parts of the country from 1926-28. All these developments could not have failed to make their impact on the young revolutionaries of the HRA.

It was against this background that a key meeting of leading revolutionaries was held at the Ferozshah Kotla Grounds in Delhi on September 8-9, 1928. A total of eight representatives attended the meeting. There were from two from Punjab, three from Uttar Pradesh, two from Bihar and one from Rajasthan. The Bengal group did not attend, but it later sent Jatin Das to Agra to train the others in manufacturing bombs.

Bhagat Singh placed the following main proposals before the meeting: (a) that the time had come to boldly declare Socialism as our ultimate goal, (b) that the name of the Party be changed accordingly to Hindustan Socialist Republican Association (HSRA) so that the people would know our ultimate aim, (c) that we should undertake only such actions which have direct relationship with the demands and sentiments of the people, and not fritter away our time and energy in killing petty police officials and informers, (d) that for funds we should lay our hands on government money and avoid actions on private houses, and (e) that the principle of collective leadership should be strictly observed. After a detailed two-day discussion on these proposals, they were adopted by a majority of six to two. The six who voted in favour were Bhagat Singh, Sukhdev, Shiv Verma, Bejoy Kumar Sinha, Jaidev Kapur and Surendra Pandey. Phanindranath Ghosh and Manmohan Banerjee, both from Bihar, and both of whom were later to turn approvers in the Second Lahore Conspiracy Case against Bhagat Singh and others, opposed the idea of socialism as well as the change in the name of the Party.

Chandrashekhar Azad did not attend the meeting for security reasons, but he had been fully consulted by Bhagat Singh, and had given his assent to the above proposals. The meeting elected a seven-member central committee. Bhagat Singh was given the charge of ideological work and Chandrashekhar Azad was elected commander-in-chief.

The HSRA Manifesto, written by Bhagwati Charan Vohra and widely distributed in the Lahore Session of the Congress in December 1929, is a remarkable document. Beginning with the sentence "The food on which the tender plant of liberty thrives is the blood of the martyr," the Manifesto lyrically explains the meaning of Revolution thus: "Revolution is a phenomenon which nature loves and without which there can be no progress either in nature or in human affairs.

Revolution is certainly not unthinking, brutal campaign of murder and incendiarism; it is not a few bombs thrown here and a few shots fired there; neither is it a movement to destroy all remnants of civilization and blow to pieces time honoured principles of justice and equity. Revolution is not a philosophy of despair or a creed of desperadoes. Revolution may be anti-God but is certainly not anti-Man. It is a vital, living force which is indicative of eternal conflict between the old and the new, between life and living death, between light and darkness. There is no concord, no symphony, no rhythm without revolution. 'The music of the spheres' of which poets have sung, would remain an unreality if a ceaseless revolution were to be eliminated from the space. Revolution is Law, Revolution is Order and Revolution is the Truth."

Analyzing the current situation, the Manifesto says, "India is writhing under the yoke of imperialism. Her teeming millions are today a helpless prey to poverty and ignorance. Foreign domination and economic exploitation have unmanned the vast majority of the people who constitute the workers and peasants of India. The position of the Indian proletariat is, today, extremely critical. It has a double danger to face. It has to bear the onslaught of foreign capitalism on one hand and the treacherous attack of Indian capital on the other. The latter is showing a progressive tendency to join hands with the former. The leaning of certain politicians in favour of dominion status shows clearly which way the wind blows. Indian capital is preparing to betray the masses into the hands of foreign capitalism and receive as a price of this betrayal, a little share in the government of the country. The hope of the proletariat is now centred on socialism which alone can lead to the establishment of complete independence and the removal of all social distinctions and privileges."

While this certainly marked a significant advance over earlier declarations of all armed freedom fighters so far, hangovers of the past legacy were not obliterated altogether. A certain amount of confusion still prevailed in the Manifesto about the role of terrorism. For instance, "We have been taken to task for our terroristic policy. Our answer is that terrorism is never the object of revolutionaries, nor do they believe that terrorism alone can bring independence. No doubt the revolutionaries think, and rightly, that it is only by resorting to terrorism alone that they can find a most effective means of retaliation. The British government exists, because the Britishers have been successful in terrorizing the whole of India. How are we to meet this official terrorism? Only counter-terrorism on the part of revolutionaries can checkmate effectively this bureaucratic bullying."

The other major document of the HSRA was called The Philosophy of the Bomb. It had an interesting background. On December 23, 1929, a bomb exploded under Viceroy Irwin's special train, from which he escaped death or serious injury. Gandhiji thanked God for the Viceroy's narrow escape and in the Lahore session of the Congress that was held the very next week, Gandhiji wanted a resolution passed unanimously 'condemning the cowardly deed of the misguided youth.' But the Congress was in no mood to oblige, and the resolution was passed by a bare majority of 81 in a house of 1713.

After this, Gandhiji wrote a piece called The Cult of the Bomb in his journal Young India. To this, Bhagwati Charan Vohra, in full consultation with Chandrashekhar Azad, wrote a reply called The Philosophy of the Bomb. That was also published in Young India. It was an outstanding document, the most mature that the HSRA produced. It polemically countered Gandhiji's attack on the armed revolutionaries, criticized his creed of nonviolent satyagraha, reiterated the aim of a socialist revolution and ended with the stirring battle-cry:

"We take this opportunity to appeal to our countrymen-to the youth, to the workers and peasants, to the revolutionary intelligentsia-to come forward and join us in carrying aloft the banner of freedom. Let us establish a new order of society in which political and economic exploitation will be an impossibility...There is no crime that Britain has not committed in India. Deliberate misrule has reduced us to paupers, has 'bled us white'. As a race and a people we stand dishonoured and outraged. Do people still expect us to forget and to forgive? We shall have our revenge-a people's righteous revenge on the tyrant. Let the cowards fall back and cringe for compromise and peace. We ask for no mercy and we give no quarter. Ours is a war to the end-to Victory or Death. Long Live Revolution!"

THE ASSASSINATION OF SAUNDERS

In 1928, the all-white Simon Commission came to India to probe the question of further constitutional reforms. The Congress decided to boycott the Commission and to hold protest demonstrations against it. The HSRA decided to actively participate in these actions. The Commission came to Lahore on October 30, 1928, less than two months after the formation of the HSRA. A huge demonstration, led by Lala Lajpat Rai, was held. Bhagat Singh and his comrades were part of it. The police ordered a lathi charge and the Superintendent of Police named Scott rained lathi blows on Lajpat Rai's head. He died on November 17. The nation was stunned and infuriated.

The HSRA decided to avenge the death of Lajpat Rai and the insult to the nation by killing Scott. On December 17, 1928, exactly a month after Lajpat Rai's death, Bhagat Singh, Chandrashekhar Azad, Rajguru and Sukhdev shot dead J P Saunders, another police officer who was also involved in the lathi charge, mistaking him for Scott.

The same night, handwritten posters in pink were pasted on the walls of Lahore. Issued by the Hindustan Socialist Republican Army, which claimed responsibility for the killing, the powerful poster said: "With the death of J P Saunders, the assassination of Lala Lajpat Rai has been avenged...This national insult was a challenge to young men. Today the world has seen that the people of India are not lifeless; their blood has not become cold. They can lay down their lives for the country's honour. The proof of this has been given by the youth who are ridiculed and insulted by the leaders of their own country." The poster continued: "We are sorry to have killed a man. But this man was a part of a cruel, despicable and unjust system and killing him was a necessity. This man has been killed as an employee of the British government. This government is the most oppressive government in the world. We are sorry for shedding human blood but it becomes necessary to bathe the altar of revolution with blood. Our aim is to bring about a revolution which would end all exploitation of man by man. Long Live Revolution!"

After the assassination of Saunders, Bhagat Singh immediately escaped to Calcutta along with Rajguru and Bhagwati Charan's wife Durga Bhabhi, who was a dedicated revolutionary in her own right. All three were in disguise. In Calcutta, Bhagat Singh met the Bengal revolutionaries Trailokya Chakravarty and Pratul Ganguly who had by that time come out of jail. He reported to them about the HSRA decisions taken in the September meeting in Delhi and obtained their assent on all the points. They agreed to send Jatin Das to train the HSRA revolutionaries in manufacturing bombs.

Bhagat Singh attended in secret the first All India Conference of the Workers' and Peasants' Parties which was held at Calcutta from December 21-24, 1928. Sohan Singh Josh and others from Punjab attended the conference as delegates. Bhagat Singh was also present during the Calcutta session of the Congress which was held from December 29, 1928 to January 1, 1929. Here, on the first day, the Communist Party made a historic intervention when it led a huge demonstration of over 50,000 workers which occupied the Congress pandal and demanded that the Congress accept the goal of complete independence instead of dominion status at this session itself. That did not happen. This long-standing demand of the Indian people, which was first raised by the Communist Party, was finally accepted one year later, at the Lahore session of the Congress on December 31, 1929.

Shiv Verma has recalled an interesting and significant anecdote of that time. He writes: "While talking to Comrade Sohan Singh Josh at Calcutta in December 1928, at the time of the Calcutta session of the Congress, Bhagat Singh had said, 'We entirely agree with the programme and activities of your Party, but there are times when the blow of the enemy has to be immediately counteracted by armed actions to inspire confidence among the masses.' That is how our minds were working then."

For four months, from December 1928 to April 1929, the British regime, in spite of desperate efforts, could not trace those responsible for the assassination of Saunders. It was the next episode in the struggle that was to provide them with the clues.

Bombs in the Central Assembly

To crack down on the rising working class movement and the increasing influence of the Communists, the British government brought the repressive Public Safety Bill and the Trade Disputes Bill in the Central Legislative Assembly at Delhi. Already, on March 20, 1929, the British regime had arrested 31 prominent Communist and labour leaders from different parts of the country in the famous Meerut Conspiracy Case.

The HSRA leadership decided to throw bombs in the Central Assembly to protest against the passage of the above two draconian Bills and also against the arrests of the Communist and labour leaders. The bombs were not meant to kill anybody; they were to serve as a warning. Those throwing the bombs would not escape, but would deliberately get arrested and then use the trial in court for propaganda so that the programme and ideology of the HSRA would become widely known throughout the country.

After considerable discussion, it was decided that Bhagat Singh and Batukeshwar Dutt should carry out this task. Bhagat Singh would put forth the views of the revolutionaries before the court and the country most effectively, and the presence of Batukeshwar Dutt would stress the All-India character of the HSRA. This decision was taken although it was fraught with grave risk, since Bhagat Singh was also involved in the Saunders case. On April 8, 1929, as planned, Bhagat Singh and Batukeshwar Dutt threw two bombs in the Assembly, immediately after the passage of the Trade Disputes Bill. No one was seriously injured. They also threw leaflets in the Assembly proclaiming why they had thrown the bombs. They did not try to run away and calmly courted arrest.

The leaflet thrown in the Assembly, in the name of the Hindustan Socialist Republican Association, began thus: "It takes a loud voice to make the deaf hear. With these immortal words uttered on a similar occasion by Valliant, a French anarchist martyr, do we strongly justify this action of ours...The Government is thrusting upon us new repressive measures like the Public Safety and the Trade Disputes Bill, while reserving the Press Sedition Bill for the next session.

The indiscriminate arrests of labour leaders working in the open field clearly indicate whither the wind blows..."

"Let the representatives of the people return to their constituencies and prepare the masses for the coming revolution, and let the Government know that while protesting against the Public Safety and Trade Disputes Bills and the callous murder of Lala Lajpat Rai, on behalf of the helpless Indian masses, we want to emphasize the lesson often repeated by history, that it is easy to kill individuals but you cannot kill the ideas. Great empires crumbled while the ideas survived. Bourbons and Czars fell.

"We are sorry to admit that we who attach so great a sanctity to human life, we who dream of a glorious future, when man will be enjoying perfect peace and full liberty, have been forced to shed human blood. But the sacrifice of individuals at the altar of the 'Great Revolution' that will bring freedom to all, rendering the exploitation of man by man impossible, is inevitable. Long Live Revolution! "

Both the above actions-the assassination of Saunders and the hurling of bombs in the Central Assembly-made Bhagat Singh and his comrades legendary heroes. The whole country acclaimed them with admiration and adulation. The acclamation was to increase even more after seeing their fearless defiance in British jails and before British courts.

AN INTELLECTUAL GIANT

By all accounts, Bhagat Singh was of a scholarly bent of mind and a deep thinker who understood the power of ideas. "The sword of revolution", he told the judges trying him, "is sharpened at the whetstone of thought". On being asked as to what set him apart from other revolutionaries, Shiv Verma, a fellow revolutionary and a close comrade-in-arms, replied thus: "I can tell you that in just one sentence: Bhagat Singh was our undisputed ideological leader. I do not remember a single moment when Bhagat Singh did not have a book in his pocket. The other virtues of Bhagat Singh like tremendous courage and so on were there in the other revolutionaries amongst us also. But his uniqueness lay in his great studiousness. The degree of clarity and integrity that he had about the aims of our movement, was not there in any of us at that time".

Well-known Indian historian Bipan Chandra has correctly observed that "Bhagat Singh was already at a young age a giant of an intellectual and thinker". Chaman Lall, who edited all of Bhagat Singh's manuscripts, noted that Bhagat Singh had command of four languages-Punjabi, Hindi, Urdu and English-without much formal training or education. He wrote in all these languages and his prison notebooks contain "... excerpts from 108 authors and 43 books including prominently Marx, Engels and Lenin, but also many others".

Bhagat Singh's quest for knowledge, his rigorous pursuit of a scientific under-pinning for his revolutionary beliefs and activity, becomes clear from the remarkable article, 'Why I am an Atheist', which he wrote shortly before his execution. In it, he explains that during the earlier period of his activity he had merely been a romantic revolutionary. Then came the time to shoulder the whole responsibility. It was a time when the very existence of the revolutionary movement appeared impossible-a time when not only "enthusiastic comrades", but even leaders began to "jeer at us". Continuing, Bhagat Singh, reveals the mental torture he went through in the following moving words:

> *"For some time I was afraid that some day I also might be convinced of the futility of our own programme. That was a turning point in my revolutionary career. 'Study' was the cry that reverberated in the corridors of my mind. Study to enable yourself to face the arguments advanced by opposition. Study to arm yourself with arguments in favour of your cult. I began to study. My previous faith and convictions underwent a remarkable modification. The romance of the violent methods alone which was so prominent amongst our predecessors was replaced by serious ideas. No more mysticism, no more blind*

faith. Realism became our cult. Use of force justifiable when resorted to as a matter of terrible necessity: nonviolence as policy indispensable for all mass movement. So much about methods. The most important thing was the clear conception of the ideal for which we were to fight. As there were no important activities in the field of action I got ample opportunity to study various ideals of the world revolution. I studied Bakunin, the Anarchist leader, something of Marx the father of Communism and much of Lenin, Trotsky and others, the men who had successfully carried out a revolution in their country".

What is more, Bhagat Singh was born at a time of the rising tide of the anti-colonial movement and widespread discontent. Alarmed by the mood of the people, Denzil Ibbetson, the Lieutenant Governor, noted in a report: "Everywhere people are sensible of a change, of a 'new air' ..., which is blowing through men's minds, and are waiting to see what will come of it. ... In the towns of Rawalpindi, Sialkot and Lyallpur, active anti-English propaganda is being openly and sedulously preached. In Lahore, the capital of the province, the propaganda is virulent and has resulted in a more or less general state of serious unrest" (quoted in K.K.Khullar, Shaheed Bhagat Singh, pp.98-110).

Far from subsiding, the wave of anti-colonial feelings and agitation gained increasing strength in the years following 1907. Growing up in this milieu, brought up on stories of the exploits of his uncle and father, Bhagat Singh could hardly have failed to imbibe patriotic and anti-colonial sentiments. He was only eight when Punjab was plunged into turmoil following the hanging of Seven Ghadar revolutionaries by the British colonial authorities on 16-17 November 1915 in the First Lahore Conspiracy Case. One of those hanged was Kastar Singh Sarabha, who was only 19 at the time of his judicial murder by the British. Sarabha's last words were: "My only ambition is to see my country free. All that I did had this objective. I have never done anything out of hatred for any person, nation, religion or race. I only desire one thing-independence. This is my only dream. If I had to live more lives than one, I would sacrifice each of them for my country's sake".

Sarabha became Bhagat Singh's hero, whose photo Bhagat Singh always carried in his pocket and was carrying at the time of his arrest in 1929. When in 1926, Bhagat Singh, along with Sukhdev and Bhagwati Charan Vohra (BCV) founded the Naujawan Bharat Sabha in Lahore, its inaugural meeting was preceded by the unveiling of Sarabha's portrait in daring and open defiance of the colonial authorities.

The Ghadar Party (party of revolt) was formed on 21 April 1913 by Indian revolutionaries then resident in Canada and the USA. The formation of the

Ghadar marked the beginning of the latest and most modern phase of India's freedom movement; with its formation, the revolutionary movement in India took a giant step forward. In its outlook the Ghadar Party was internationalist and secular; it stressed the importance of revolutionary work in the army with the aim of inciting the latter to rise in rebellion against the British imperialist rule; it drew its ranks from the peasants turned factory workers, unlike earlier revolutionaries who had by and large hailed from the lower middle-class intelligentsia.

The Ghadar movement, though cruelly suppressed by the British imperial authorities, left a rich revolutionary legacy and made an indelible mark on the freedom movement, inspiring in the process an entire generation of revolutionaries with its courage, outlook and death-defying heroism.

Just over three years after the martyrdom of the leaders of the Ghadar movement came the Amritsar (Jallianwala) massacre, which claimed the lives of over a thousand innocent men, women and children, and left many more wounded. This senseless massacre on the orders of the butcher of Amritsar, General Dyer, on 13 April 1919, left a lasting impression on Bhagat Singh, who was just twelve year old then.

According to records, enraged by the dastardly deed of the colonial government, Bhagat Singh went straight from his school to Amritsar, kissed the earth sanctified by the blood of Dyer's victims, and brought back with him a little of the blood-soaked soil which he kept in a bottle as a permanent reminder of the injustice, injury and humiliation perpetrated by the colonial rulers on the Indian people.

Bhagat Singh and his comrades were not the first fighters against British colonialism; nor were they the first to take up arms against the British Raj. What distinguished them from the several thousands of armed fighters for Indian freedom over a period of nearly two centuries is, first, that the revolutionary activities of Bhagat Singh and his comrades happened to coincide with the tumultuous arrival of the Indian masses into the arena of political life and, second, that they were irresistibly driven to accept the ideology of Marxism.

October Revolution

In this regard, the Great October Socialist Revolution in Russia played a most crucial role. Such was the liberating effect of the Russian Revolution that even some Congress leaders, such as Bal Gangadhar Tilka, Lala Lajpat Rai and Bipin Chandra Pal, greeted with joy the Bolshevik victory and the Bolshevik programme.

The Russian Revolution, by laying bare the contrast between the compromising bourgeois Congress leadership of the Indian freedom struggle, on the one hand, and the uncompromising revolutionary Bolshevik leadership, on the other, had an even bigger impact on the young armed freedom fighters in India and elsewhere.

The October Revolution, with its earth-shattering ramifications, had a triple effect on the young Indian revolutionaries in particular. First, it instilled confidence in them that imperialism and the system of exploitation of one man by another, and one nation by another, could be got rid of. Second, it forced them to seriously ponder the meaning-the economic and social content-of independence.

Third, it prompted a serious study of Marxism as the only reliable weapon and ideological tool for the attainment of the freedom of the Indian people from British colonialism and the system of exploitation alike.

Bhagat Singh in particular was deeply influenced by the triumphant march of the October Revolution. Less than two months before his execution, in what can only be called his last testament, this is how he exposes, by an implicit reference to the events of the 1920s, the compromising capitulationist and cowardly leadership of the Congress, above all Gandhi, as the enemy of the Indian proletariat and peasantry and a friend of the exploiting bourgeois and landlord classes:

"The real revolutionary armies are in the villages and in factories, the peasantry and the labourers. But our bourgeois leaders do not and cannot dare to tackle them. The sleeping lion once awakened from its slumber shall become irresistible even after the achievement of what our leaders aim at. After his first experience with the Ahmedabad labourers in 1920 Mahatma Gandhi declared: 'We must not tamper with the labourers. It is dangerous to make political use of the factory proletariat' (The Times, May 1921). Since then, they never dared to approach them. There remains the peasantry. The Bardoli resolution of 1922 clearly defines the horrors the leaders felt when they saw the gigantic peasant class rising to shake off not only the domination of an alien nation but also the yoke of the landlords. It is there that our leaders prefer surrender to the British than to the peasantry".

It was also in the aftermath of the October Revolution, and under its direct impact, that the Communist Party of India was formed at Tashkent on 17 October 1920, and the All India Trade Union Congress (AITUC) established on 31 October 1920 in Bombay. Both these bodies were to play an important role in the anti-colonial and revolutionary movement.

Kakori Trial

In 1924, still in his teens, Bhagat Singh left Lahore for Kanpur, where he completed his study of Marx's Capital, met many revolutionaries, including Batukeshwar Dutt, who taught him Bengali, and Chandrashekar Azad, and joined the Hindustan Republican Association (HRA), which had been formed in 1923, with Sachindra Nath Sanyal being it moving spirit. The object clause of the HRA's Rules and Regulations stated: "The object of the Association shall be to establish a Federal Republic of the United States of India by an armed revolution". It was to be a republic in which exploitation of one person by another would be outlawed.

The HRA was to be "not national but international" in its outlook and follow in the footsteps of "Bolshevik Russia". Funds for the HRA were to be raised, among other things, through armed robberies. It was to this end that the HRA revolutionaries stopped a train on 9 August 1925 at Kakori near Lucknow, looted a government safe containing the modest sum of Rs4,679, in the process killing one person accidentally.

Most of the participants in the train robbery were arrested and tried in the Kakori Conspiracy Case. Four of the accused in this case, including the famous poet Ram Prasad Bismil, were hanged, two received life imprisonment and eleven others varying prison terms. Only two, including the legendary Chandrashekar Azad, managed to evade arrest. Although a heavy blow to the HRA, the Kakori case acquired the proportions of a legend in view of the display of courage and manhood by the accused during the trial. The four sentenced to be hanged cheerfully mounted the gallows while singing the following legendary song, which was from then on to be on the lips of literally every Indian:

"Sarfaroshi ki tamanna ab hamare dil mein hai,
"Dekhna hai zor kitna basu-e katil mein hai".
"We are burning with a longing to be denuded of our heads,
"We shall see how much strength can the executioner's arms wield".

Thanks to the strenuous work of Azad and the second line of leadership, which included Shiv Verma and many others, the HRA was able to recover from the setback following the Kakori Conspiracy Case.

Naujawan Bharat Sabha (NBS)

Meanwhile, after a six-month stay in Kanpur, Bhagat Singh returned to Lahore. He had only gone to Kanpur to escape pressure from his father and grandmother to get married. His correspondence with his father on this question clearly brings out Bhagat Singh's lofty ideals in the service of which he was ready to renounce all worldly comforts and sacrifice his life. "Now is not the time for marriage. The country is calling me. I have taken oath to serve the country physically, mentally and monetarily", he wrote to his father. Alluding to his family's patriotism and its sacrifices in the service of the freedom struggle, he continued "I am only following your footprints ... you will kindly not tie me in matrimony but give me your blessings so that I may succeed in my mission". In response to a letter from his father saying that "We have already settled your marriage ... you should not create any difficulty", Bhagat Singh wrote a firm, but respectful reply. "I am astonished to read the contents of your letter. When you, who are a staunch patriot and brave personality, can be influenced by such trifles, then what will happen to ordinary men?

"You are caring for Dadi [my grandmother], but in how much trouble is our Mother of 33 crores [330 million], the Bharat Mata [Mother India]. We will have to sacrifice everything for her sake".

At the time of leaving for Kanpur, he left this note: "Revered Father, ... I have dedicated my life to the lofty goal of service to the Motherland. Hence there is no attraction in me for home and fulfilment of worldly desires. ... I hope you will forgive me".

Six months later, when assured that his father would no longer insist on him getting married, Bhagat Singh returned to Lahore, only more ardent than ever before, to continue along a path in the service of which he had dedicated his life. While remaining in touch with his fellow revolutionaries in the United Provinces (UP) after his return to Lahore, Bhagat Singh extended and deepened his contacts in Punjab. In March 1926, along with Sukhdev, B.C.Vohra and Ram Krishan, he formed the Naujawan Bharat Sabha (NBS) [Indian Youth Association], which took up the unrealised mission of the HRA. In addition to the youth, the NBS's membership included such eminent people as Saifuddin Kitchlew, Satyapal, Mir Abdul Majid, Sardul Singh Caveeshar and the poet Lal Chand Falaq. Ram Krishan was the NBS's President and Bhagat Singh, its Secretary.

The progress of the NBS was truly phenomenal. Its branches spread throughout the Punjab, and similar organisations were set up in other provinces. An All-India NBS was established in Delhi, which soon thereafter forged links with the HRA and the Kirti Kisan [Workers and Peasants] Party founded by the veteran communist leader Sohan Singh Josh. The NBS was to function openly as a legal arm of the revolutionary movement and undertake political work in the ranks of the youth as well as among workers and peasants. As such, recognising as it did the importance of political work among the broad masses of people, the NBS, its aims and programme, marked a very important step forward in the political and ideological development of Bhagat Singh and his close comrades and the acceptance by them of Marxist methods of work as well as Marxist ideology.

The political aims of the NBS included, inter alia, the establishment of a completely independent workers' and peasants' republic in India; the organisation of labourers and peasants; instilling the sprit of patriotism in the country's youth; and fighting against communalism (the pitting of one religious group against another). "Revolution by the masses and for the masses" was the motto of the NBS's Manifesto, written by B.C.Vohra. The masses must be made to realise, said the Manifesto, that "... the revolution which is to come will mean more than a change of masters. It will, above all, mean the birth of a new order of things, a new state", requiring decades of "matchless self-sacrifice", adding that a "... revolutionary does not necessarily mean a man of bombs and revolvers".

The rules of the NBS were written by Bhagat Singh. Such was the importance attached by Bhagat Singh to the need for fighting the corrosive disease of communalism that two out of its six rules called for the creation of "... the spirit of general toleration among the public concerning religion as a matter of personal belief of man", and to "... have nothing to do with communal bodies or other parties which disseminate communal ideas". Believing religion to be the private concern of an individual, Bhagat Singh was firmly of the view that the moment it intruded into politics and donned the garb of communalism, religion had to be fought like an enemy. He was of the view that communalism was no less an enemy than colonialism. More than any other contemporary leader, Bhagat Singh worked tirelessly to free the masses from the servitude of religion and superstition. As is clear from his wonderful article 'Why I am an Atheist', he rightly poured scorn and ridicule on the concept of a world created by a supreme being.

So strong was Bhagat Singh's hatred of communalism that he went to the extent of publicly denouncing, though without naming him, the eminent Congress leader in Punjab, Lal Lajpat Rai, for avenging whose death at the hands of British colonialism he was to pay for with his own life. As Lajpat Rai's politics took a markedly communal turn in the mid-twenties, Bhagat Singh printed, as a pamphlet, Robert Browning's famous poem, 'The Lost Leader', in which Browning subjected Wordsworth to trenchant criticism for his renegacy against the French Revolution and the spirit of liberty. In the words of Dr. Bipin Chandra: "... The opening line of the poem was 'Just for a handful of silver he left us;, a few other lines were 'We shall march prospering-not thro' his presence; songs may inspire us-from his lyre'; and 'Blot out his name, record one lost soul'-in fact, his name appeared nowhere in it-only the front cover carried Lajpat Rai's photograph".

In 1928 Bhagat Singh successfully argued that young persons belonging to religious-communal organisations be barred from the membership of the NBS.

From HRA to HSRA

In the aftermath of the Kakori trial, which was intended by the colonial authorities to smash the Hindustan Republican Association (HRA), the latter began regrouping under the leadership of Azad. At the same time, global and national political and economic developments were increasingly pushing the HRA revolutionaries in the direction of Marxism. In their never-ceasing thirst for knowledge, the HRA revolutionaries, especially Bhagat Singh, devoured voluminous amounts of literature, including Marxist literature.

Their enlightenment through literature was supplemented by lessons driven home by the various conspiracy cases, especially the Kanpur Conspiracy Trial of 1923-24 against the communists, the world economic crisis which made its appearance in the colonies as early as 1926, the historic British General Strike of 1926, and a wave of unprecedented and momentous strikes of the Indian proletariat under communist leadership in several parts of the country.

These developments left their stamp on the HRA revolutionaries and furnish the background to the crucial meeting of the HRA held at Ferozeshah Kotla ground in Delhi on 8-9 September 1928. Present at this meeting were representatives from Punjab, UP, Bihar and Rajasthan.

The Punjab group was led by Bhagat Singh, who played a leading role. He put forward at this meeting the following major proposals: First, that socialism be accepted as the ultimate goal of the organisation; second, that consequently the name of the party, in order to reflect the goal of socialism, be changed to Hindustan Socialist Republican Association (HSRA); third, that only such actions be undertaken by the party as those bearing a direct relationship with the desires, demands and interests of the people, so as not to waste time and effort in killing petty police functionaries and informers; fourth, that the principle of collective leadership be accepted as the basis of the party's functioning and be strictly adhered to; and, finally, that for securing funds, the target should be government resources and not private houses. These proposals were accepted by a majority of six against two (the two dissidents-Phanindranath Ghosh and Manmohan Bannerjee-were to turn approvers in the Second Lahore Conspiracy Case against Bhagat Singh and others) and the meeting elected a seven-member Central Committee. Bhagat Singh was made responsible for ideological work and Azad was elected to be the Commander-in-chief of the HSRA.

The Manifesto of the HSRA, drafted by B.C.Vohra, is an extraordinary panegyric in praise of revolution-almost lyrical in form, powerful in its content and uplifting in its effect. Having stated that without revolution "... there can be no progress in nature or in human affairs", it carries on thus:

> *"Revolution is certainly not unthinking, brutal campaign of murder and incendiarism; it is not a few bombs thrown here and a few shots fired there; neither is it a movement to destroy all remnants of civilization and blow to pieces time honoured principles of justice and equity. Revolution is not a philosophy of despair or a creed of desperadoes. Revolution may be anti-God but is certainly not anti-Man. It is a vital, living force which is indicative of eternal conflict between the old and the new, between life and living death, between light and darkness. There is no concord, no symphony, no rhythm without revolution. 'The music of the spheres' of which poets have sung, would remain an unreality if a ceaseless revolution were to be eliminated from the space. Revolution is Law, Revolution is Order and Revolution is Truth".*

The Manifesto goes on to portray the miserable lot of the Indian masses, who suffered the double yoke of foreign capitalism as well as the attack of Indian capital. It laid bare the capitulatory and cowardly role played by the Indian capitalist class and its political representatives, warning the Indian masses against their treachery and bringing home to them the truth that their only hope lay in socialism, which alone could accomplish the establishment of true independence and remove all social distinctions and privileges.

"India", says the Manifesto, "is writhing under the yoke of imperialism. Her teeming millions are today a helpless prey to poverty and ignorance. Foreign domination and economic exploitation have unmanned the vast majority of the people who constitute the workers and peasants of India. The position of the Indian proletariat is, today, extremely critical. It has a double danger to face. It has to bear the onslaught of foreign capitalism on one hand the treacherous attack of Indian capital on the other. The latter is showing a progressive tendency to join hands with the former. The leaning of certain politicians in favour of dominion status shows clearly which way the wind blows. Indian capital is preparing to betray the masses into the hands of foreign capitalism and receive as a price of this betrayal, a little share in the government of the country. The hope of the proletariat is now centred on socialism which alone can lead to the establishment of complete independence and the removal of all social distinctions and privileges".

Role of Revolutionary Terror

While emphasising the need for mobilising the broad masses in their fight against colonial bondage and class oppression and exploitation, the Manifesto correctly goes on to stress the need for, and the place of, armed revolutionary struggle in pursuit of the ideals of freedom and emancipation. It says:

> *"We have been taken to task for our terroristic policy. Our answer is that terrorism is never the object of revolutionaries, nor do they believe that terrorism alone can bring independence. No doubt the revolutionaries think, and rightly, that it is only by resorting to terrorism alone that they can find a most effective means of retaliation. The British government exists because the Britishers have been successful in terrorizing the whole of India. How are we to meet this official terrorism? Only counter-terrorism on the part of revolutionaries can checkmate effectively this bureaucratic bullying".*

Certain writers, even some who call themselves communist, have put on record their disapproval of the lines quoted immediately above, allegedly betraying the partiality of Bhagat Singh and his comrades to terrorist methods of struggle. Only by misunderstanding, or worse, deliberately distorting, the meaning of these lines and dogmatically objecting to the use of the words 'terror' and 'terrorism' can one criticise their authors as being trigger happy terrorists. In our view, these lines express no more than that counter-revolutionary terror can only be answered by revolutionary terror. And of this, Bhagat Singh and his comrades were fully, and rightly, convinced. It would not be difficult to cite many examples of similar expressions of thought, and similar use of language, from the writing of V.I.Lenin, against whom it would occur to no one to level the accusation of terrorism.

The attempt to smear Bhagat Singh and his comrades by sticking on them the label of terrorism bears an uncanny resemblance to the shameful characterisation of the 1916 Easter uprising in Ireland, not only by the imperialist bourgeoisie but also by the overwhelming majority of the working-class parties of Europe at the time, as a mere putsch. No less a person than V.I.Lenin poured derision on such a "monstrously doctrinaire and pedantic opinion". "The term putsch", he said, "in its scientific sense, may be employed when the attempt at insurrection has revealed nothing but a circle of conspirators or stupid maniacs, and has aroused no sympathy among the masses". This, he went on, was not the case insofar as the Irish rebellion was concerned, for the centuries-old Irish liberation movement, "having passed through various stages and combinations, expressed itself, among other things, in a mass Irish National Congress in America, which called for Irish independence; it also expressed itself in street fighting conducted by a section of the urban petty bourgeoisie and a section of the workers after a long period of mass agitation, demonstrations, suppression of papers, etc. Whoever calls such a rebellion a 'putsch' is either a hardened reactionary, or a doctrinaire who is hopelessly incapable of envisaging a social revolution as a living phenomenon."

Without in the least impugning the strength and vitality of the Irish liberation movement in 1916, one can confidently say that the anti-imperialist and anti-colonialist struggle of the Indian people during the time that Bhagat Singh and his comrades were carrying out their revolutionary activities had developed to an incomparably higher level-Bhagat Singh and his comrades were inseparably connected with, and an extension of, the powerful national movement of the Indian people, which was shaking the very foundations of British rule in India. Far from revealing them to be "... a circle of conspirators or stupid maniacs", their actions aroused mass sympathy among the Indian masses, who took up the cause and slogans of these revolutionary heroes as their own and, who through their love and adoration for the self-sacrificing heroism of the revolutionaries in the cause of the emancipation of the Indian masses, turned them into living legends. Only those who are hardened reactionaries, "hopelessly incapable of envisaging a socialist revolution as a living phenomenon" can condemn them as terrorists. In fact such was the popular acclaim for the courageous acts of Bhagat Singh and his comrades that even a hardened reactionary like Gandhi who, as we shall reveal later on, played such a dirty and complicity role in the judicial murder of these brave and wonderful sons of India, was obliged, under mass pressure, to shower praise on them-no matter how grudgingly and meanly.

Even today, seventy six years after their martyrdom, there are some who continue to accuse Bhagat Singh and his comrades of being infatuated with the ideology of anarchistic terrorism, in isolation from the masses. This, notwithstanding clear statements to the contrary by Bhagat Singh such as these, in which, while emphasising the significance and role of revolutionary violence, he forswears the use of terrorism as a method of struggle:

> *"Apparently I have acted like a terrorist. But I am not a terrorist. I am a revolutionary who has got definite ideas of a lengthy programme as is being discussed here ... Let me announce with all the strength at my command, that I am not a terrorist and I never was, except perhaps in the beginning of my revolutionary career. And I am convinced that we cannot get anything through these methods. ... I do not mean that bombs and pistols are useless,*

rather the contrary. But I mean to say that mere bomb-throwing is not only useless, but sometimes harmful. The military department of the Party should always keep ready all the war material at its command for any emergency. It should back the political work of the Party. It cannot and should not act independently".

In a message from his prison cell, this is how Bhagat Singh laid stress on the seizure of state power as an instrument for uprooting the existing social order based on exploitation:

"We mean by revolution the uprooting of the present social order. For this capture of state power is necessary. The state apparatus is now in the hands of the privileged class. The protection of the interests of the masses, the translation of our ideal into reality, that is, laying the foundation of society in accordance with the principles of Karl Marx, demand our seizure of this apparatus" (October 1930).

On 2 February 1931, less than two months before his judicial murder, Bhagat Singh wrote his memorable appeal 'To Young Political Workers', which has justly been deemed as his last testament. Having analysed the then prevailing political and social conditions and the cowardly and capitulatory programme and tactics of the Congress Party, he exhorted the youth to embrace the ideology of Marxism, join the Communist Party, work among the people and do everything in their power to organise the working class and the peasantry, and went on to lay before it (the youth) the following Leninist programme on maters of organisation:

"We require-to use the term so dear to Lenin-the 'professional revolutionaries'. The whole time workers who have no other ambition or life-work except the revolution. The greater the number of such workers organized into the Party, the greater the chances of your success. ... The name of the Party should be the Communist Party. This Party of political workers, bound by strict discipline, should handle all other movements. It shall have to organize the peasants' and workers' parties, labour unions, and may even venture to capture the Congress and kindred political bodies. And in order to create political consciousness, not only of national politics but class politics as well, the Party should organize a big publishing campaign".

In 1928, the British government sent the Simon Commission to India to look into the question of further constitutional reforms-a mere hoax to delay India's independence. Indians had neither been consulted over the constitution and the remit of this mockery of a Commission, nor did India have any representation on it. In the circumstances the Congress leadership decided to boycott the Commission and stage protest demonstrations against it. The revolutionaries of the HSRA resolved to actively support the boycott and the demonstrations. On the occasion of the arrival of the Commission in Lahore on 30 October 1928, hardly two months after the formation of the HSRA, a mammoth protest demonstration was held under the leadership of Lala Lajpat Rai.

The police subjected the participants to a baton charge. During this brutal action, Lala Lajpat Rai received several blows on his head from a baton wielded by a superintendent of police by the name of Scott. Lajpat Rai died on 17 November 1928 from his injuries. The entire country was astounded, with everyone feeling the pain and humiliation resulting from the brutal and senseless murder of Lajpat Rai by the colonial authorities. The youth of the country were particularly infuriated and burned with a desire to avenge Lajpat Rai's murder.

It was in these circumstances that the HSRA decided to kill Scott. One month to the day after Lajpat Rai's death, on 17 December 1928, Bhagat Singh, Rajguru, Sukhdev and Chandrashekar Azad shot dead another police officer, J.P.Saunders, who too had taken part in the attack on the demonstration of 30 October, mistakenly believing him to be Scott. Handwritten bills pasted on the walls of Lahore the same night, in which the HSRA claimed responsibility for the killing of Saunders, stated, inter alia: "With the death of J.P.Saunders, the assassination of Lala Lajpat Rai has been avenged. ... This national insult was a challenge to young men. Today the world has seen that the people of India are not lifeless; their blood has not become cold. They can lay down their lives for the country's honour. The proof of this has been given by the youth who are ridiculed and insulted by the leaders of their own country".

Continues the HSRA statement: "We are sorry to have killed a man. But this man was a part of a cruel, despicable and unjust system and killing him was a necessity. This man has been killed as an employee of the British Government. This government is the most oppressive government in the world.

"We are sorry for shedding human blood but it becomes necessary to bathe the altar of revolution with blood. Our aim is to bring about a revolution which would end all exploitation of man by man.

"Long Live Revolution!"

For nearly four months, all the efforts of the colonial authorities in tracing those who killed Saunders proved utterly fruitless. Only the next episode in the revolutionary struggle provided them with the clues that led to Bhagat Singh and his comrades, their trial by a specially constituted tribunal and their judicial murder by the colonial authorities. Let us turn to this episode.

The colonial government had introduced the draconian Public Safety Bill and the Trade Disputes Bill in the Central Legislative Assembly at Delhi, with the twin aims of suppressing the vibrant rising working-class movement and checking the increasing influence of the communists within this movement. As a prelude to this, on 20 March 1929, the colonial regime had arrested 31 prominent labour and communist leaders in various parts of India and brought them to court to face conspiracy charges in the notorious Meerut Conspiracy Case.

The HSRA resolved to dramatically interrupt the proceedings of the Assembly by lobbing bombs into the Chamber for the sole purpose of registering a protest against the passage of the above-mentioned Bills and the arbitrary and unjust incarceration of the communist and labour leaders. Never meant to kill anyone, the bombs were merely to serve as a warning to the authorities. Those given the responsibility to throw the bombs were to make no attempt to escape; instead they were to court arrest and use the inevitable court trial for propagating and popularising the programme and ideology of the HSRA among the wider masses of India.

After long discussion, the task of throwing the bombs was assigned to Bhagat Singh and Batukeshwar Dutt. While the former, as its most ideologically equipped member, was to explain the views and programme of the HSRA before the court and, through it, to the wider masses, Batukeshwar was included to emphasise the national, all-India, character of the revolutionary organisation.

The inclusion of Bhagat Singh was fraught with extreme risk as he had been a participant in the killing of J.P.Saunders. Be that as it may, as per the decision of the HSRA, on 8 April 1929, Bhagat Singh and Batukeshwar Dutt threw two bombs in the Central Assembly Hall, immediately following the passage of the Trade Disputes Bill.

Hardly anyone was seriously injured. All the same, pandemonium broke out on the official benches. Bhagat Singh also fired two unaimed shots from a pistol. Bhagat Singh and Dutt began shouting their favourite slogans: "Inquilab Zindabad" and "Down with British Imperialism" and threw copies of a leaflet into the Assembly Chamber.

This leaflet, under the name of the HSRA, together with the joint statement of Bhagat Singh and Dutt (whose author was Bhagat Singh alone), read out on their behalf by their lawyer Asaf Ali on 6 June 1929 in Sessions Court, gives us an accurate picture of the motive and extent of intention of the HSRA in executing the Assembly bomb plan, as well as its views on the significance of the use of force in pursuit of revolutionary goals, and the meaning and content of the word 'Revolution' as understood by Bhagat Singh and his comrades. It is well worth our while quoting extensively from these two documents and, in view of their significance, hopefully the reader will forgive us the use of lengthy quotations.

The leaflet thrown in the Assembly boldly announces that "It takes a loud voice to make the deaf hear...", adding that ".. while the people are expecting some more crumbs of reforms from the Simon Commission, ... the Government is thrusting upon them new repressive measures like the Public Safety and the Trade Disputes Bill, ... reserving the Press Sedition Bill for the next session. The indiscriminate arrests of labour leaders working in the open field clearly indicate wither the wind blows". It was these provocative conditions which had forced the HSRA to instruct its army to undertake the action it had, emphasising that while the government might succeed in killing a few individuals it will never succeed in stamping out the ideas concerning the liberation of the masses. Let the leaflet speak for itself:

> *"In these extremely provocative circumstances, the Hindustan Socialist Republican Association, in all seriousness, realizing their full responsibility, had decided and ordered its army to do this particular action, so that a stop be put to this humiliating farce and to let the alien bureaucratic exploiters do what they wish, but they must be made to come before the public eee in their naked form.*
>
> *"Let the representatives of the people return to their constituencies and prepare the masses for the coming revolution, and let the Government know that while protesting against the Public Safety and Trade Disputes Bills and the callous murder of Lala Lajpat Rai, on behalf of the helpless Indian masses, we want to emphasize the lesson often repeated by history, that it is easy to kill individuals but you cannot kill the ideas. Great empires crumbled while the ideas survived. Bourbons and Czars fell.*
>
> *"We are sorry to admit that we who attach so great a sanctity to human life, we who dream of a glorious future, when man will be enjoying perfect peace and full liberty, have been forced to shed human blood. But the sacrifice of individuals at the altar of the 'Great Revolution' that will bring freedom to all, rendering the exploitation of man by man impossible, is inevitable.*
>
> *"Long Live the Revolution".*

The 6 June statement of the accused in the court of judge Leonard Middleton, methodically and scientifically answers the charges laid against Bhagat Singh and Dutt, while throwing great light on their motivation and ideals. The question was raised in the court: Were bombs thrown into the

Assembly Chamber and Why? To the first half of the question, the accused replied in the affirmative. As to the second half of the question, the accused found it necessary "to go into some detail to offer a full and frank explanation of [their] motive and the circumstances leading up to what has become a historic moment.

"When we are told by some of the police officers, who visited us in jail that Lord Irwin in his address to the joint session of the two houses described the event as an attack directed against no individual but against an institution itself, we readily recognised that the true significance of the incident had been correctly appreciated.

"We are next to none in our love for humanity. Far from having any malice against any individual, we hold human life sacred beyond words.

"We are neither perpetrators of dastardly outrages, and, therefore, a disgrace to the country, as the pseudo-socialist Dewan Chaman Lal is reported to have described us, nor are we 'Lunatics' as 'The Tribune' of Lahore and some others would have it believed".

The statement goes on to say that the action of the revolutionaries was a "... practical protest against the institution, which, since its birth, has eminently helped to display not only its worthlessness but its far-reaching power for mischief", an institution which existed only "to demonstrate to the world India's humiliation and helplessness", and which symbolised "... the overriding domination of an irresponsible and autocratic rule". While resolutions such as those concerning the repeal of the repressive and arbitrary measures, passed the by House were routinely and "contemptuously trampled under foot on the floor of the so-called Indian Parliament", the government proposals, "rejected as unacceptable by the elected members of the legislatures, have been restored by a mere stroke of the pen".

Continues the statement: "In short, we have utterly failed to find any justification for the existence of an institution which, despite all its pomp and splendour, organized with the hard earned money of the sweating millions of India, is only a hollow show and a mischievous make-believe. Alike, have we failed to comprehend the mentality of the public leaders who help the Government to squander public time and money on such a manifestly stage-managed exhibition of India's helpless subjection.

"We have been ruminating upon all these matters, as also upon the wholesale arrests of the leaders of the labour movement. When the introduction of the Trade Disputes Bill brought us into the Assembly to watch its progress, the course of the debate only served to confirm our conviction that the labouring millions of India had nothing to expect from an institution that stood as a

menacing monument to the strangling of the exploiters and the serfdom of the helpless labourers.

"Finally, the insult of what we consider, an inhuman and barbarous measure was hurled on the devoted head of the representatives of the entire country, and the starving and struggling millions were deprived of their primary right and the sole means of improving their economic welfare. None who has felt like us for the dumb driven drudges of labourers could possibly witness this spectacle with equanimity. None whose heart bleeds for them, who have given their life-blood in silence to the building up of the economic structure could repress the cry which this ruthless blow had wrung out of our hearts."

In view of the above circumstance, the bomb had been dropped on the floor of the Assembly Chamber "... to register our protest on behalf of those who had no other means left to give expression to their heart-rending agony. Our purpose was 'to make the deaf hear' and to give the heedless a timely warning". That "... from under the seeming stillness of the sea of Indian humanity, a veritable storm is about to break out. We have only hoisted the 'danger-signal' to warn those who are speeding along without heeding the grave danger ahead ... " Taking a swipe at the apostles of Gandhian nonviolence, the statement says: "We have only marked the end of an era of utopian nonviolence, of whose futility the rising generation has been convinced beyond the shadow of doubt".

By way of an explanation on this question, the statement adds: " ... Force when aggressively applied is 'violence' and is, therefore, morally unjustifiable, but when it is used in furtherance of a legitimate cause, it has its moral justification. The elimination of force at all costs is utopian. ..."

6

Bhagat Singh Views on Violence and Non-violence

Recent events, particularly the congress resolution on the attempt to blow up the Viceregal Special on the 23 December, 1929, and Gandhi's subsequent writings in Young India, clearly show that the Indian National Congress, in conjunction with Gandhi, has launched a crusade against the revolutionaries. A great amount of public criticism, both from the press and the platform, has been made against them. It is a pity that they have all along been, either deliberately or due to sheer ignorance, misrepresented and misunderstood. The revolutionaries do not shun criticism and public scrutiny of their ideals or actions. They rather welcome these as chances of making those understand, who have a genuine desire to do so, the basic principles of the revolutionary movement and the high and noble ideals that are a perennial source of inspiration and strength to it. It is hoped that this article will help the general public to know the revolutionaries as they are and will prevent it from taking them for what interested and ignorant persons would have it believe them to be.

VIOLENCE OR NON-VIOLENCE

Let us, first of all, take up the question of violence and non-violence. We think that the use of these terms in itself, is a grave injustice to either party, for they express the ideals of neither of them correctly. Violence is physical force applied for committing injustice, and that is certainly not what the revolutionaries stand for. On the other hand, what generally goes by the name of non-violence is in reality the theory of soul force, as applied to the attainment of personal and national rights through courting, suffering and hoping thus to finally convert your opponent to your point of view. When a revolutionary believes certain things to be his right he asks for them, pleads for them, argues for them, wills to attain them with all the soul-force at his command, stands the greatest amount of suffering for them, is always prepared to make the highest sacrifice for their attainment, and also back his efforts with all the physical force he is capable of. You may coin what other word you like to describe his methods but you cannot call it violence, because that would constitute an outrage on the dictionary meaning of that word. Satyagraha is insistence upon truth. Why press, for the acceptance of truth, by soul-force alone? Why not add physical force also to it? While the revolutionaries stand for winning independence by all the forces, physical as-well as moral, at their command, the advocates of soul-force would like to ban the use of physical force. The question really, therefore, is not whether you will have violence, but whether you will have soul-force plus physical force or soul-force alone.

VIOLENCE AND MILITARY EXPENDITURE

Gandhi is of opinion that as violence has been practiced in the country it has resulted in an increase of military expenditure. I fhis reference is to revolutionary activities during the last twenty-five years we dispute the accuracy of his statement and challenge him to prove his statement with facts and figures. If, on the other hand, he had the wars that have taken place in India since the British came here in mind, our reply is that even his modest experiment in Ahimsa and Satyagraha which had little to compare in it with the wars for independence produced its effect on the finances of the bureaucracy. Mass action, whether violent or non-violent, whether successful or unsuccessful, is bound to produce the same kind of repercussion on the finances of a state.

THE REFORMS

Why should Gandhi mix up the revolutionaries with the various constitutional reforms granted by the governemtn? They never cared or worked for the Morely-Minto Reforms, Montague Reforms and the like. These the British government threw before the constitutionalist agitators to lure them away from the right path. This was the bribe paid to them for their support to the government in its policy of crushing and uprooting the revolutionaries. These toys - as Ganghi calls them - were sent to India for the benefit of those, who, from time to time, raised the cry of 'Home Rule', 'Self-Government', 'Responsible', 'Full Responsible Government', 'Dominion Status' and such other constitutional names for slavery. The revolutionaries never claim the Reforms as their achievements. They raised the standard of independence long ago. They have lived for it. They have ungrudgingly laid their lives down for the sake of this ideal. They claim that their sacrifices have produced a tremendous change in the mentality of the people. That their efforts have advanced the country a long way on the road to independence, is granted by even those who do no see eye to eye with them in politics.

THE WAY OF PROGRESS

As to Gandhi's contention that violence impedes the march of progress and thus directly postpones the day of freedom, we can refer him to so many contemporary instances where violence has led to the social progress and political freedom of the people who practiced it. Take the case of Russia and Turkey for example. In both countries the party for progress took over the state organization through an armed revolution. Yet social progress and political freedom have not been impeded. Legislation, backed by force, has made the masses go 'double march' on the road of progress. The solitary example of Afghanistan cannot establish a political formal. It is rather the exception that proves the rule.

FAILURE OF NON-COOPERATION

Gandhi IS of opinion that the great awakening in the people, during the days of non-cooperation, was a result of the preaching of non-violence. It is wrong to assign to nonviolence the widespread awakening of the masses which, in fact, is manifested wherever a programme of direct action is adopted. In Russia, for instance, there came about widespread awakening in the peasants and workers when the communists launched forth their great programme of Militant Mass Action, though nobody preached nonviolence to them. We will even go further and state that it was mainly the mania for non-violence and Gandhi's compromise mentality that brought about the disruption of the forces that had come together at the call of Mass Action. It is claimed that nonviolence can be used as a weapon for righting political wrongs. To say the least, it is a novel idea, yet untried. It failed to achieve what were considered to be the just rights of Indians in south Africa. It failed to bring 'Swaraj within a year' to the Indian masses in spite of the untiring labours of an army of national workers and one and a quarter crores of rupees. More recently, it failed to win for the Bardoli peasants what the leaders of the Satyagraha movement had promised them - the famous irreducible minimum of Gandhi and Patel. We know of no other trials non-violence has had on a country-wide scale. Up to this time non-violence has been blessed with one result - Failure. Little wonder, then, that the country refuses to give it another trial. In fact Satyagraha as preached by Gandhi is a form of agitation - a protest, leading up invariably, as has already been seen, to a compromise. It can hardly be of any use to a nation striving for national independence which can never come as the result of a compromise. The sooner we recognize that there can be no compromise between independence and slavery, the better.

IS IT A NEW ERA

'We are entering upon a new era', thinks Gandhi. The mere act of defining Swaraj as Complete Independence, this technical change in the Congress constitution, can hardly constitute a new era. It will be a great day indeed when Congress will decide upon a country-wide programme of Mass Action, based on well recognized revolutionary principles. Till then the unfurling o fthe flag of Independence is a mockery and we concur with the following remarks of Sarla Devi Chaudharani which she recently made in a press interview.

'The unfurling of the Flag of Independence', she says, 'at just one minute after midnight of the 31 December, 1929, was too stagy for words - just as the GOC and the assistant GOC and others in gaudy uniforms were card board Grand Officers Commanding.

'The fact that the unfurling of ht eflag of Independence lay hanging in the balance till midnight of that date, and that the scales might have been turned at even the eleventh hour fiftyninth minute had a message from the viceroy or the secretary of state come to the Congress granting Dominion Status, proves that Independence is not a heart hunger (sic) of the leaders but that the declaration of it is only like a petulant child's retort. It would have been a worthy action of the Indian National Congress if Independence was achieved first and declared afterwards.' It is true that the Congress orators will henceforth harangue the masses on Complete Independence instead of Dominion Status. They will call upon the people to prepare for a struggle in which one party is to deliver blows and the other is simply to receive them, till beaten and demoralized beyond hope of recovery. Can such a thing be named a struggle and can it ever lead the country to Complete Independence? It is all very well to hold fast to the highest ideal worthy of a nation, but it is nonetheless necessary, to adopt the best, the most efficacious and tried means to achieve it, are you became the laughing stock of the whole world.

NO BULLYING PLEASE

Gandhi has called upon all those who are not past reason to withdraw their support from the revolutionaries and condemn their actions so that 'our deluded patriots may, for want of nourishment to their violent spirit, realize the futility of violence and the great harm that violent activities have every time done'. How easy and convenient it is to call people deluded, to declare them to be past reason, to call upon the public to withdraw its support and condemn them so that they may get isolated and be forced to suspend their activities, specially when a man hold the confidence of an influential section of the public.

It is a pity that Gandhi does not and will not understand revolutionary psychology in spite of the life-long experience of public life. Life is a precious thing. It is clear to everyone. If a man becomes a revolutionary, if he goes about with his life in the hollow 'of his hand ready to sacrifice it at any moment, he does not do so merely for the fun of it. He does not risk his life merely because sometimes, when the crowd is in a sympathetic mood, it cries 'Bravo' in appreciation.

He does it because his reason forces him to take that course, because his conscience dictates it. A revolutionary believes in reason more than anything. It is to reason, and reason alone, tha the bows. No amount of abuse and condemnation, even if it emanates from the highest of the high can turn him from his set purpose. To think that a revolutionary will give up his ideas if public support and appreciation is withdrawn from him, is the highest folly. Many a revolutionary has, ere now, stepped on the scaffold and laid his life down for the cause, regardless of the curses that the constitutionalist agitators rained plentifully upon him. If you will have the revolutionaries suspend their activities, reason with them squarely. That is the one and the only way. For the rest let there be no doubt in anybody's mind. A revolutionary is the last person on earth to submit to bullying.

AN APPEAL

We take this opportunity to appeal to our countrymen - to the youth, to the workers and peasants, to the revolutionary intelligentsia - to come forward and join us in carrying a loft the banner of freedom. Let us establish a new order of society in which political and economic exploitation will be an impossibility. In the name of those gallant men and women who willingly accepted death so that we, their descendants, may lead a happier life, who toiled ceaselessly and perished for the poor, the famished, and exploited millions of India, we call upon every patriot to take up the fight in all seriousness. Let nobody toy with the nation's freedom which is her very life, by making psychological experiments in non-violence and such other novelties. Our slavery is our shame. When shall we have courage and wisdom enough to be able to shake ourselves free of it? What is our great heritage of civilization and culture worth if we have not enough self-respect left in us to prevent us from bowing surveillance to the commands of foreigners and paying homage to their flag and kind?

OUR IDEAL

The revolutionaries believe that the deliverance of their country will come through revolution. The revolution, they are constantly working and hoping for, will not only express itself in the form of an armed conflict between the foreign government and

its supporters and the people, it will also usher in a new social order. The revolution will ring the death knell of capitalism and class distinctions and privileges. It will bring joy and prosperity to the starving millions who are seething today under the terrible yoke of both foreign and Indian exploitation. It will bring the nation into its own. It will give birth to a new state - a new social order. Above all, it will establish the dictatorship of the proletariat and will for ever banish social parasites from the seat of political power.

TERRORISM

The revolutionaries already see the advent of the revolution in the restlessness of youth, in its desire to break free from the mental bondage and religious superstitions that hold them. As the youth will get more and more saturated with the psychology of revolution, it will come to have a clearer realization of national bondage and a growing, intense, unquenchable thirst for freedom. It will grow, this feeling of bondage, this insatiable desire for freedom, till, in their righteous anger, the infuriated youth will begin to kill the oppressors. Thus has terrorism been born in the country. It is a phase, a necessary, an inevitable phase of the revolution. Terrorism is not the complete revolution and the revolution is not complete without terrorism. This thesis can be supported by an analysis of any and every revolution in history. Terrorism instills fear in the hearts of the oppressors, it brings hopes of revenge and redemption to the oppressed masses, it gives courage and self-confidence to the wavering, it shatters the spell of the superiority of the ruling class and raises the status of the subject race in the eyes of the world, because it is the most convincing proof of a nation's hunger for freedom. Here in India, as in other countries in the past, terrorism will develop into the revolution and the revolution into independence, social, political and economic.

REVOLUTIONARY METHODS

This then is what the revolutionaries believe in, that is what they hope to accomplish for their country. They are doing it both openly and secretly, and in their won way. The experience of a century long and world-wide struggle, between the masses and the governing class, is their guide to their goal, and the methods they are following have never been known to have failed.

THE CONGRESS AND THE REVOLUTIONARIES

Meanwhile, what has the Congress being doing? It has changed its creed from Swaraj to Complete Independence. As a logical sequence to this, one would expect it to declare a war on the British government. Instead, we find, it has declared war against the revolutionaries. The first offensive of the Congress came in the form of a resolution deploring the attempt made on the 23 December, 1929, to blow up the Viceroy's Special. It was drafted by Gandhi and he fought tooth and nail for it, with the result that was passed by a trifling majority of 81 in a house of 1,713.

Was even this bare majority a result of honest political convictions? Let us quote the opinion of Sarla Devi Chaudharani who has been a devotee of the Congress all her life, in reply. She says: 'I discovered in the course of my conversation with a good many of the Mahatma's followers that it was only their sense of personal loyalty to him that was keeping them back from an expression of the independence views and preventing them from voting against nay resolution whatsoever that was fathered by Mahatmaji.'

As to Gandhi's arguments in favour of his proposition, we will deal with them later, when we discuss his article The Cult of the Bomb which is more or less an amplification of his speech in the Congress. There is one fact a bout this deplorable resolution which we must not lose sight of, and that is this. In spite of the fact, that the Congress is pledged to non-violence and has been actively engaged in carrying on propaganda in its favour for the last ten years, and in spite of the fact also that the supporters of the resolution indulged in abuse, called the the revolutionaries 'cowards' and described their actions as 'dastardly' - and one of them even threateningly remarked that if they wanted to be led by Gandhi, they should pass this resolution without any opposition - in spite of all this, the resolution could only be adopted by a dangerously narrow majority.

That demonstrates, beyond the shadow of a doubt, how solidly the country is backing the revolutionaries. In a way Gandhi deserved our thanks for having brought the question up for discussion and thus having shown to the world at large that even the Congress - that stronghold of non-violence - is at least as much, if not more, with the revolutionaries as with him.

GANDHI ON WAR PATH

Having achieved a victory which cost him more than a defeat, Gandhi has returned to the attack in his article The Cult of the Bomb. We will give it our closest attention before proceeding further. That article consists of three things - his faith, his opinion and his arguments. We will not discuss what is a matter of faith with him because reason has little in common with faith. Let us then take such of his opinion as are backed by arguments and his arguments proper, against what he calls violence and discuss them one by one.

DO THE MASSES BELIEVE IN NON-VIOLENCE

He thinks that on the basis of his experience during his latest tour in the country, he is right in believing that the large masses of Indian humanity are yet untouched by the spirit of violence and that non-violence has come to stay as a political weapon. Let him not delude himself on the experiences of his latest tour in the country. Though it is true that the average leader confines his tours to places where only the mail train can conveniently land him while Gandhi has extended his tour limit to where a motorcar can take him, the practice of staying only with the richest people in the places visited, of spending most of his time on being complimented by his devotees in private and public, and of granting Darshan now and then to the illiterate masses whom he claims to understand so well, disqualifies him from claiming to know the mind of the masses.

No man can claim to know a people's mind by seeing them from the public platform and giving them Darshan and Updesh. He can at the most claim to have told the masses what he thinks about things. Has Gandhi, during recent years, mixed in the social life of the masses?

Has he sat with the peasant round the evening fire and tried to know what he things? Has he passed a single evening in the company of a factory labourer and shared with him his vowes? (sic).

We have, and therefore we claim to know what the masses think. We assure Gandhi that the average Indian, like the average human being, understands little of the fine theological niceties about Ahimsa and loving one's enemy. The way of the world is like this. You have a friend: you love him, sometimes so much that you even die for him. You have an enemy: you shun him, you fight against him and, if possible, kill him. The gospel of the revolutionaries is simple and straight. It is what has been since the days of Adam and Eve, and no man has any difficulty about understanding it. We affirm that the masses of India are solidly with us because we know it from personal experience. The day is not far off when they will flock in their thousands to work the will of the Revolution.

THE GOSPEL OF LOVE

Gandhi declares that his faith in the efficacy of non-violence has increased. That is to say, he believes more and more, that through his gospel of love and self-imposed suffering, he hopes someday to convert the foreign rulers to his way of thinking. Now, he has devoted his whole life to the preaching of his wonderful gospel and has practiced it with unwavering constance, (sic) as few others have done. Will he let the world know how many enemies of India he has been able to turn into friends? How many O'Dwyers, Readings and Irwins has he been able to convert into friends of India? If none, how can India be expected to share his 'growing faith' that he will be able to persuade or compel England to agree to Indian Independence through the practice of non-violence?

WHAT WOULD HAVE HAPPENED

If the bomb, that burst under the Viceroy's Special, had exploded properly, one of the two things suggested by Gandhi would have surely happened. The viceroy would have either been badly injured or killed. Under such circumstances there certainly would have been no meeting between the leaders of political parties and the viceroy. The uncalled for and undignified attempt on the part of these individuals, to lower the national prestige by knocking at the gates of the government house with the beggar's bowl in their hands and dominion status on their lips, in spite of the clear terms of the Culcutta Ultimatum, would have been checkmated and the nation would have been the better off for that.

If, fortunately, the explosion had been powerful enough to kill the viceroy, one more enemy of India would have met a well deserved doom. The author of the Meerut prosecutions and the Lahore and Bhusawal persecutions can appear a friend of India only to the enemies of her freedom. In spite of Gandhi and Nehru and their claims to political sagacity and statesmanship, Irwin has succeeded in shattering the unity between different political parties in the country, that had resulted from the boycott of the Simon Commission. Even the Congress today is a house divided against itself. Who else, except the viceroy and his olive tongue, have we to thank for our grave misfortunes? And yet, there exist people in our country who proclaim him a Friend of India.

THE FUTURE OF THE CONGRESS

There might be those who have no regard for the Congress and hope nothing from it. If Gandhi thinks that the revolutionaries belong to the category, he wrongs them grievously. They fully realize the part played by the Congress in awakening among the ignorant masses a keen desire for freedom. They expect great things of it in the future. Though they hold firmly to their opinion, that so long as persons like Sen Gupta whose wonderful intelligence compels him to discern the hand of the CID in the late attempt to blow up the Viceroy's Special, and persons like Ansari, who think abuse the better part of argument and know so little of politics as to make the ridiculous and fallacious assertion that no nation had achieved freedom by the bomb, have a determining voice in the affairs of the Congress, the country can hope little from it; they are hopefully looking forward to the day, when the mania of non-violence would have passed away from the Congress, and it would march arm in arm-with the revolutionaries to their common goal of complete Independence. This year, it has accepted the ideal which the revolutionaries have preached and live upto more than a quarter of a century. Let us hope the next year will see it endorse their methods also.

VICTORY OR DEATH

There is no crime that Britain has not committed in India. Deliberate misrule has reduced us to paupers, has 'bled us white'. As a race and a people we stand dishonoured and outraged. Do people still expect us to forget and to forgive? We shall have our revenge - a people's righteous revenge on the tyrant. Let cowards fall back and cringe for compromise and peace. We ask not for mercy and we give no quarter. Ours is a war to the end - to Victory or Death.

7

Views and Legacy of Bhagat Singh

WHY I AM AN ATHEIST?

A new question has cropped up. Is it due to vanity that I do not believe in the existence of an omnipotent, omnipresent and omniscient God? I had never imagined that I would ever have to confront such a question. But conversation with some friends has given me, a hint that certain of my friends, if I am not claiming too much in thinking them to be so-are inclined to conclude from the brief contact they have had with me, that it was too much on my part to deny the existence of God and that there as a certain amount of vanity that actuated my disbelief.

Well, the problem is a serious one. I do not boast to be quite above these human traits. I am a man and nothing more. None can claim to be more. I also have this weakness in me. Vanity does form a part of my nature. Amongst my comrades I was called an autocrat. Even my friend Mr. B.K. Dutt sometimes called me so. On certain occasions I was decried as a despot. Some friends do complain and very seriously too that I involuntarily thrust my opinions upon others and get my proposals accepted. That this is true up to a certain extent, I do not deny. This may amount to egotism. There is vanity in me in as much as our cult as opposed to other popular creeds is concerned. But that is not personal. It may be, it is only legitimate pride in our cult and does not amount to vanity. Vanity or to be more precise "Ahankar" is the excess of undue pride in one's self. Whether it is such an undue pride that has led me to atheism or whether it is after very careful study of the subject and after much consideration that I have come to disbelieve in God, is a question that I, intend to discuss here. Let me first make it clear that egotism and vanity are two different things.

In the first place, I have altogether failed to comprehend as to how undue pride or vain-gloriousness could ever stand in the way of a man in believing in God. I can refuse to recognize the greatness of a really great man provided I have also achieved a certain amount of popularity without deserving it or without having possessed the qualities really essential or indispensable for the same purpose.

That much is conceivable. But in what way can a man believing in God cease believing due to his personal vanity? There are only two Ways. The man should either begin to think himself a rival of God or he may begin to believe himself to be God. In neither case can he become a genuine atheist. In the first case he does not even deny the existence of his rival. In the second case as well he admits the existence of a conscious being behind the screen guiding all the movements of nature.

It is of no importance to us whether he thinks himself to be that supreme being or whether he thinks the supreme conscious being to be somebody apart from himself. The fundamental is there. His belief is there. He is by no means an atheist. Well, here I am I neither belong to the first category nor to the second.

I deny the very existence of that Almighty Supreme being. Why I deny it shall be dealt with later on. Here I want to clear one thing, that it is not vanity that has actuated me to adopt the doctrines of atheism. I am neither a rival nor an incarnation nor the Supreme Being Himself. One point is decided, that it is not vanity that has led me to this mode of thinking. Let me examine the facts to disprove this allegation. According to these friends of mine I have grown vain-glorious perhaps due to the undue popularity gained during the trials-both Delhi Bomb and Lahore conspiracy cases. Well, let us see if their premises are correct. My atheism is not of so recent origin. I had stopped believing in God when I was an obscure young man, of whose existence my above mentioned friends were not even aware. At least a college student cannot cherish any short of undue pride which may lead him to atheism. Though a favorite with some professors and disliked by certain others, I was never an industrious or a studious boy. I could not get any chance of indulging in such feelings as vanity. I was rather a boy with a very shy nature, who had certain pessimistic dispositions about the future career. And in those days, I was not a perfect atheist.

My grandfather under whose influence I was brought up is an orthodox Arya Samajist. An Arya Samajist is anything but an atheist. After finishing my primary education I joined the DAV. School of Lahore and stayed in its Boarding House for full one year. There, apart from morning and evening prayers, I used to recite "Gayatri Mantra" for hours and hours. I was a perfect devotee in those days. Later on I began to live with my father. He is a liberal in as much as the orthodoxy of religions is concerned. It was through his teachings that I aspired to devote my life to the cause of freedom. But he is not an atheist. He is a firm believer. He used to encourage me for offering prayers daily. So, this is how I was brought up. In the Non-Co-operation days I joined the National College. it was there that I began to think liberally and discuss and criticize all the religious problems, even about God. But still I was a devout believer. By that time I had begun to preserve the unshorn and unclipped long hair but I could never believe in the mythology and doctrines of Sikhism or, any other religion. But I had a firm faith in God's existence.

Later on I joined the revolutionary party. The first leader with whom I came

in contact, though not convinced, could not dare to deny the existence of God. On my persistent inquiries about God, he used to say, "Pray whenever you want to". Now this is atheism less courage required for the adoption of that creed. The second leader with whom I came in contact was a firm believer. Let me mention his name-respected comrade Sachindra Nath Sanyal, now undergoing life transportation in connexion with the Karachi conspiracy case. From the every first page of his famous and only book, "Bandi Jivan" (or Incarcerated Life), the Glory of God is sung vehemently. In the last page of the second part of that beautiful book his mystic-because of Vedantism - praises showered upon God form a very conspicuous part of his thoughts.

"The Revolutionary leaflet" distributed- throughout India on January 28th, 1925, was according to the prosecution story the result of his intellectual labor, Now, as is inevitable in the secret work the prominent leader expresses his own views, which are very dear to his person and the rest of the workers have to acquiesce in them-in spite of differences, which they might have. In that leaflet one full paragraph was devoted to praise the Almighty and His rejoicings and doing. That is all mysticism. What I wanted to point out was that the idea of disbelief had not even germinated in the revolutionary party. The famous Kakori martyrs -all four of them-passed their last day in prayers. Ram Prasad Bismil was an orthodox Arya Samajist. Despite his wide studies in the field of Socialism and Communism, Rajen Lahiri could not suppress his desire, of reciting hymns of the Upanishads and the Gita. I saw only one man amongst them, who never prayed and used to say, "Philosophy is the outcome of human weakness or limitation of knowledge". He is also undergoing a sentence of transportation for life. But he also never dared to deny the existence of God.

UP to that period I was only a romantic idealist revolutionary. Uptil then we were to follow. Now came the time to shoulder the whole responsibility. Due to the inevitable reaction for some time the very existence of the Party seemed impossible. Enthusiastic comrades - nay leaders - began to jeer at us. For some time I was afraid that some day I also might not be convinced of the futility of our own program. That was a turning point in my revolutionary career. "Study" was the cry that reverberated in the corridors of my mind. Study to enable yourself to face the arguments advanced by opposition. Study to arm yourself with arguments in favor of your cult. I began to study. My previous faith and convictions underwent a remarkable modification. The Romance of the violent methods alone which was so prominent amongst our predecessors, was replaced by serious ideas. No more mysticism, no more blind faith. Realism became our cult. Use of force justifiable when resorted to as a matter of terrible necessity: non-violence as policy indispensable for all mass movements. So much about methods.

The most important thing was the clear conception of the ideal for which we were to fight, As there were no important activities in the field of action I got ample opportunity to study various ideals of the world revolution. I studied Bakunin, the Anarchist leader, something of Marx the father of Communism and much of Lenin, Trotsky and others the men who had successfully carried out a revolution in their country. They were all atheists. Bakunin's "God and State", though only fragmentary, is an interesting study of the subject. Later still I came across a book entitled 'Common Sense' by Nirlamba Swami. It was only a sort of mystic atheism. This subject became of utmost interest to me. By the end of 1926 I had been convinced as to the baselessness of the theory of existence of an almighty supreme being who created, guided and controlled the universe. I had given out this disbelief of mine. I began discussion on the subjects with my friends. I had become a pronounced atheist. But, what it meant will presently be discussed.

In May 1927 I was arrested at Lahore. The arrest was a surprise. I was quite unaware of (he fact that the police wanted me. All of a sudden while passing through a garden I found myself surrounded by police. To my own surprise, I was very calm at that time. I did not feel any sensation, neither did I experience any excitement. I was taken into police custody. Next day I was taken to the Railway Police lock-up where I was to pass full one month. After many day's conversation with the Police officials I guessed that they had some information regarding my connexion with the Kakori Party and my other activities in connexion with the revolutionary movement. They told me that I had been to Lucknow while the trial was going on there, that I had negotiated a certain scheme about their rescue, that after obtaining their approval, we had procured some bombs, that by way of test one of the bombs was thrown in the crowd on the occasion of Dussehra 1926. They further informed me, in my interest, that if I could give any statement throwing some light on the activities of the revolutionary party, I was not to be imprisoned but on the contrary set free and rewarded even without being produced as an approver in the Court. I laughed at the proposal. It was all humbug.

People holding ideas like ours do not throw bombs on their own innocent people. One fine morning Mr. Newman, the then Senior Superintendent of CID., came to me. And after much sympathetic talk with me imparted-to him-the extremely sad news that if I did not give any statement as demanded by them, they would be forced to send me up for trial for conspiracy to wage war in connexion with Kakori Case and for brutal murders in connexion with Dussehra Bomb outrage. And he further informed me that they had evidence enough to get me convicted and hanged.

In those days I believed - though I was quite innocent - the police could do it if they desired. That very day certain police officials began to persuade me to offer my prayers to God regularly both the times. Now I was an atheist. I wanted to settle for myself whether it was in the days of peace and enjoyment alone that I could boast of being an atheist or whether during such hard times as well I could stick to those principles of mine. After great consideration I decided that I could not lead myself to believe in and pray to God. No, I never did. That was the real test and I came, out successful. Never for a moment did I desire to save my neck at the cost of certain other things. So I was a staunch disbeliever : and have ever since been. It was not an easy job to stand that test.

'Belief' softens the hardships, even can make them pleasant. In God man can find very strong consolation and support. Without Him, the man has to depend upon himself. To stand upon one's own legs amid storms and hurricanes is not a child's play. At such testing moments, vanity, if any, evaporates, and man cannot dare to defy the general beliefs, if he does, then we must conclude that he has got certain other strength than mere vanity. This is exactly the situation now. Judgment is already too well known. Within a week it is to be pronounced. What is the consolation with the exception of the idea that I am going to sacrifice my life for a cause ? A God-believing Hindu might be expecting to be reborn as a king, a Muslim or a Christian might dream of the luxuries to be- enjoyed in paradise and the reward he is to get for his sufferings and sacrifices. But what am I to expect? I know the moment the rope is fitted round my neck and rafters removed, from under my feet. That will be the final moment, that will be the last moment. I, or to be more precise, my soul, as interpreted in the metaphysical terminology, shall all be finished there. Nothing further.

A short life of struggle with no such magnificent end, shall in itself be the reward if I have the courage to take it in that light. That is all. With no selfish motive, or desire to be awarded here or hereafter, quite disinterestedly have I devoted my life to the cause of independence, because I could not do otherwise. The day we find a great number of men and women with this psychology who cannot devote themselves to anything else than the service of mankind and emancipation of the suffering humanity; that day shall inaugurate the era of liberty.

Not to become a king, nor to gain any other rewards here, or in the next birth or after death in paradise, shall they be inspired to challenge the oppressors, exploiters, and tyrants, but to cast off the yoke of serfdom from the neck of humanity and to establish liberty and peace shall they tread this-to their individual selves perilous and to their noble selves the only glorious imaginable-path. Is the pride in their noble cause to be - misinterpreted as vanity? Who dares to utter such an abominable epithet? To him, I say either he is a fool or a knave. Let us forgive him for he can not realize the depth, the emotion, the sentiment and the noble feelings that surge in that heart. His heart is dead as a mere lump of flesh, his eyes are-weak, the evils of other interests having been cast over them. Self-reliance is always liable to be interpreted as vanity. It is sad and miserable but there is no help.

You go and oppose the prevailing faith, you go and criticize a hero, a great man, who is generally believed to be above criticism because he is thought to be infallible, the strength of your argument shall force the multitude to decry you as vainglorious. This is due to the mental stagnation, Criticism and independent thinking are the two indispensable qualities of a revolutionary. Because Mahatamaji is great, therefore none should criticize him. Because he has risen above, therefore everything he says-may be in the field of Politics or Religion, Economics or Ethics-is right. Whether you are convinced or not you must say, "Yes, that's true". This mentality does not lead towards progress. It is rather too obviously, reactionary.

Because our forefathers had set up a faith in some supreme, being - the Almighty God - therefore any man who dares to challenge the validity of that faith, or the very existence of that supreme being, he shall have to be called an apostate, a renegade. If his arguments are too sound to be refuted by counter-arguments and spirit too strong to be cowed down by the threat of misfortunes that may befall him by the wrath of the Almighty, he shall be decried as vainglorious, his spirit to be denominated as vanity. Then why to waste time in this vain discussion? Why try to argue out the whole thing? This question is coming before the public for the first time, and is being handled in this matter of fact way for the first time, hence this lengthy discussion.

As for the first question, I think I have cleared that it is not vanity that has led me to atheism. My way of argument has proved to be convincing or not, that is to be judged by my readers, not me. I know in the present, circumstances my faith in God would have made my life easier, my burden lighter and my disbelief in Him has turned all the circumstances too dry and the situation may assume too harsh a shape. A little bit of mysticism can make it poetical. But I, do not want the help of any intoxication to meet my fate. I am a realist. I have been trying to overpower the instinct in me by the help of reason. I have not always been successful in achieving this end. But man's duty is to try and endeavor, success depends upon chance and environments.

As for the second question that if it was not vanity, then there ought to be some reason to disbelieve the old and still prevailing faith of the existence of God. Yes; I come to that now Reason there is. According to. me, any man who has got some reasoning power at his command always tries to reason out his environments. Where direct proofs are lacking philosophy occupies the important place. As I have already stated, a certain revolutionary friend used to say that Philosophy is the outcome of human weakness. When our ancestors had leisure enough to try to solve out the mystery of this world, its past, present and the future, its whys and wherefores, they having been terribly short of direct proofs, everybody tried to solve the problem in his own way. Hence we find the wide differences in the fundamentals of various religious creeds, which some times assume very antagonistic and conflicting shapes. Not only the Oriental and Occidental philosophies differ, there are differences even amongst various schools of thoughts in each hemisphere. Amongst Oriental religions, the Moslem faith is not at all compatible with Hindu faith. In India alone Buddhism and Jainism are sometimes quite separate from Brahmanism, in which there are again conflicting faiths as Arya Samaj and Sanatan Dharma. Charwak is still another independent thinker of the past ages. He challenged the authority of God in the old times. All these creeds differ from each other on the fundamental question., and everybody considers himself to be on the right. There lies the misfortune. Instead of using the experiments and expressions of the ancient Savants and thinkers as a basis for our future struggle against ignorance and to try to find out a solution to this mysterious problem, we - lethargical as we have proved to be - raise the hue and cry of faith, unflinching and unwavering faith to their versions and thus are guilty of stagnation in human progress.

Any man who stands for progress has to criticize, disbelieve and challenge every item of the old faith. Item by item he has to reason out every nook and corner of the prevailing faith. If after considerable reasoning one is led to believe in any theory or philosophy, his faith is welcomed. His reasoning can be mistaken, wrong, misled and sometimes fallacious. But he is liable to correction because reason is the guiding star of his life. But mere faith and blind faith is dangerous: it dulls the brain, and makes a man reactionary.

A man who claims to be a realist has to challenge the whole of the ancient faith. If it does not stand the onslaught of reason it crumbles down. Then the first thing for him is to shatter the whole down and clear a space for the erection of a new philosophy. This is the negative side. After it begins the positive work in which sometimes some material of the old faith may be used for the purpose of reconstruction. As far as I am concerned, let me admit at the very outset that I have not been able to study much on this point. I had a great desire to study the Oriental Philosophy but I could not get any chance or opportunity to do the same. But so far as the negative study is under discussion, I think I am convinced to the extent of questioning the soundness of the old faith. I have been convinced as to non-existence of a conscious supreme being who is guiding and directing the movements of nature. We believe in nature and the whole progressive movement aims at the domination of man over nature for his service. There is no conscious power behind it to direct. This is what our philosophy is.

As for the negative side. we ask a few questions from the 'believers'.

If, as you believe, there is an almighty, omnipresent, omniscient and omnipotent God-who created the earth or world, please let me know why did he create it ? This world of woes and miseries, a veritable, eternal combination of numberless tragedies: Not a single soul being perfectly satisfied.

Pray, don't say that it is His Law: If he is bound by any law, he is not omnipotent. He is another slave like ourselves. Please don't say that it is his enjoyment. Nero burnt one Rome. He killed a very limited number of people. He created very few tragedies, all to his perfect enjoyment. And what is his place in History? By what names do the historians mention him? All the venomous epithets are showered upon him. Pages are blackened with invective diatribes condemning Nero, the tyrant, the heartless, the wicked.

One Changezkhan sacrificed a few thousand lives to seek pleasure in it and we hate the very name. Then how are you going to justify your almighty, eternal Nero, who has been, and is still causing numberless tragedies every day, every hour and every minute? How do you think to support his misdoings which surpass those of Changez every single moment? I say why did he create this world - a veritable hell, a place of constant and bitter unrest? Why did the Almighty create man when he had the power not to do it? What is the justification for all this ? Do you say to award the innocent sufferers hereafter and to punish the wrong-doers as well? Well, well: How far shall you justify a man who may dare to inflict wounds upon your body to apply a very soft and soothing liniment upon it afterwards? How far the supporters and organizers of the Gladiator Institution were justified in throwing men before the half starved furious lions to be cared for and well looked after if they could survive and could manage to escape death by the wild beasts? That is why I ask, 'Why did the conscious supreme being created this world and man in it? To seek pleasure? Where then is the difference between him and Nero'?

You Mohammadens and Christians : Hindu Philosophy shall still linger on to offer another argument. I ask you what is your answer to the above-mentioned question? You don't believe in previous birth. Like Hindus you cannot advance the argument of previous misdoings of the apparently quite innocent sufferers? I ask you why did the omnipotent labor for six days to create the world through word and each day to say that all was well. Call him today. Show him the past history. Make him study the present situation. Let us see if he dares to say, "All is well". From the dungeons of prisons, from the stores of starvation consuming millions upon millions of human beings in slums and huts, from the exploited laborers, patiently or say apathetically watching the procedure of their blood being sucked by the Capitalist vampires, and the wastage of human energy that will make a man with the least common sense shiver with horror, and from the preference of throwing the surplus of production in oceans rather than to distribute amongst the needy producers…to the palaces of kings built upon the foundation laid with human bones.... let him see all this and let him say "All is well".

Why and wherefore? That is my question. You are silent.

All right then, I proceed. Well, you Hindus, you say all the present sufferers belong to the class of sinners of the previous births. Good. You say the present oppressors were saintly people in their previous births, hence they enjoy power. Let me admit that your ancestors were very shrewd people, they tried to find out theories strong enough to hammer down all the efforts of reason and disbelief. But let us analyze how far this argument can really stand.

From the point of view of the most famous jurists punishment can be justified only from three or four ends to meet which it is inflicted upon the wrongdoer. They are retributive, reformative and deterrent. The retributive theory is now being condemned by all the advanced thinkers. Deterrent theory is also following the same fate. Reformative theory is the only one which is essential, and indispensable for human progress. It aims at returning the offender as a most competent and a peace-loving citizen to the society. But what is the nature of punishment inflicted by God upon men even if we suppose them to be offenders. You say he sends them to be born as a cow, a cat, a tree, a herb or a best. You enumerate these punishments to be 84 lakhs. I ask you what is its reformative effect upon man? How many men have met you who say that they were born as a donkey in previous birth for having committed any sin? None. Don't quote your Puranas. I have no scope to touch your mythologies. Moreover do you know that the greatest sin in this world is to be poor. Poverty is a sin, it is a punishment.

I ask you how far would you appreciate a criminologist, a jurist or a legislator who proposes such measures of punishment which shall inevitably force man to commit more offences? Had not your God thought of this or he also had to learn these things by experience, but at the cost of untold sufferings to be borne by humanity? What do you think shall be the fate of a man who has been born in a poor and illiterate family of say a chamar or a sweeper. He is poor, hence he cannot study. He is hated and shunned by his fellow human beings who think themselves to be his superiors having been born in say a higher caste. His ignorance, his poverty and the treatment meted out to him shall harden his heart towards society. Suppose he commits a sin, who shall bear the consequences? God, he or the learned ones of, the society? What about the punishment of those people who were deliberately kept ignorant by the haughty and egotist Brahmans and who had to pay the penalty by bearing the stream of being led (not lead) in their ears for having heard a few sentences of your Sacred Books of learning-the Vedas? If they committed any offence-who was to be responsible for them and who was to bear the brunt?

My dear friends: These theories are the inventions of the privileged ones: They justify their usurped power, riches and superiority by the help of these theories. Yes: It was perhaps Upton Sinclair, that wrote at some place, that just make a man a believer in immortality and then rob him of all his riches, and possessions. He shall help you even in that ungrudgingly. The coalition amongst the religious preachers and possessors of power brought forth jails, gallows, knouts and these theories.

I ask why your omnipotent God, does not stop every man when he is committing any sin or offence? He can do it quite easily. Why did he not kill war lords or kill the fury of war in them and thus avoid the catastrophe hurled down on the head of humanity by the Great War? Why does he not just produce a certain sentiment in the mind of the British people to liberate India? Why does he not infuse the altruistic enthusiasm in the hearts of all capitalists to forgo their rights of personal possessions of means of production and thus redeem the whole laboring community - nay the whole human society from the bondage of Capitalism. You want to reason out the practicability of socialist theory, I leave it for your almighty to enforce it.

People recognize the merits of socialism in as much as the general welfare is concerned. They oppose it under the pretext of its being impracticable. Let the Almighty step in and arrange everything in an orderly fashion. Now don't try to advance round about arguments, they are out of order. Let me tell you, British rule is here not because God wills it but because they possess power and we do not dare to oppose them. Not that it is with the help of God that they are keeping us under their subjection but it is with the help of guns and rifles, bomb and bullets, police and millitia and our apathy that they are successfully committing the most deplorable sin against society- the outrageous exploitation of one nation by another. Where is God ? What is he doing? Is he enjoying all I these woes of human race ? A Nero; A Changez : Down with him.

Do you ask me how I explain the origin of this world and origin of man? Alright I tell you. Charles Darwin has tried to throw some light on the subject. Study him. Read Soham Swami's "Commonsense". It shall answer your question to some extent. This is a phenomenon of nature. The accidental mixture of different substances in the shape of nebulae produced this earth. When? Consult history. The same process produced animals and in the long run man. Read Darwin's 'Origin of Species'. And all the later progress is due to man's constant conflict with nature and his efforts to override it. This is the briefest possible explanation of this phenomenon.

Your other argument may be just to ask why a child is born blind or lame if not due to his deeds committed in the previous birth? This problem has been explained away by biologists as a more biological phenomenon. According to them the whole burden rests upon the shoulders of the parents who may be conscious or ignorant of their own deeds led to mutilation of the child previous to its birth.

Naturally you may ask another question though it is quite childish in essence. If no God existed, how did the people come to believe in him? My answer is clear and brief. As they came to believe in ghosts, and evil spirits; the only difference is that belief in God is almost universal and the philosophy well developed. Unlike certain of the radicals I would not attribute its origin to the ingenuity of the exploiters who wanted to keep the people under their subjection by preaching the existence of a supreme being and then claiming an authority and sanction from him for their privileged positions. Though I do not differ with them on the essential point that all faiths, religions, creeds and such other institutions became in turn the mere supporters of the tyrannical and exploiting institutions, men and classes. Rebellion against king is always a sin according to every religion.

As regards the origin of God my own idea is that having realized the limitations of man, his weaknesses and shortcoming having been taken into consideration, God was brought into imaginary existence to encourage man to face boldly all the trying circumstances, to meet all dangers manfully and to check and restrain his outbursts in prosperity and affluence. God both with his private laws and parental generosity was imagined and painted in greater details. He was to serve as a deterrent factor when his fury and private laws were discussed so that man may not become a danger to society. He was to serve as a father, mother, sister and brother, friend and helpers when his parental qualifications were to be explained. So that when man be in great distress having been betrayed and deserted by all friends he may find consolation in the idea that an ever true friend was still there to help him, to support him and that He was almighty and could do anything. Really that was useful to the society in the primitive age.

The idea of God is helpful to man in distress.

Society has to fight out this belief as well as was fought the idol worship and the narrow conception of religion. Similarly, when man tries to stand on his own legs, and become a realist he shall have to throw the faith aside, and to face manfully all the distress, trouble, in which the circumstances may throw him. That is exactly my state of affairs. It is not my vanity, my friends. It is my mode of thinking that has made me an atheist. I don't know whether in my case belief in God and offering of daily prayers which I consider to be most selfish and degraded act on the part of man, whether these prayers can prove to be helpful or they shall make my case worse still. I have read of atheists facing all troubles quite boldly, so am I trying to stand like a man with an erect head to the last; even on the gallows.

Let us see how I carry on : one friend asked me to pray. When informed of my atheism, he said, "During your last days you will begin to believe". I said, No, dear Sir, it shall not be. I will think that to be an act of degradation and demoralization on my part. For selfish motives I am not going to pray. Readers and friends, "Is this vanity"? If it is, I stand for it.

- Bhagat Singh (1930)

THE BRITISH VIEW

"The word Ghadar means mutiny...it is aimed at bringing about a revolution in India in order to secure liberation from British Control. The headquarters of the Ghadar Party were established in San Francisco and the Party published their own paper known as the Ghadar, and founded an institution known as the Yugantar Ashram, the object of the institution being to instill patriotic feelings in young Indians and train them for a rising in India."-Director of the Intelligence Bureau, Home Department, New Delhi 1934

"The Ghadar, or Mutiny, conspiracy derived its origin from the Pacific Coast of America, its centre being at San Francisco...the object of the paper (Ghadar) was to bring about a rising in India within few years because the people could no longer bear the oppression and tyranny practiced under English rule.

It was stated that the Yugantar Ashram had been founded in San Francisco, and that in this institution books would be compiled, young preachers trained, and preparations for a rising would be taken in hand.

The paper amply fulfilled the worst anticipations that could have been formed from such an introduction. It was violently anti-British in nature, playing on every passion that it could possibly excite...and urging all Indians to go to India with the express intention of committing murder, causing revolution and expelling the British Government by any means."-Account of Ghadr Conspiracy Punjab Police, Lahore 1919.

"...That these defendants in the year 1914, about the beginning of the European war, entered into a conspiracy the object of which was to produce mutiny and rebellion and the overthrow of the British Government in India...that in order to produce this rebellion and mutiny in India, these defendants did certain things in the United States of America... that these defendants conspired to recruit men in America, to give them training in the use of arms and explosives in America, to dispatch them to India to places on the border line of the Indian territory, there to be assembled and trained further by officers in part at least sent from America; that likewise in this country funds were provided,...that men were to be dispatched from here to carry these funds that were to be expanded in other places than America; that these men were to go themselves, some of them, and engage in this rebellion; that arms and ammunitions were to be purchased and shipped from our shores and from our borders; that passage was to be engaged in large numbers for returning persons desiring to enter into this military enterprise."-Prosecution of Gadharites in the US San Francisco 1917

(The British government spent $2.5 million on this trial, an enormous sum indicating the degree to which the Empire feared this movement.) The Ghadar Movement was a movement of patriotic, progressive, democratic, and enlightened Indians living abroad, working for the emancipation of India from the yoke of British colonialism and the birth of a new India based on national and social emancipation. They organized themselves in 1913 among communities throughout the world, adopting the following goals and means:

1. To liberate India with the force of arms from British servitude and to establish a free and independent India with equal rights for all.
2. To establish their headquarters in San Francisco, that would serve as a base to coordinate all the activities for achieving these aims and objectives.
3. To publish a weekly paper, Ghadar, in Urdu, Hindi, Punjabi and in other languages of India.
4. To hold organisational elections every year to elect a coordination committee from the different committees to carry out all the work.
5. To organize cells amongst Indian railway, industrial, and farm workers, as well as students who would be directly linked to the centre.
6. The coordination committee would elect a three-member commission to supervise the political and underground work.
7. Revenue would be drawn from each member through a monthly contribution of one dollar.
8. No discussion or debate was to take place on religion within the organization. Religion was considered a personal matter and that it had no place in the organization.
9. Every member was duty bound to participate in the liberation struggle of that country in which they were resident.

At the initial gathering in Astoria in 1913, Sohan Singh Bhakna was elected President, Kesar Singh Thathgarh, Vice President, Lala Hardayal, General Secretary, Lala Thakur Das Dhuri, Joint Secretary, and Pandit Kanshi Ram Mardauli, Treasurer.

In a conference held in Sacramento, California in December 1913, new members were included in the executive committee: Santokh Singh, Kartar Singh Sarabha, Arur Singh, Pirthi Singh, Pandit Jagat Ram, Karm Singh Cheema, Nidhan Singh Chugha, Sant Vasakha Singh, Pandit Munshi Ram, Harnam Singh Kotla, Nodh Singh. To carry out the secret and underground work of the party, a three-member commission was also constituted by Sohan Singh Bhakhna, Santokh Singh and Pandit Kanshi Ram.

Publication of Ghadar also began after this conference. On its masthead the paper had inscribed in bold letters-Enemy of the British Rule in India. It included articles on the conditions of the people of India under British hegemony, and it also dealt with the problems that confronted Indians abroad such as racial attacks and discrimination. It called upon the Indian people to unite and rise up against British rule and throw the British out of India. Ghadar was published in Urdu, Punjabi, Hindi and in other languages of India. Besides Ghadar, the Yugantar Ashram, the headquarters of the Ghadar Party, also brought out various publications to raise the consciousness of the people and organize them to revolt against the British. A poster entitled, "Jang Da Hoka" (Declaration of War), which was distributed widely, read as following:

CLARION CALL FOR THE GHADAR ARMY

The British have occupied our dear land. Our commerce and industry has been ruined. They have plundered and looted the wealth of Hindustan and brought famine and plague. More than 90 million Hindustanis do not even have one square meal a day. Thirty million have died due to famine and plague. They are sending all our produce and grains to England. It is due to these conditions of misery that Hindustanis have started going to far off lands such as Australia, Canada, America, and Africa and when they have begun to fill their stomachs, it has poked needles and pins in the heart of the British. Because it has opened the eyes of the Hindustanis and they are understanding all the schemes of the British, these British strangle us in India. And when we come abroad here they also make our lives miserable. They have closed Australia and Canada for us. Our mothers, sisters and children are treated like animals in Africa by the British.

Now the British are pressuring the American government to stop us from coming to the shores of America. The American government has said that if the British government is stopping the Hindus from coming to their own-ruled countries, Australia and Canada, why should we allow them to come here. This bill is in their parliament (Congress). If this bill is passed we will be ruined. Other countries will also make such laws. Now is the time to do something about this condition.

Brave Hindis! Awaken from your sleep. The British are getting you thrown out from everywhere. Let us unite and fight so such laws are not passed here. We should also think about, whether or not these laws pass, what should we do? What is our duty at this time? Our duty at this time is to prepare an army to fight against British rule in India which is the root of all our problems. This is not the time for talk. This is the time for war. How long will you wait? How long will the world keep calling you slaves? On Sunday, February 15, a huge gathering will take place in Stockton. All Hindus and Muslims of America are called upon to join. No more petition to the oppressors. Now we have to take our rights with sword. AN ARMY WILL BE RECRUITED FOR THE GHADAR IN INDIA.

Come brothers, you have earned plenty of dollars! Take the ship back to our motherland! Come let us go back to our motherland and raise the banner of revolt! Come to the gathering in Stockton and take a vow to go back to Hindustan and fight in the Ghadar! Just as this call is written in blood in the same fashion the letter of freedom will be written in ours and the blood of the British on the soil of Hindustan. For this oath, this call is being sent out from the Yugantar Ashram. This is not a paper, but a declaration of war! Stop everything and come! Do not delay! ONLY HE IS A BRAVE FIGHTER WHO FIGHTS FOR HIS COUNTRY. EVEN IF HE IS CUT INTO PIECES, HE DOES NOT LEAVE THE BATTLEFIELD. ______________

AN OPEN LETTER TO THE PEOPLE OF INDIA

Dear Friends,

We do not have to remind you; you all know how much we have suffered under the British rule. We all wish to get rid of this foreign tyrant who has been bleeding us white. The time is coming when our united efforts will be able to throw off the yoke of this aggressor.

Another world war is approaching. We must take advantage of this opportunity. England is sure to get involved in the coming war. Political wisdom demands that we must utilize this rare opportunity for our good. We must put forward our demand for complete independence when our enemy, British imperialism, is engaged in a life and death struggle.

To save her life, Britain will need India's friendship more than anything else. We must demand complete independence as the price of our friendship.

We must let the British rulers know in clear terms right that if they care for the friendship of India, they must be prepared to give India full independence at once. Otherwise India will resist to limit their effort to get any help from India. It is beside the point how we will resist, but resist we will.

Complete independence means India's control over treasury, foreign affairs, and military forces. Nothing short of that will do.

We must remember that we can no longer trust any more promises from the British imperialists. To our sorrow, we have found out many times that we can not rely upon their words. We must stand pat on our demands; we must one way or another unite until our demands are met. The world situation is such that the British will think twice before refusing India's demand. We must not miss this golden opportunity.

To get full advantage of the situation, we must put up a strong united front. All those Hindustanis who really work for independence must come together in a united front. Personal differences must be forgotten. Unity of purpose is essential for our cause. All of us who hold India's freedom dear to us, must work to establish a formidable united front. Our demands backed by our united front will have a telling effect. Our demands must be popularized among our countrymen. Our people must be made to act in case our demands are not met.

Now is the time to educate our people: tomorrow may be too late. During the war, martial law will make things difficult. Unless the masses are made ready to act, our demands will not have much weight. The British imperialists care little for empty resolutions unless they are backed by united might of the masses.

War may start any day. We have not a moment to lose. We must do our best to educate and organize the Indian masses while we have time. Our slogans must be such as:

Complete Independence or Noncooperation! Freedom or Nothing Else! No Freedom, No Soldiers from India! No Freedom, No Money from India! Freedom or Resistance!

Yours for the cause

Soldiers of Independence ______________

FACTS AND FIGURES-THE BALANCE SHEET

(Bilan, Complete Rendu, Translated from the Hindustan Ghadar)

(1) Englishmen drain from India and take to England every year 50 crore rupees ($167 million); consequently the Hindus have become so poor that the daily average income per capita is only 5 paise (2.5 cents).

(2) The land tax is more than 65% of the net produce.

(3) The expenditure on the education of 240 million persons is about 0.02 percent per head per annum, about $40,000,000 on sanitation $6,000,000 but on the army $330,000,000

(4) Under the British rule, the famines are ever on the increase and in the last ten years 20 million men, women, and children have died of starvation.

(5) From the plagues that have occurred, during the sixteen years past,

8 million deaths have resulted. And the death rate during the last thirty years has steadily increased from 24 per mile to 34 per mile.

(6) Means are employed to spread disunion and disorder in the native states and to increase British influence there.

(7) Englishmen are not punished for murdering Hindus or for insulting Hindu women.

(8) With money taken form the Hindus, aid is given to English Christian priests.

(9) Attempt is always made to create enmity between people of different religious denominations.

(10) The arts and crafts (Industries) of India have been destroyed for England's benefit.

(11) Employing India's money, and sacrificing the lives of the Hindus as soldiers, China, Afghanistan, Burma, Egypt and Persia have been conquered.

(12) For the sake of the almighty dollar, the British government has forced poppy cultivation in India, thereby creating the drug menace for India and the world.

The Ghadarites wanted to establish a Democratic Republic of India in which all peoples, irrespective of their race, religion, gender, language, or national origin, would have equal rights. They envisioned a United States of India as a federation of all the nations, nationalities and tribal people of Hindustan. This was illustrated by the poster of United States of India issued by the Ghadar Party (see illustration). According to Bhagat Singh Bilga one of the few Ghadarites still alive, Ghadarites were influenced by the First War of India's Independence of 1857 (the oiriginal Great Ghadar), and the American, French, and Bolshevik Revolutions. They wanted a completely independent, secular, and democratic India in which there would be no exploitation of man by man.

A precursor of Ghadar, The Talvar, which was printed in Berlin, had on its front page in a April-May 1910 issue a couplet from Bhadur Shah Zafar, one of the leaders of the Ghadar of 1857, and the lead article was dedicated to May 10, 1857, the date of the uprising. The article concludes:

In memory of
Rani Lakshmi Bai and her comrades
Mandar and Kashi
Rana Kunwar Singh
Maulvi Ahmad Shah

Tantia Tope

Kuar Khuda Baksh

Ghulam Ghose Khan

Mangal Pandey

and of those tens of thousand men and women who perished in 1857 in the sacred attempt to wrench the mother from the hands of the Faranghi.

A March 19,1917 issue of Ghadar proclaimed in bold letters "RUSSIA HAS BECOME FREE, SOON INDIA WILL BE FREE", following the fall of the Czarist regime in Russia and the beginning of the revolution there.

In their publications, the Ghadarites dealt with the problems and issues of the day. In Nia Zamana, they urged all Indians to unite and fight for a new India and spare no sacrifice for the freedom of their land and work tirelessly for liberty and the rights of all. They also engaged in polemics against various organisations and tendencies that they regarded as diversions from the most important task at hand, namely revolution:

It is the duty of all to use every endeavor to improve the condition of India, but it is also necessary to act intelligently...there are several wrong movements in the country which are of no value upon which money, time and moral power are being wasted. The founders of these movements are fools or selfish men, who hope to obtain a reward from Government by misleading the young men of the country...The following are some of the movements:

The Congress

All wise men know that the Congress is an official assembly. The founder of this assembly of ignorant persons was an Englishman named Mr. Hume. Almost every year an Englishman is appointed as its president. Mr. Gokhale, who takes a great part in it, is a titled man and member of the Imperial Legislative Council. Messrs. Mehta and Nauroji are also titled men...In short, all its members are flatterers and timid men. They do not think of measures for the prevention of famine and plague.

They have learnt certain sentences which they repeat every year...They beg government to give them their rights merely by begging...These empty shows can not result in preventing famines, reducing taxes, spreading industry, introducing administration of real justice, filling the stomachs of cultivators and removing plague. The appointment of a few young men to Legislative councils can not result in any good to the country, even though they may be able to deliver very eloquent speeches. The acceptance of government service by able Indians only causes great harm to the nation...This is not the way to free country from the calamities which are devastating it...great courage and wisdom are required to awaken the country. The flattery of Englishmen can be of no avail...Congress is in the hands of Englishmen and conducted by them from London...Avoid it.

Religious Movements

Several new creeds and religious associations are coming into existence in India, everyone of which boasts of liberating India from Slavery...Religious disputes among different sections are considered by some as signs of the activity and energy of the Hindu nation...They think that when there is one religion throughout India no foreign nation can aspire to become her ruler. But this is not borne out by history and is opposed to common sense.

Every person can have his/her own philosophical or religious principles. Nobody should be compelled to act upon a particular principle and thought...Social organisations should not be based upon religion...India has produced patriots like Ram Singh, Nana Sahib, Tantia, The Rani of Jhansi, Mr. Tilak, Amba Prasad Sufi, and Ajit Singh, but the religion of these men was not the same. So it is not necessary that there should be one religion throughout the country...It is foolish to think that a single religious association would be sufficient for all purposes. Education and social reform should not be based on religion...The prosperity and happiness of a people does not depend on a particular creed...To abandon efforts for liberty and equality and to devote one's entire zeal to religion is to degrade one's self below the status of man. Duty, knowledge and happiness depend on liberty and equality and upon these also depends the deliverance of a country, and in fact of the whole world.

Hindu Sabha

An association called by this name exists in Northern India. Its business is to celebrate certain festivals and to send congratulatory messages to the Lieutenant Governor. The members of this society are rich and titled sycophants...As the supporters of this movement are mostly flatterers and sycophants who have no idea of liberty it can not be conducive to any good to the country.

Temperance

This movement is also unnecessary, for a very low percentage of Hindus drink liquor. It is a foolish movement, for drink is not ruining India. It is not the cause of famine or plague. It does not rob people of their money, nor is it the cause of injustice being done to them. If you really want to do some work, you should work against the British Government: otherwise do not make useless noise.

Protection of Cows

This also is a useless movement, for the Hindus do not kill cows and they have no control over the Muhammadans or the Christians who do so...To obtain liberty should be the first aim of every person and one must have a greater regard for the rights and interests of human beings than for those of the cow...

Education

When the Hindus have nothing else to do they turn their attention to establishing colleges and universities...True education can not be imparted in any country before it has acquired liberty, for in such country all schools of the people possess no rights, their education will be wholly under the control of the government...

Social Reforms

Some Hindus lay great stress upon such minor matters as the age of marriage, the re-marriage of widows, the raising of the depressed classes and so on.

These reforms are good but do not limit great movements to these objects...It is not due to any social custom that 75 Lakhs of men have died and that plague and famine visit the country so frequently...Try to include liberty and equality in the politics of your country and then you will find true knowledge and happiness everywhere...

Spread of Hindi Language

The Urdu-Hindi controversy misleads many lovers of the nation. As regards such movements it should be remembered that the proper time for them will be when we have obtained our goal...It is childish to ask government to introduce Hindi in courts or to have Hindi inscriptions on coins and currency notes.

Do you consider government courts permanent that we ask government to introduce Hindi there?...whilst there is so much clamour against Urdu, why is there none against English, which is a foreign language?"

The Ghadarites saw social and national emancipation of the peoples of India as the most decisive condition for a prosperous and happy life. Therefore they concentrated all their efforts and energies and urged all the peoples of Hindustan to do so irrespective of their creed, colour, language, or caste. They wanted dignity and honour for all in and outside of Hindustan, and the necessary condition for this was the liberation of India from the rule of the

British and their collaborators. To liberate India from the shackles they called upon all the Indians to return to India and overthrow the British rule.

Through the pages of Ghadar Di Goonj they spread their message in poetic form. Ghadar Di Goonj was published in Shahmukhi and Gurmukhi. This poetry was hard hitting and simple:

Kuli Kuli Pukarda Jag Saanun
Saada Jhulda Kitey Nishan Kiyon Nahin
Kikoon Bachangey Sada Ghulam Rahkey
Saanun Rajniti Wala Giyan Kiyon Nahin
Dhayi Totru Kha Gaye Khet Sada
Hindustan da Koi Kisan Kiyon Nahin
(We are called coolies in countries abroad
We do not have a flag of our own
Will we always live the life of slaves?
Why do we not know the science of politics?
A handful people have taken control of our land
Why is not there a caretaker of Hindustan?)
Marna Bhala Ghulami di Zindagi Ton
Nahin Sukhan eh Man Bhulaavney Da
Mulk Jaagyaya Cheen Jo Ghook Suta
Dhol Vajyaya Hind Jagaawanney Da
Saanun Lord Na Panditan Kazian Di
Nahin Shok Hai Berda Dubavaney Da
Jap Jaap Da Waqt Bateet Hoya
Vella Aa Giya Teg Uthavney Da
Pardhkey Ghadr Akhbar Nun Khabar Lagi
Vela Aa Giya Ghadr Machavaney Da
(It is better to die than live a life of servitude
We should never forget this saying
China has awakened from its sleep
Battle drums of Hindustan's awakening are raging
We do not need Pandits or Kazis
As we do not want our ship to sink
The time for prayers and Puja is past
This is the time to pick up the sword
The Ghadar paper is proclaiming
That the time for revolt is here)

It also stated which organisational steps people must take:

Khufiya Raj Societiyan Karo Kaayam
Rall Marhatey Bengali De Yaar Ho Jayo
Hindu Sikh Te Momno Karo Jaldi
Ik Dusrey De Madadgar Ho Jayo
(Establish secret political organizations
Bengalis and Marathis all should get together
Hindu, Sikh and Muslims all should unite
And stand together with each other)
Ghar Ghar Gupti Sabha Banayo
Logan Ko Mantar Sikhlayo
Har Aik Dil Main Jot Jagayo
Binan Joot Yeh Bhoot Na Jaayi
Jaldi Ghadar Macha Diyo Bhai
(Form secret societies in every household
Arouse the people with the Mantra of freedom
Start the spark in every heart
Without force the scourge of British colonialism will not leave
Hurry to the call of revolution)

They described the conditions of Hindustan:

Bhukhey Marnn Bacchey Kaall Vich Sadey
Khatti Khann Saadi Englistan Walley
Kannak Beejkey Khann Nun Jaun Mildey
Paisa Chhadadey Nahin Laggan Valley
Laayiya Tax Firangiyan Bahut Yaaro
Bhukhey Marann Gharib Dukaan Valley
Karo Paltan Nun Khabardar Jaakey
Sutey Payey Kiyon Teg Chalaan Valley
Musalmaan Pathan Balwan Dogar
Singh Soormey Yudh Machaann Valley
Hindustaniyan Morchey Fatey Keetey
Burma, Misar Te Cheen Sudan Valley
(Our children are dying in famines
The English are enjoying the fruit or our toil
We sow wheat but we get barley to eat
We are not left with a penny, all is taken by the tax collectors

The English have levied heavy taxes
Poor shopkeepers are dying of hunger
Go and arouse the army
Why those who wield the sword are asleep?
Brave Muslims, Pathans and Dogras
Valiant Sikhs in the battlefield
Hindustanis fighting on fronts in
Burma, China, Egypt and Sudan)

They exposed the so-called leaders of the Hindustanis, the collaborators of the British:

Jattan Sidhiyan Nun Koi Dosh Nahin
Sadey Leaderan Da Manda Haal Singho
Rai Bandran Mulk Veeran Kita
Piyar Rakhdey Bandran Nal Singho
Sanun Paas Angrez De Bechaya Hai
Aap Mulk De Banney Dalal Singho
(The common folk is not to be blamed
Our 'leaders' are traitors
Rai Bhadurs, copy cats of the British, have ruined our land
They have sold us to the British
And have become pimps of the British)

They called upon the people of Hindustan to see through the illusions spread by the leaders of Indian National Congress such as Gandhi, Nehru and others:

Ghairat Annakh Wala Je Khoon Hunda
Dehli Takht Zaalam Saathon Khasade Naan
Banner, Bipin, Gandhi, Madanmohan Varge
Eh Firangiyaan De Boot Jhasde Naan
(If our leaders had fought for our self respect
We would not have lost our country and rule
The kind of Bannerji, Bipin Chander Pal, Gandhi
And Madanmohan Malviya would not
Have Licked the Boots of the British)
Deputationaan Te Resolutionaan Te
Muft Dhan Kharab Karaaya Kiyon
Naram Dil Congressi Leadraan Nun

Tusin Sutiyo Leader Banyaya Kiyon
(Deputations and resolutions are waste of money
These leaders of Congress who have soft corner
for the British have become leaders
Because you are asleep and not conscious)

They also pointed out the old Indian tradition:

Kade Mangyian Milann Azadiyan Na
Hunde Tarliyan Naal Na Raj Loko
(Freedom is not obtained by begging
By appeals political power is not won)
Karo Na Minnat Ainwe Bano Na Kaiyar
Fardo Talwar Ehnan Nahin Rahnna
Agge Veero Arjiyan Ne Ki Banna Liya
Zalam Firangyian Ne Desh Kha Liya
(Do not petition like cowards
Take the sword and they will run
What have all the petitions done?
Brutal British have plundered our land)

They called upon the Hindustani soldiers to revolt:

Tusin Lardo Jaa Key Khaatar Goriyan De
Singho Bholiyo Karde Khyal Kiyon Nahin
Desan Dujiyan Te Nit Karo Dhaavey
Mulk Apna Laindey Sambhaal Kiyon Nahin
Tibet, Cheen, Africa Nun Fateh Kardey
Dita Dushmanan Hath Dakhal Kiyon Nahin
Utho Azadi Da Lavo Jhaaka
Ralke Kheddey Kiyon Gulal Nahin
(You go and fight for the British
You brave lions just think about it
You fight in far and distant lands
Why not take charge of your own land?
You have subdued Tibet, China, Africa for the British
Why not show your valor to our enemy the British?
Arise and breathe the fresh air of Freedom
Why do you not play Holi with the blood of British?)
Faujan Waliyo Tusaan Di Matt Maari

Lokaan Waste Karo Lardayian
Vairi Tusan Da Gheriya Vich Europe
Vaila Saanbh Layo Dheriyan Dhayian Kiyon
(Soldiers awaken and come to your senses
Why are you fighting for the others, the British
Our enemy is caught in Europe
Take advantage of this situation and revolt)

They also exposed those 'religious leaders' who collaborated with the British in dividing the people on the basis of religion:

Kazi, Pandatan, Ate Giyaniyan Ne
Yudh Karan Da Vachan Sunawnna Na
Bhaunkan Raat Diney Bhukhye Tukrdiaan De
Khali Rahannge Dhidh Bharavanna Na
Haddi Pun Pai Ju Thode Khalsa Ji
Murdu Dhan Puja Wala Khawna Na
Vaja Mominan Di Kam Luchyian De
Deel Dol Nun Vaikh Bhul Jawana Na
Saanun Lord Na Amayan Afayan Di
Ilam Ragard Forde Uttey Lawnna Na
(Kazis, Pandits and Giyanis of Gurudwara
Will not speak of fighting the British
They bark like dogs day and night
Looking for the crumbs from the British
If you listen to them your bellies will remain empty
Your bones will be eaten by cancer
If you eat the crumbs that they give
They wear garb of holy men but
Their deeds are those of devil
Do not be fooled by their garb
We do not need useless degrees of BA and MA
We want solutions to our problems)

To organize the Hindustanis abroad and in India for revolution was the chief aim of the Ghadar Party. Ghadar, and other publications of the Yugantar Ashram became tools for this organizing activity. Soon there were Ghadar Party branches in China, Malaya, Siam, Europe, the Philippines, Africa, Hongkong, Singapore, Panama, Argentina, Brazil, Iran, Afghanistan, Japan,

Russia, amongst other locations. Wherever there were Hindustanis, there were Ghadar Party branches. By 1916, it is estimated that one million copies of Ghadar were published per week.

Special issues of Ghadar were also printed in Nepali, Bengali, Pashto, Gujrati, as well as many other languages. The British government used every means to stop the circulation of Ghadar and other publications of the Yugantar Ashram, mainly to stop it from reaching India, but they were not successful. The Ghadarites always found ways and means of distributing their publications in India in spite of proscription and efforts by the British to stop the distribution of Ghadar.

The British Government also tried with all its might to slander, suppress, and eradicate the Ghadar Movement abroad by conniving with the Governments of Canada and the USA and by recruiting spies and their agents such as Hopkinson and others to closely watch the activities of the Ghadarites. For this purpose they also recruited a temple priest in San Francisco and some Granthis in Gurudwaras. As a result of this pressure, Lala Hardyal was arrested on March 25, 1914. Because of Hopkinson's reposts, he was forced to leave the USA in April 1914.

IDEAS AND THOUGHTS OF BHAGAT SINGH

With the sabarmati in flames with communal frenzy, remembering Bhagat Singh has a special relevance. The history of our freedom struggle is a tale of sacrifice of many. All communities, seets and regions participated in it, Now that history has faded.

The present has become rootless. The future is in peril. Bhagat Singh could become a rallying point to fight these ills, Not only did he give his life for the country's freedom but he has left a message for the country's future.

SHORT LIFE

Even otherwise, India's Independence movement was never confined to wresting power. It was a struggle for emancipation 'to wipe every tear from every eye' as the pledge of Independence on 26 January 1930 spelt out. Though that pledge is now nearly forgotten or mortgaged with the World Bank to get new loans to make a few rich, the consensus that developed during the freedom struggle was clear.

That consensus that developed during the freedom struggle was clear. That consensus was for secularism, socialism and self-reliance as opposed to communalism, capitalism and foreign dependence. Now we are crawling in a reptile era where greed is good and borrowing is best. To put the country on right track, a Bhagat Singh is needed.

It was a short life of 24 years from 1907 to 1931 with the last two years in jail. In 1925 at the age of 18 Bhagat Singh founded Bharat Navjawan Sabha and in 1927 the Hindustan republican association to which he added the word 'socialist' the following year. In Indian politics that was the first use of the term 'socialist' in the name of any organization. In 1928 there was a nationwide call to boycott the Simon Commission, and all white Commission to decide the political fate of India. On 30 October 1928, Lala Lajpat Rai was assaulted by the police while demonstrating against the Simon Commission in Lahore in Lahore. He succumbed to his injuries on 13 November.

SCIENTIFIC IDEOLOGY

The revolutionaries of those days under the leadership of Bhagat Singh and Chandra Shekhar Azad resolved to avenge the murder. The police officer, Mr. Saunders who had led the assault on Lala Lajpat Rai was shot dead on 17 December before his office itself.

What is striking is that even during these waves of events, Bhagat Singh's pen did not rest. What is more, he pointed out in clear terms the danger of communal divide and peril of mixing religion with politics in his two famous articles after the communal riot in Lahore. One of the brightest sides of Bhagat Singh was the that he did not become a revolutionary because he was swayed by emotion as was expected at his age and in his era but because he was committed to some scientific ideology and with a rational thinking. This was evident in his speeches and writing. So Bhagat Singh did not remain a Shaheed but became a Shaheed-a-Azam.

Tolstoy

In an article written in May 1928 at the age of 21 under the heading?Religion and our freedom struggle?, Bhagat Singh brilliantly analysed the views of Tolstoy dividing religion into three parts: ethics, theology and rituals.

He interpreted their implications in the contemporary political reality of that day which can be a guide to the political leaders even today. In that article Bhagat Singh stressed the need of communal harmony and feeling of communal harmony and feeling of brotherhood amongst communities concluding,?the meaning of our full independence is not only to get out of the grip of the British but to create a condition where all communities would live like brothers and be free from mental slavery (to all orthodox and blind faith)?.

This is the theme, which Tagore enshrined, in his famous poem,?where mind is without fear and head is held high, where the knowledge is free, where the clear stream of reason has not lost its way in the dreary desert sand of dead habits.? However, the country is now going in the opposite direction practicing religious bigotry and under economic reforms deforming the society to get wealth quick.

THE HUMANITARIAN EVEN WITH BOMBS

In another article,?Communal riots and the way out? In June 1928, Bhagat Singh wrote,?If we search the root of communal riots we find economic reason. We further see the hand of section of press and the communal leaders behind that?.

It sounds as if this is written today after the Ayodhya episode. Referring to Russian history Bhagat Singh pointed out in the same article,?in the period of the tsar, the situation there was as is now in India. After the rule of working class was established the whole picture got changed?.

Tracing the root of communalism to capitalism and offering the political leadership of the working class as the way out, Bhagat Singh maintained that class-consciousness was a correct way to combat communal riots. This thinking has been proved correct gain with the return of communal and ethnic strife in Russia after the fall of socialism there and a sudden spurt in communalism and terrorism in India after the decontrolling of capitalism in the nineties.

COMMUNALISM AND COMMUNISM

Bhagat Singh believed in separating religion from politics and state. In his article referring to the Ghadar movement, Bhagat Singh wrote:?the martyrs of 1941-15 kept religion outside politics. Their conception was that religion was the private matter of individuals. Other should not interfere in that nor should it be injected into politics.? So the movement of the Ghadar party remained united both in mind and heat where the Sikh took the lead in making sacrifices and the Hindu and Muslims did not lag behind. Today after, mixing religion with politics we get Khalistan in Canada in place of the Ghadar party.

In the country secularists are defensive and communalist are aggressive. This is because only class struggle can resist communal riots which even the communists have abandoned long ago, except for a symbolic exercise before wage and bonus negotiations. There was a time when Congress, the party of the ruling bourgeoisie, had to talk of socialistic pattern of society but now even the Marxists are shy of mentioning socialism in their election manifesto and name their youth organization democratic.

Bhagat Singh was very forthright in his views. Unlike the apologetic secularists Bhagat Singh was aggressive in accusing the exploitative system and declared:?Producers and Labourers are robbed by the exploiter of the fruits of their labour and deprived of their elementary sights. Radical change, therefore, is needed and it is the duty of those who realize this to reorganize society on a socialist basis in accordance with the principle of Karl Marx?. Bhagat Singh dropped a bomb when the Delhi Assembly was discussing the Trade Dispute Bill to chain the working class in the British days. In these days of WTO many bills are waiting in Parliament to facilitate the 'exit policy' for the workers and to liquidate the public sector but there is no Bhagat Singh to thunder.

ATHEIST TO THE LAST

The martyrdom of Bhagat Singh, Raj Guru and Sukhdev was a moving issue from the beginning. Netaji Subhash Bose has recorded his reactions in his book The Indian Struggle after he received that shocking news while in a train proceeding to Karachi congress, Anger and emotion swept through the country, Bose referred to his insistence on Gandhiji that he should not sign the pact with the then Viceroy, Lord Irwin, withdrawing the civil disobedience movement till the death sentence on Bhagat Singh and his colleagues was commuted.

The pact was signed on 18 March 1931 only five days before the hanging. It should be recalled that Bhagat Singh and Batu Keshwar Datta were arrested after dropping the bomb in the Delhi Assembly on 4 April 1929. It was a grim decision, which was taken not suddenly at the spur of the moment but after a long debate. Dropping the bomb in the Assembly meant sure arrest and arrest meant death for Bhagat Singh who had already been named the accused in the Saunders murder case. The expected happened. Bhagat Singh and Batu Keshwar Datta were awarded life imprisonment for dropping bomb in the Assembly and the death sentence on Bhagat Singh was pronounced in the Lahore conspiracy case.

What was astounding was even in such condition Bhagat Singh did not forget the problems of communalism in the country and the complicated question of religion and politics. Whereas many staunch atheists became believers of God before death, Bhagat Singh wrote his last and perhaps his best article, 'why I am an Atheist'? on 6 October 1930 i.e., hardly five months before his hanging. His last article was a unique combination of politics, theology and science, which referred even to Darwain's Origin of species, which can educate many social scientists even today. This was written not in a cool library room but in a condemned cell of a jail.

FROM THE VOLGA TO THE GANGA

In sharp contrast to the terrorist of these days causing death to hundreds, including women and children, to serve the design of the communal and imperialist forces, Bhagat Singh and his colleagues were extremely humanitarian eve with bombs. The blast he caused in the assembly spread his message but did not hurt anybody. After the killing of Saunders, a poster written in red ink was pasted on the walls of Lahore, which read: We consider human life sacred. We believe in a bright future where each man will enjoy freedom to all and to end exploitation of man by man, sometimes it becomes inevitable to shed some blood.

Then came that fateful day; 23 March 1931, Hanging of Bhagat Singh, Raj Guru and Sukhdev was suddenly decided ahead of schedule to avoid agitation, When the sentry appeared unexpectedly in the cell to take them to the gallows, recalls Mr. KPS Menon, the celebrated ICS of those days and the ambassador to Moscow afterwards, Bhagat Singh was found reading Lenin's state and revolution.

It is said that Bhagat Singh asked the sentry to stop for a moment as one revolutionary was in 'communication' with another. The sentry did not stop. But history has stopped today to look back. Time and tide wait for none. The Volga and the Ganga also have changed their course with socialism destroyed and swadeshi perished leaving a wild world around. But that communication, that message of Bhagat Singh, still resonates from the Ravi to Cauvery, from the Jamuna to Ganga, reminding one of the goal and the pledge. We have 'miles to go before we sleep' as the way out of the present mess. So from the Sabarmati to Ayodhya there is hectic search of Bhagat Singh.

RETURN TO INDIA

The Ghadarites decided that the time was ripe to organize a revolt in the army against the British, as the first world war was approaching and it was only through armed force that the British were able to subjugate Hindustan. With men and materiel flowing out of India to aid in the war effort, the forces of occupation were perched precariously, depleted and vulnerable to attack. Therefore they decided to organize and return to Hindustan.

In August 1914 huge rallies and public meetings were organized, where it was decided that all the Hindus abroad should return to Hindustan and participate in the armed revolt against the British. The Executive Committee of the Ghadar Party met and decided to call upon all the Ghadarites everywhere to return to India and organize the revolt. Kartar Singh Sarabha, one of the youngest Ghadarites, was a student at Berkeley and left right away with other Ghadarites. The president of Ghadar Party, Sohan Singh Bhakhna, who was in Japan, also organized to return home with others. Similarly, the Ghadarites planned to return from other parts of the world. They left a few organizers abroad to carry on the work. They worked out the following plan:

1. To contact all the revolutionary groups in India on their return and unite with them.
2. The Ghadarite organizers should travel from village to village and prepare the people for the revolt against the British.
3. To propagate amongst the soldiers in the cantonments and arouse them to revolt against the British. A special committee was elected for this work.
4. For acquisition of weapons, a special group was organized.
5. A special group to carry on the work of publishing literature to distribute amongst the people and soldiers.
6. To further strengthen relations with all those movements who were fighting against colonialism for their national liberation and seek their help.
7. To seek possibilities of help from Germany and Turkey who were fighting against the British.

To get help from enemies of the British, Barakatullah was sent to Kabul to organize this work. Kapur Singh Mohi met with Sun Yat Sen to seek the help of the Chinese revolutionaries. Sohan Singh Bhakhna also met with the German Counselor in Tokyo in this regard. Teja Singh Sutantar had joined the Turkish Military Academy for military training to prepare for the revolutionary storms. Ghadarites returned to India through sea and land. The Komagata Maru, SS Korea, and the Namsang were some of the ships on which thousands of Ghadarite returned home:

> *"The most important vessel to leave San Francisco was the SS Korea, which left for Hong Kong on the 29th August...Before the ship left San Francisco Maulvi Barkatullah, Ram Chand and Bhagwan Singh came aboard and gave the following advice, 'your duty is clear. Go to India and stir up rebellion in every corner of the country. Arms will be provided for you on your arrival in India."*

It is estimated that close to 8000 Ghadarites returned to Hindustan to aid in the revolt by 1916. In a speech in Dehra Dun Bhai, Parmanand declared that five thousand Ghadarites had returned with him.

The British authorities knew about the plans of the Ghadarites. They had also seen the Declaration of War in Ghadar and also had information through their agents.

They issued an ordinance in September 1914, according to which provincial governments were empowered to intern people entering India from abroad even if they were Indian citizens. Bengal and Punjab governments were given these powers first because a great deal of ships on which the Ghadarites were returning were to dock at Calcutta.

They also established a detention centre in Ludhiana where those passengers who were suspected of being Ghadarites were interned. The passengers of Komagatu Maru were the first victims of this ordinance. Sohan Singh Bhakhna and others were arrested from the ship Namsang and brought to Ludhiana. Ghadarites traveling in Tosha Maru were also arrested and taken to different jails such as Montgomery and Multan. But the Ghadarites made it through Colombo, Madras, and Bombay.

In India the Ghadarites developed close working relationships with other revolutionary groups such as the revolutionaries of Bengal, Uttar Pradesh, etc., who later formed the Revolutionary Party of India which declared in 1917:

> *"The immediate object of the revolutionary party in the domain of politics is to establish a Federal Republic of the United States of India by an organized armed revolution. The final constitution of this Republic shall be framed and declared at a time when the representatives of India shall have the power to carry out their decisions. But the basic principles of this Republic shall be universal suffrage, and the abolition of all systems which make the exploitation of man by man possible;...In this Republic the electors shall have the right to recall their representatives if so desired, otherwise the democracy shall become a mockery. In this Republic, the legislature shall have the power to control the executives and replace them whenever necessity will arise.*
>
> *The Revolutionary Party is not national but international in the sense that its ultimate object is to bring harmony in the world by respecting and guaranteeing the diverse interests of the different nations; it aims not at competition but at cooperation between the different nations and states, and in this respect it follows the footsteps of the great Indian Rishis and of Bolshevik Russia in the modern age. Good for humanity is no vain and empty word for Indian revolutionaries."*

Vishnu Ganesh Pingley, Kartar Singh Sarabha, Ras Bihari Bose, Bhai Parmanand, Hafiz Abdullah, Sachinder Nath Sanyal, and others played very important roles in developing these close relationships with other revolutionary groups. They aimed to overthrow the British rule by force of arms and build a new society. For this aim they were willing to unite and work together with all those forces that were working for this common aim of liberating Hindustan.

Amritsar was established as the control centre for the activity of the Ghadar party which had to be changed to Lahore on February 6,1915 due to security considerations. After analyzing all the reports from the organizers amongst the army and civilians, it was decided on February 12,1915 that the date of uprising will be February 21,1915. The plan was to occupy the cantonments of Mian Mir, Ferozepur, Meerut, Lahore, and Delhi and proclaim the Republic of India. Garrisons in Kohat, Bannu and Dinapur were also to revolt on the same day. Kartar Singh Sarabha was to take control of Ferozepur and Pingle to march to Delhi from Meerut with the 128th Battalion.

Dr. Mathura Singh was sent to the frontier areas of the Northwest to organize the Afridis and others. Nidhan Singh Chugha, Gurmukh, Singh and Harnam Singh were sent to Jhelum, Rawalpindi, and Hoti Mardan. Parmanand went to Peshawar. Others were sent to Ambala, Meerut, Lucknow, Allahabad, Benares, Dinapur, and Faizabad to raise the banner of revolt.

They also decided that the flag of this revolt and republic would be a tricolor of Red, Green and Yellow with two swords crossing in the centre. The organization of revolt in the eastern part of India, such as in Bengal and Assam, was to be coordinated by the Bengali revolutionaries. The rebellion was to engulf the British Empire from Peshawar to Hongkong.

Unfortunately the British government got wind of the uprising through their agents. The Ghadarites changed the date of uprising to February 19 instead of February 21, after they determined that the authorities knew of their plans. But the British authorities acted swiftly and disarmed the Indian troops in the above mentioned garrisons and interned them. Several leaders of Ghadar Party and organizers were arrested and imprisoned in Lahore; 82 of them were charged for sedition in Lahore Conspiracy Case on April 26,1916 and 17 Ghadarites were declared absconding and international non-bailable warrants for their arrest were issued.

Michael O'Dwyer, the governor of Punjab, asked the British government to remove all provisions of appeal in the legal provisions of the courts. The British government brought in "Defence of India Rule" to carry out summary trials of the Ghadarites. This ordinance was opposed by all the Indian members of the legislative assembly. A special tribune was set up which held its hearings in camera in a Lahore jail. On September 13,1915, 24 Ghadarites were sentenced to death and the rest were given life imprisonment. This judgment of the tribunal raised a wave of protest and demonstrations against the British all over India. As a result the Viceroy Lord Hardinge himself intervened and converted the death sentence of 17 Ghadarites into life imprisonment and reduced the term of imprisonment for 7 Ghadarites. On November 16, seven Ghadarites were hanged.

After Lahore, arrests took place in Benaras and Delhi. Sachinder Nath Sanyal was exiled to Andaman jail known as Kala Pani and others were given varying rigorous sentences by the special tribunal. The Tribunal declared that they were all part of the same movement with its centre in Lahore.

The Ghadarites did not get disheartened by this set back and continued carrying on their work. Arrests and imprisonments followed them. In the second Lahore Conspiracy case, 102 Ghadarites were tried. This case began on October 25, 1915 and sentences were handed down on March 30, 1916. Seven Ghadarites were sentenced to death, 45 were given life sentences and the rest were given rigourous imprisonment varying from 8 months to four years. Eleven were let free. Several Ghadarites were hanged, sentenced for life and given rigorous imprisonment in the third, fourth and fifth Lahore Conspiracy Cases. According to one estimate, a total of 145 Ghadarites were hanged, 308 were given sentences longer than 14 years.

Outside India the Ghadarites had organized revolts amongst the Indian soldiers. They started organizing the soldiers of the 26th Punjabi regiment in Hongkong. This regiment had been brought in 1912 to suppress the Chinese democratic revolution led by Sun Yat Sen.

The British officer could go home on vacations but the Hindustani soldiers had to remain on duty. Besides the 26th Punjabi, the 25th Punjabi, 126th Baluchi and 50th Artillery was also stationed here. The Ghadar Party had carried out work amongst them. Especially after the Komagata Maru incident, they had a great deal of anti-British sentiment and Ghadar was regularly distributed amongst them. On June 14, several of the soldiers in these regiments were arrested and court-martialed for distributing Ghadar and sent back to India and imprisoned.

In Singapore two regiments, Fifth Holly Light and Malaya State Guide, were garrisoned. The Ghadarites started their work in 1914 in Singapore and through Ghadar, called upon the soldiers to revolt against the British and not participate in the war on the British side. The British authorities, suspecting something was amiss, transferred the Malaya State Guide to Penang. On the night of February 15,1914, the soldiers were ordered to deposit their ammunition and arms in the depot. As a result the officers refused to obey this order and shot several of the officers. The British reinforcements arrived by the 18th of February and crushed this rebellion. Two leaders of the mutiny were hanged and 38 were shot dead, and on the side of the British 8 officers, 9 soldiers and 17 civilians were killed.

In Rangoon in January 1915, the 130th Baluchi regiment revolted. They did not want to fight in the war for the British. On January 15, 200 soldiers of this regiment were court-martialed. Four soldiers were hanged, 69 were given life imprisonment and 126 were given rigorous imprisonment for varying terms. Pandit Sohan Lal Pathak, one of the outstanding leaders of the Ghadar Party was hanged on February 10,1916 in Mandalay jail for inciting rebellion against the British rule. At his martyrdom another Ghadarite Amar Singh wrote:

Chadha Mansoor Phansi Par Pukara Ishk Bazon Ko
Yeh Beeda Hai Tabahi Ka Uthaye Jiska Ji Chaahey
(From the Gallows Mansoor called those who dared to love
This path of self-sacrifice, those who march on it, should do so with complete free will)

Burma had also become an important centre of the Ghadarites. Several Ghadarites were tried and sentenced in two Mandalay Conspiracy Cases.

In December 1915, a government-in-exile of Free Hindustan was established in Kabul, Afghanistan, with Raja Mohinder Pratap as President, Maulavi Barkatullah, Prime Minister, Maulavi Abaidullah Sindhi, Home Minister, Maulavi Bashir, War Minister and Champakaran Pillai, Foreign Minister. All of them were members of the Ghadar Party except Raja Mahendra Pratap. This government-in-exile carried on work on various fronts including the diplomatic fronts by establishing relationships with anti-British governments such as Turkey, Germany, Japan, China, etc.

The Ghadarites also organized the Hindustani prisoners of war in Turkey, Germany, Mesopotamia, and the Middle East. The Ghadarites in Turkey fought against the British in Iran, Baluchistan and Turkey. In Constantinople, they decided that they will attack the British soldiers in Iran, move on to Baluchistan and then enter Punjab from there. They also worked amongst the Hindustani soldiers in the British army in Iran and Iraq, especially in Basra and Bushahir. It is here that the Indian Independence Army was organized by the Ghadarites to invade British India from Iran. Amba Prasad Sufi was the leader of the Ghadar Party in Shiraz. He was joined by Kedar Nath, Rishi Kesh Letha and Amin Chaudhry. This army of the Ghadarites reached the borders of Baluchistan where the British army was very weak. General Sykes tried to recruit the help of the Baluchi tribal chiefs. This Ghadarite army attacked the frontier city of Karman and arrested the British Counsel and turned Karman into its base of operations.

The British pressed into their service the Aga Khan and his brother. Aga Khan's brother was captured by the Ghadarite army and shot dead. The army of the Ghadarites also defeated the British forces in the province of Sistan in Afghanistan. The Ghadar army chased the British forces into the Karamshir area of Baluchistan. Here they heard the news and declaration of the Free Hindustan by the government-in-exile headed by Mohendra Pratap. From here the Ghadar army advanced towards Karachi and took over the coastal towns of Gawador and Dawar. The Baluch chief of Bampur declared his independence from the British rule and joined the Ghadar forces. Meanwhile, however, the war in Europe took a turn for the better for the British. Turkey was defeated and Baghdad came under British control, cutting the supply lines of for the Ghadar army, which finally led to its defeat. They retreated to regroup in Shiraz. The British army, reinforced by their victory in Turkey and Iraq, attacked Shiraz. The Ghadar army fought very bravely but was defeated. Amba Prasad Sufi, the leader of the Ghadarites was killed in this battle. The Ghadarites carried on Guerrilla warfare along with the Iranian partisans but when the Iranian patriots were defeated, they left Iran in 1919.

Ghadar was sent through China to Russia and then through Russia, it used to go through Iran and Mesopotamia to the Indian troops stationed there. The 15th Lancers, stationed in Basra revolted and 64 soldiers were court-martialed. Similarly, the 24th Punjabi and 22nd Pahari also revolted.

Before returning to India in 1914-15, the Ghadar Party had elected a new collective to carry on the work. The following were elected to the executive committee:

1. Bhai Bhagwan Singh---President
2. Bhai Santokh Singh---General Secretary
3. Munshi Ram---Treasurer
4. Ram Chand---Manager of the paper
5. Gobind Bihari Lal---Editor
6. Godha Ram---Urdu Editor
7. Gopal Singh Sohi---Punjabi Editor
8. Hari Singh Fakir---Assistant Editor

9. Sundar Singh Ghali---Office Secretary
10. Ram Singh Dhuleta---Staff
11. Mahadev Aboj---Staff
12. Imamdin---Staff
13. Nidhan Singh---Staff
14. Bishan Singh Hindi---Staff

As it has been mentioned, one million copies of the Ghadar were published every week by 1916. On January 22,1917, the movement was officially registered as the Hindustan Ghadar Party in San Francisco to comply with the American law, with its headquarters at 5 Wood Street.

The Ghadarites were defeated but they were not crushed. They regrouped and decided to carry on their work to fight another battle and yet another until Hindustan was free. On the international scene, the defeat of Turkey and Germany had created new difficulties and an unfavorable situation. The end of war had also given rise to another event of great international significance: the Bolshevik revolution in Russia, which had tremendous effect on the Ghadar Party's work and direction. The news of the triumph of the workers' and peasants' revolution in Russia inspired the people of Hindustan tremendously. There was great enthusiasm on the part of workers, peasants, intellectuals, and enlightened individuals to find out more and in detail about the achievements of this revolution.

The Ghadarites had been working closely with all the revolutionaries internationally such as the Irish revolutionaries, the Chinese revolutionaries, the Russian revolutionaries, as well as with the Egyptian, African, Latin American, and Algerian revolutionaries. They had also been influenced by socialist ideas and movements, and had close working relations with the trade union movement.

In North America they had aclose association with the IWW. Agnes Smedley, Emma Goldman, Mary Lyon Howzer, Mrs. Carrington Lewis, Freida Birch, and Chas Lester were some of the famous socialist and trade union leaders with whom the Ghadarites had good working relations.

These leaders of the working class and democratic public opinion had assisted the Ghadarites tremendously in their fight in the courts of Seattle and San Francisco. Agnes Smedley and her friends including Tarak Nath Das, formed Friends of Freedom of India in 1919, to popularize and support the cause of the Ghadarites in North America. Friends of Freedom of India, had many socialists, communists, and labour organizers as well as well-known writers and artists such as Upton Sinclair. Tarak Nath's paper, Free Hindustan, which was published in Seattle in 1907, declared in bold letters on its masthead, "Workers of the World Unite, You Have Nothing to Lose But Chains."

The triumph of the Bolshevik revolution naturally attracted their attention and drew them to the Soviet Union and its experience, just as the French revolution, American revolution, and the Mexican revolution of 1911 had drawn their attention earlier. They were anxious to meet and learn from the leaders of the October revolution who had overthrown the rule of exploiters, and who had established a state of the exploited and the oppressed.

The Ghadarites called the Russian revolutionaries the Russian Ghadarites and considered them as their Ghadarite brothers fighting for the same cause of national and social liberation. In turn the Bolsheviks and the newly formed Soviet state had declared unconditional support for the people of Hindustan in their struggle against the British colonialism.

Several Ghadarites had been in Russia during the period of the Bolshevik revolution and the Russian revolutionaries had assisted them in distributing Ghadar. By now these revolutionaries had succeeded in overthrowing their oppressors and formed their own state and were charting a new path hitherto unknown. Ghadarites were greatly excited by these prospects.

The Ghadar Party sent Rattan Singh and Santokh Singh as its representatives to the Soviet Union to learn from the Bolsheviks. Talso attended the 4th Congress of the Communist International (Comintern) as the Hindustani representatives:

"The IV Congress of the Communist International, which met in Moscow in November 1922, was attended by two representatives deputed by the Ghadar Party in California, one being Santokh Singh as a 'delegate from India' and the other Rattan Singh. Both of these men were thorough going Ghadar supporters."

..."Santokh Singh it may be said, had also attended the Second World Congress of the R.I.L.U., held in Moscow in November 1922...at a formal meeting of the Ghadar Party to welcome him, he said that Russia, America and Turkey had secured freedom through revolution, and that India would have to do the same."

The fourth congress of the Comintern sent a telegram to the All Indian Trade Union Congress, Lahore, and had advised them;

"No amelioration of living conditions is possible while imperialist exploitation exists. It is for this reason that you will play an important part in the struggle for national independence. Prepare for this historic role. The advanced proletariat of fifty-two countries represented at this Congress is entirely on

your side. Beware of the false friendship and the misleading advice of labour leaders that are subservient to imperialism."

Comintern also pointed out:

"Only an agrarian revolution committed to the expropriation of the great landowners can arouse the vast peasant masses, who will be a key factor in the struggle against imperialism. The bourgeois nationalists fear of agrarian demands and their efforts to water them down in every possible way (as in India, Persia, Egypt) are an indication of the close connection between the native bourgeoisie and the great feudal bourgeois landowners, and the former's intellectual and political dependence on the latter. The revolutionary forces must use these hesitations and uncertainties to make a thorough, ongoing criticism and exposure of the compromises made by the bourgeois leaders of the nationalist movement. It is precisely these compromisers that hinder the organization and rallying of the working masses, as is shown by the bankruptcy of the tactic of passive resistance."

Rattan Singh and Santokh Singh had the opportunity to exchange opinions and views with the Bolshevik leaders including Lenin. They were deeply and profoundly influenced by the fight that the Soviet Union was waging to consolidate the gains of revolution and the fight that it was carrying on against the 18 imperialist countries including, the US, Britain, Canada, France, and Germany, who had invaded the Soviet Union. They visited various parts of Soviet Union, met with workers, peasants, and intellectuals, and were convinced that the path that was being charted out in the Soviet Union would be helpful in the national and social emancipation of India. They were deeply moved by the unconditional support of the Soviet Union and Soviet Ghadarites (Bolsheviks) for the emancipation of Hindustan.

In India after the war, a great revolutionary upsurge had gained momentum. This movement had become a forest fire in Punjab and Northwestern Provinces due to the repression of the Rowlatt Act and Crawling orders. The British government had carried out massacres in Jalianwala Bagh in Amritsar and strafed with Royal Air Force planes in Gujjranwala, killing hundreds of people and injuring thousands. In Afghanistan, Ammanullah had declared Afghanistan's independence from the British and the anti-colonial movement of Khilafat in Turkey stirred them a great deal. Barkatullah, a Ghadarite, and Ammanullah had collaborated greatly in their anti-British activities in Afghanistan. With Ammanullah at the head of Independent Afghanistan, gave tremendous boost and status to the work of Ghadar Party. The news of the Bolshevik revolution and the state of workers and peasants had tremendously inspired these insurgent people. They were not cowed down by the repression of the British. After the British had killed several people in a firing in Lahore one of the poets expressed the sentiments of this movement in the following lines:

Shaheed ki jo maut hai wo kaum ki hayat hai
Shaheed ka jo hai lahu wo kaum ki zakat hai
Katain jo chand daaliyan to chaman ho hara bhara
Katain jo chand gardanain to kaum ki hayat hai
(The death of the martyrs is life of the nation
The blood of the martyrs is the offering of the nation
Few branches fall so that the garden can bloom
Few heads fall so that the nation can have life)

Rattan Singh, Santokh Singh and Barkatullah were representatives of the Ghadar Party who traveled in various countries to consolidate and strengthen the work of the Ghadar Party. Rattan Singh traveled to India, America, Latin America, Europe, Russia and the Middle East. Teja Singh Sutantar was leading the Ghadar Party in Turkey. Santokh Singh undertook the work of organizing the Kirti group of Communists in India and the publication of the paper Kirti, "Rattan Singh while still in America, had suggested the starting of the Kirti and in his first letter wrote...'business could only be successful if the Kirti was successful...we are trying to send money soon for this paper.'" In January 1926 the Kirti was advertised as follows:

"This journal will be the voice of Indian workers in America and Canada and will be dedicated to the sacred memory of those heroes and martyrs who awakened sleeping India...In February following the first issue appeared, bearing on its title page the picture of a dead labourer lying on his funeral pyre, amidst factories, fields, etc.,...the sense of his labours when alive and surrounded by tools such as the hammer and pickax, the whole obviously intended to convey the idea that the deceased had succumbed to the hard tasks he had to perform during his lifetime. The paper has ever since its appearance consistently advocated the cause and ideals of the Ghadar conspirators of 1914 and 1915, it has glorified the Babbar Akalis as martyrs and heroes...The magazine has been welcomed by the Hindustan Ghadar, which issued an appeal for subscriptions for it."

Another intelligence report points out:

"the Ghadar Party in 1925 established a Workers and Peasant Party (Kirti Kisan Party) in the Punjab. Its organ, the Kirti, a purely communistic production, was subsidized by the Ghadar Party in America. The aims of the Kirti Kisan Party were (1) to achieve complete independence from British Imperialism by every possible method in order to liberate the workers and

peasants from political, economic and social serfdom and to establish their democratic power; and (2) to organize the workers and peasants. The Kirti Kisan Party was a counter part in India of the Ghadar Party organization in America and it professed communist creed."

The Kirti Party also organized the youth and had close relations with Naujawan Bharat Sabha, with Bhagat Singh as one of its leaders. Bhagat Singh also worked for some time on the Kirti Urdu edition. Bhagat Singh's uncle, Ajit Singh, who was in exile was very closely connected to the Ghadarites in Argentina and Brazil. At one time it was intended by the Ghadar Party to invite Ajit Singh to be the editor of Ghadar. In Britain the Ghadar Party could not exist legally because the British had outlawed it in their empire. Therefore Rattan Singh founded the Indian Workers Association with the same aims of the Ghadar Party.

Barkatullah played a very important role in the Muslim parts of the Soviet Union working with the Hijris, and also cooperating with the Bolsheviks. After the declaration of Afghanistan's independence, Ammanullah sent an official delegation with Barkatullah at its head to Soviet Union. This mission known as the Barkatullah mission was received very warmly by the Soviet government.

A treaty of peace and friendship was signed between the two governments. Barkatullah went to the Soviet Union during the civil war, and exposed the dastardly deeds of the British and the French amongst the eastern regions of the Soviet Union, where the colonial powers were using their tested weapon of divide and rule on the religious basis by inciting the Muslim inhabitants against the gains of the revolution and the Soviet Union. Barkatullah's work in the Soviet Union in support of the revolution and its gains was an expression of the Ghadar Party's deep-seated internationalism.

As a result of their internationalism, they had developed close ties with other revolutionaries and revolutionary governments such as the government of Ammanullah in Afghanistan, Fakhri Pasha in Turkey and the Soviet government. Barkatullah also attended the congress of the League Against Imperialism in Brussels in 1928 as a delegate, which passed a resolution on India stating:

"The general council of the League against Imperialism declares its complete solidarity with the Indian peoople in the latter's opposition to the British government's proposal of a commission of the British Parliament to investigate India's fitness for self government.

The appointment of this commission of the exploiters to the grant 'reforms' to the peoples whom they exploit is nothing but an impudent farce, and the general council heartily supports the Indian national movement's resolve to boycott the commission.

The general council notes with disgust that the British Labour party leaders and members of parliament have made common cause with the British imperialists on this question, by supporting the conservative government's proposals of a commission an by endorsing without any but the weakest support to comrade Saklatvala in Parliament, the participation of two labour representatives.

The general council declares that this open united front of the British capitalists and British labour leaders in defence of British imperialism which has no parallel since the black days of August 1914, is as harmful to the workers of the oppressor countries, since they are exploited by the same ruling class. The league against Imperialism pledges the wholehearted support of all its adherent organisations and sections to the Indian national movement in this struggle. At the same time it urges all genuine enemies of imperialist oppression in India to concentrate on rallying the masses around the positive slogan of complete independence for India-the sole real threat to the power of British imperialism...and on election of a constituent assembly to consider the entire question of the political future of India, which should be prepared by the creation of local committees, mass demonstrations and the widest possible participation of the masses of people generally."

Rattan Singh in this period travelled on an Afghan passport issued by the Afghan government as the British government had impounded his passport. During his travels Rattan Singh visited the branches of Ghadar Party in Mexico, Cuba, Central America, Panama, Brazil and Argentina and met with Bujha Singh and Bhagat Singh Bilga. After his visit to Argentina, it was decided that Bujha Singh would take the first group of Ghadarites from Argentina back to India via Moscow. They were to receive political training and education in Moscow. The Ghadar Party had issued a second "Return to India Call" and said that the Ghadarites should return to India via Moscow. The intelligence bureau reported that, "there are at present 35 students of the Ghadar Party undergoing training in Moscow."

The Kirti Party had its independent and separate organization from other communist groups in India and had direct links with the Comintern. They also published Lal Jhanda and Lal Dhandora papers besides Kirti. They assigned Kisan Sabhas to organize the peasantry and the trade unions of workers in towns and cities. Overseas the Hindustan Ghadar propagated the cause of the liberation of India and popularized the work of the Kirti Party and other revolutionaries. To lead the work of the Kirti Party, a revolutionary committee was elected with Santokh Singh its secretary, Karam Singh Cheema, Rattan Singh, Udham Singh Kasel and Gurmukh Singh as members.

The last three members were in exile and could not enter India and were based abroad. One by one they would come to India secretly while others travelled to the Ghadar Party headquarters in San Francisco, as well as other parts of the world including the Soviet Union.

On the first anniversary of the Kirti paper this revolutionary committee pointed out in its report:

1. The objective for which the publication of Kirti was started, we have made all the efforts to fulfil that goal.
2. The objective of Kirti is neither Swaraj or Home Rule but complete independence of Hindustan and rule of workers and peasants. We stand on this unwaveringly and will stand for these objectives in future.
3. India can achieve complete independence by those means only by which other enslaved countries have gained their independence. It can not be achieved by any other means such as boycott, Satyagrah etc. We stand for revolutionary methods and will do so in future.
4. In Kirti's view the struggle of the people of Hindustan for liberation and socialism is a link in the chain of the struggle of all the peoples of the world for liberation. Therefore we will inform all the revolutionaries of the world about the struggles of Hindustan's people and inform the people of Hindustan of their struggles as we are part of one struggle. In the past one year we have been writing about the liberation struggle of the people of China and Afghanistan.We have written about the coal miners struggle in Britain, danger of fascism in Italy and the invasion of Abyssinia by fascist Italy and other international events. In future we will continue to do so.
5. A workers' and peasants' state has come into being in Russia and the people of Russia are building a new system and are marching towards socialism. We have provided full information to our readers about these matters and we will continue to do so in future.
6. Martyrs of a nation are its fundamental heritage. We have been writing about their deeds and life. In coming times we will continue to write about the Ghadarite martyrs of 1914-1916, including Babbar Akali and other young revolutionaries who have sacrificed their lives for our nation.

In 1929 a great wave of peasant unrest gripped Hindustan from Kanya Kumari to Kashmir. Also, many workers strikes were taking place at this time.

Demonstrations and rallies against British rule were being organized all over the country. Bhagat Singh and his comrades had thrown a bomb in the Assembly to awaken the masses. The Army refused to open fire on a demonstration in Peshawar. The whole country was in fervor. The Ghadarites of the Kirti Party tirelessly organized against the British rule and guided the people. They were also instrumental in organising the Naujawan Sabha led by Bhagat Singh. The constitution of the Naujavan Bharat Sabha defined the main aims and objectives of the Sabha as follows:

1. To establish a complete independent republic of labourers and peasants throughout India.
2. To inspire in the hearts of the young men of the country the feelings of patriotism and spirit of sacrifice for forming a united nationality in India.
3. To create the spirit of general toleration among the public considering religion as a matter of personal belief of man's and to act upon the same fully.
4. To show interest for and help every economic and social movement which is quite free from communal feelings and which is calculated to take us near our goal to establish a complete independent republic of labourers and peasants throughout India.
5. To organise labourers and peasants

Along with Kisan Sabhas, Naujawan Sabha, workers and other people were in the front ranks of these agitations and struggles. They published in Kirti the full text of the statement issued by Bhagat Singh and Dutt in their defence. Kirti fully supported the revolutionary youth and at the same time it advised them through its pages against the dangers of individual terrorism. In 1928 Abdul Majid started Mahnatkash which was also an organ of the Kirti Party.

In March 1931, Rajguru, Sukhdev, and Bhagat Singh were hanged by the British. This further fuelled the fire against the British. The Kirti Party decided to bring out a weekly paper Mazdoor Kisan (Workers and Peasants) in Hindi and Urdu. It organized conferences and rallies along with Nau Jawan Sabha in Shekhupur, Multan, Gujaranwala, Layalpur, Rohtak, Jullundhur and other places. The writings of Ferozuddin Mansur and Munshi Ahmed Din, dealt with the burning questions of the day. Mazdoor Kisan also published the statements and speeches of communists arrested in the Meerut Conspiracy Case and also exposed all those who collaborated with the British. They openly opposed the Communal Suffrage.

In 1942 the Kirti party merged with the Communist Party of India feeling the need for unity of all the communists. After the partition of the Hindustan and transfer of the power to the Congress government, the Nehru government declared the Communist Party illegal. The communists had to go underground. This was the reward that the workers, peasants and communists had harvested. The communists had to go underground, and they thought about the wisdom of policy that the leadership of the CPI was following by supporting the Congress and Nehru government. In 1948, the Ghadarites who had joined the CPI in 1942 formed their own Lal Party (Red Party), because they did not feel that the leadership of the CPI was revolutionary, instead of revolution they felt that the leadership of the CPI was tailing behind the leadership of Congress. The Ghadarites wanted national liberation with social revolution. The leaders of both Congress and the CPI were interested in national liberation without social revolution. They were on the social democratic path. They wanted to manage the British system with Indian faces. Ghadarites were also opposed to the partition of the country on a religious basis, whereas both Congress and CPI were in the favour of dividing the country on the basis of religion and the creation of Pakistan. The Kirti party had vehemently opposed the Pakistan Resolution of the CPI in 1944, which divided the country on the basis of religion.

They also supported the Telangana uprising and the peasants uprising in Punjab and Eastern Punjab States Union (PEPSU), while the leadership of CPI was opposed to both of these struggles.

In 1952 the Ghadarites of the Lal Party once again rejoined the CPI after the change of the leadership of CPI, hoping that the new leadership would carry out the social revolution to the end and not tail behind Congress and Nehru. But these hopes were to be dashed to the ground. In 1958, the communists were elected in Kerala and formed the government and attempted to carry out serious land reforms. The Congress government headed by the Nehru government dissolved the Kerala government in 1959 at the insistence of the Landlords of Kerala. The period of 1960-1964 saw one of the worst famines in India with millions of people starving to death. It created a great wave of discontent in the country leading to the defeat of the Congress party in the 1967 general elections in many states.

A peasant uprising broke out in Naxalbari, which found its resonance in many parts of the country. Baba Sohan Singh Bhakhna, the first president of the Ghadar Party declared that the aims and objectives for which the Ghadar Party had been formed in 1913 and for which the Ghadarites had made countless sacrifices. Those aims, namely the social revolution in India had not been carried out. Baba Bujha Singh, a Ghadarite who was one of the leaders of the Ghadar Party in Argentina had returned to India via Moscow, echoed his sentiment and threw his full support behind the Naxalbari uprising. And when the Communist Party of India (Marxist-Leninist) was formed, he was elected its leader in Punjab at the age of 78.

The Indian patriots, democrats and enlightened people abroad also echoed Baba Sohan Singh Bhakhna's call and fully supported the Naxalbari uprising. In Britain the Indian Workers Association had continued its work. A meeting was held in London around the time of the "Necessity for Change Conference" in November 1967 and it was decided to reactivate the Hindustani Ghadar Party in support of Naxalbari. An ad hoc committee was formed to reorganize the Ghadar Party for the social revolution in India. Manchanda was elected its president and Hardial Bains was elected to be in charge of work in North America. When the Communist Party of India (Marxist-Leninist) was formed in 1969, the Ghadar Party became its external wing. The Ghadarites were advised by CPI(M-L) and Charu Mazumdar, its General Secretary, to propagate the cause of the Indian revolution in the countries where they were resident. Ghadarites defended the cause of the Indian revolution through their paper Chingari and also organized people against racist attacks in Canada and Britain in close connection with the Canadian and British working class:

> *"There were two reasons why the Ghadar Party was founded in 1913; first to achieve the true aspirations of the Indian people to defeat the British Colonialism in India and to build a free and prosperous India, and secondly to fight racial discrimination in North America and other places where fascists organized by the British Colonialists were bullying the Indian residents...The two reasons on which the Ghadar Party was founded still remain. India is yet to gain her true independence and the Indians residing in the USA, Canada, Britain and other places have yet to achieve racial equality. It is for this that we have organized the new Ghadar Party."*

The Ghadarites once again raised the slogan, "Blame the Canadian State for Racist Attacks", "Unite with the Canadian People to Fight Against Racist Attacks" and they also followed the slogan "Self-Defence is the Only Way." Amongst the students and intelligentsia the Indian Progressive Study Groups came into being in Canada and the US as part of this trend. At the time of the founding of the Ghadar Party, resolutions were passed in support of the Palestinian people, people of Indo-China, against US Imperialism, black people in their struggle against racism in the USA, and the people of Canada and Quebec in their struggle against the domination of USA. They also developed close working relations with the revolutionaries from Asia, Africa, and Latin

America where great uprisings had taken place. Ghadarites considered liberation of India as an integral part of the liberation of the world's people and supported the just struggles of all the peoples for liberation, dignity and honour whether in the Eastern or Western blocks.

They participated in international gatherings and conferences to exchange views and learn from the experience of other revolutionaries. In this context the Internationalist Rally held in Montreal in April 1978 was very important in which revolutionaries from all continents participated. The new Ghadarites like their earlier predecessors were harassed, persecuted and attacked for their views, convictions and activities. The diplomatic offices of the Indian government also collaborated with the Canadian government in their persecution. Harsh Chaddha, a young man in his twenties was deported from Canada for his political activities. Hardial Bains was not given Canadian citizenship for more than two decades because of his political views, was denied entry into the United States, and the Indian government withdrew his Passport in 1975 which was never reinstated, while they were giving calls for his deportation to India. Like the old Ghadarites, the new Ghadarites were not frightened by these threats and attacks. They carried on doing their work.

After the assassination of Charu Mazumdar and other revolutionary leadership of the CPI(M-L), the CPI(M-L) split into various factions. The Ghadar Party worked closely with all the groups who aimed to bring about social revolution. A delegation of the Ghadar Party participated in a conference of CPI(M-L) in India in 1973 to discuss various problems of the Indian revolution. The Ghadarites emphasized the need for all revolutionaries to unite for the cause of Indian revolution.

In 1973 the then Prime Minister of India, Indira Gandhi, came to visit Britain and North America. The Ghadarites organized rallies and demonstrations against her visit in cooperation with several other organizations and groups condemning the torture and killing of thousands of youth branded as terrorists and extremists in false police encounters in Punjab, Bengal, Bihar, Kerala, Tamil Nadu, Andhra Pradesh, Kashmir, etc. The Ghadarites through the pages of Chingari, Lok Awaz, and other publications brought to light the violation of human rights, political persecution, killing and torture of the Naxalites, youth, and others.

In 1975, Indira Gandhi declared a state of emergency, which resulted in the dissolving of Parliament. A widespread movement in India and abroad started against this naked dictatorship. Workers, women, peasants, students, shopkeepers all were galvanized into a big storm.

The CPI supported the declaration of emergency while there were others who wanted to oppose Emergency in order to come to power themselves. The Ghadarites pointed out that the Emergency was one of the symptoms of colonial rule without colonialists. They believed that the Indian people should not be fooled by this or any party that would come into power and preserve the same rule under a different name. The Ghadarites hoped that Indians would develop a people's movement against this rule.

They called upon the people to develop their unity and not be fooled by the "United Front" of Jan Sangh, CPI(M) and others because they all wanted to preserve the old rule. They brought the truth of the matter under the slogan "Indira Gandhi, Morarji Desai, Chor Chor Mauserey Bhai," that both Indira Gandhi and Morarji Desai represented the same forces and that they were brother and sister in preserving neo-colonial rule. Congress and Indira Gandhi were thoroughly defeated in the elections held in 1977 and a coalition of several other parties came to power in the centre. One of the first acts of this coalition government of "restoring democracy" was the firing of striking workers of Kanpur in which several workers were killed. This act revealed how the new coalition was not interested in the social transformation of Indian society, but were perpetuating the rule of the ruling elites with hook or crook.

In October 1977 the Ghadarites held a congress in which they issued a call to all Ghadarites to return to India to further consolidate and strengthen the unity of the revolutionary forces who wanted to take up the problems of India and search for real solutions. This was the third return of the Ghadarites to India since 1913. The Ghadarites started a paper People's Voice in India to develop discussion for the unity of the revolutionary forces. Like the old Ghadarites, they built ties and working relations with other revolutionary, democratic, and progressive organizations and forces.

As a result of this work the Communist Ghadar Party of India came into being in 1980. Communist Ghadar Party declared at its founding that only the people of India, workers, peasants, women, youth, students, all the nations, and nationalities by their united forces can liberate India from medieval darkness and bring about prosperity, freedom, enlightenment and dignity to India. They would have to rely on their own forces to carry out such a transformation. They must all unite irrespective of their religious, political, ideological, caste, linguistic, and regional differences. Only they could establish a democratic India in which the rights of all the peoples will be respected and honoured. It called upon all the people of India to support the just struggles of all the oppressed and exploited abroad such as the struggle of the Palestinian people, South African people, workers struggle in Europe and Latin America, etc. It also condemned the racist attacks on the Indian people residing abroad in Britain, Canada, Australia, the US, and other places. They called upon the Indian residents in these countries to unite with the people of their countries to fight against the racist and fascist attacks.

On the cultural front, the Ghadarites also took various initiatives. Along with other organizations, they helped to organize the International Sports and Cultural Festivals in Canada, Britain and India, which were attended by thousands of people. The first international sports and cultural festival took place in Vancouver in 1981 and was attended by more than 40,000 people. It was during this festival that the first World Cup Kabbadi matches were held. In 1982 the festival was held in India and in 1983 it was held in Britain. These festivals were held under the slogan of 'Sports and Culture in service of the people."

Thousands of people participated and supported these festivals, which helped to develop friendly relations between the people of South Asia as well as with South Asians living abroad. Kabbadi teams and other sportsmen from India, Pakistan, Bangladesh, the USA, Canada, etc. participated in these festivals. Cultural personalities and performers from different parts of South Asia also participated. They also organized annual sports tournaments and cultural events to honour heroic martyrs such as Bhagat Singh, Mewa Singh, Udham Singh, etc., in cooperation with other groups and associations such as the East Indian Defence Committee and the Desh Bhagat Sports and Cultural Society. Just like the old Ghadaries, the new Ghadarites also conveyed their message through poems, songs, plays, dramas, stories, etc., in the various languages of India such as Hindustani, Punjabi, Bengali, Tamil, Malayalam, and Marathi.

The Ghadarites concluded the need for the renovation of Indian society and presented democratic renewal of India as the agenda of the day. They concluded that this renewal and renovation could only be achieved by the empowerment and affirmation of the people, and it can only be built by the people themselves. They analyzed that the present political process, representative democracy, actually disenfranchises the people. Political parties have become gatekeepers of power and have usurped the power of the people, often in the people's name:

> *"The parliamentary system is in deep crisis not only in India but all over the world. The party in power, Congress (I) and the party in opposition, the BJP, openly declare they will abide by nothing and they are a law unto themselves. There are other political parties who think in the same way. How else is it possible to have riots, disappearances, murders and false encounters*

if these parties were not a law unto themselves? The present system, besides not solving any of the problems for the benefit of the people, also appears unable to provide a smooth transfer of governance from one political party to the other. The main cause of this is not that the Congress (I) or BJP are deviants, but that the system demands the existence of such parties for its perpetuation. People are putting forward their demands and all sections of the people are discontented with the situation, but the system can not satisfy them. There is a real pressure for the creation of a new kind of party, a party which would ensure that these political parties do not keep the people out of power."

It further analyzed:

"The origin of the political system that exists in India and the roots of the crisis of this system can be traced to the Government of India Act of 1935, the transfer of power that took place in 1947 and the constitution that was adopted in 1950...While the democracy that came into being was objectively and advance for the Indian people, it did not lead to their empowerment. This was because this democracy was based on the theory of concentrating power in the executive, in order to deprive the masses of power. The role of the president of India, the frequent declaration of President's Rule at the advice of the cabinet, the ruling party's power to define and redefine state boundaries, the very notion of 'cabinet rule', are all different features of this concentration of power in the hands of the executive."

On the present social development, they state:

"Today, on the eve of the 21st century, nobody can deny that people are born to society and society has a responsibility to look after their well being. This corresponds to the modern definition of rights and is also one of the central aspects of Indian political thought. However according to present day 'Western' ideologues, society has no obligation to anyone except to the financial oligarchy. The so-called individual interest is given primacy over the collective interest and the general interest of society. This imposition of imperialist theories on the soil of India is creating grave complications. It is contributing to the further deepening of the capitalist crisis and causing great resentment amongst the people. The big capitalists and big landlords are using these theories to create serious danger to the very well-being of the people and the future of society."

Following the tradition of the old Ghadarites, they seek the unity of all the peoples to deal with problems facing the society:

"The critical task is to build the political unity of all workers and people of the middle strata who are opposed to the existing state of affairs, especially to the criminalisation of the polity; to the use of state terrorism; to all the

attacks on the freedoms of the people; and most importantly who stand for the economic well being of he workers and broad masses of the people. Declaration of this or that phrase from the classics of Marxism-Leninism, without seeking the same afresh from the objective and subjective conditions that confront the people will not contribute to progress whatsoever."

They also point out the reason for the miserable conditions of the people of India;

"Tragically for the working class and the toiling masses of India, emancipation has eluded them. This has happened because the propertied classes have bound them hand and foot to capitalism and to the remnants of feudalism. More importantly, the communist and workers movement has been undermined by social democracy. The fact that European social democracy presents itself in the colours of socialism and communism in India. The aspirations of the propertied classes created by colonialism and imperialism have dug their poisonous claws into the healthy body of the working class movement for emancipation..."

In the realm of theoretical considerations, the Ghadarites point out the necessity of Indian theory rather than Eurocentric ideas and theories for the liberation of India from hunger and starvation, oppression and exploitation, because these Eurocentric ideas and theories had only served to enslave India, mentally, politically, and economically:

"The starting point, the first step, the most immediate question and the long-term task that appears in India for the victory of the revolutionary movement is that of theory. It expresses itself most succinctly in the necessity for Indian theory, a theory emerging out of the conditions of India..."

The British colonialists attacked the Indian philosophy to the point of denying its existence or distorting it to serve their own ends by imposing irrationalism on Indian philosophy.

The Ghadarites point out:

"The stagnation of the philosophy of Darshan is inextricably linked with the stagnation of Indian thought, and of the economic and political theories in our country. The Darshandharis, ensconced within the comfortable walls of Indian, America and British universities, pontificate about Indian philosophy, as if it has no relevance or link with the present conditions in India, with the illumination of the road to progress for the Indian people at this time in history. Idealist and religious interpretations are given of Darshan, to make it lifeless and useless for the Indian people. Meanwhile, deprived of philosophy and outlook to deal with the problems of today, the Indian people are left floundering helplessly, at the mercy of the bourgeoisie and imperialism."

On the task of Democratic Renewal and completing the anti-colonial revolution the Ghadarites point out:

> *"A thorough going anti-colonial revolution necessarily means ending the capitalist system and its democracy, which has deprived people of their economic and political power. An anti-colonial revolution, which is merely a matter of formal independence and not a social revolution has become anachronistic.*
>
> *The entire experience from the time of 'transfer of power' to the Indian bourgeoisie in 1947, with the division of the Indian subcontinent, especially Bengal and Punjab, has proven that this has not led to deep-going transformations. On the contrary, the bourgeoisie has completely obstructed the social revolution. It has been proven that it is capitalism that is the defender of the remnants of feudalism; it is capitalism that is protecting imperialists and colonialist interests; it is capitalism that is the motor behind bourgeoisie in its globalisation of capital and production. Furthermore it is capitalism that has caused disaster in the countryside, deepening the agrarian problems, and trampling underfoot the slogan of the patriotic forces of ' Land to the Tiller'.*
>
> *Festering at the base of Indian society at this time are capitalism and remnants of feudalism, with the superstructure of imperialism and colonial domination. This has made the conditions of life and work for the working classes and toiling masses extremely miserable. More than fifty percent of Indian people live in abysmal conditions of poverty, victims of malnutrition, ill health, illiteracy and every kind of disease. The government of India's entire program of 'poverty alleviation' has concentrated on juggling the figures prove that the percentage of the Indian people living below the poverty line has been decreasing. Official figures now claim that it is less than 20% of the population. This juggling itself shows the callousness of the Indian state and its rulers, who define poverty levels on the basis of whether people receive a certain amount of calories a day. It distorts the reality that human beings can not exist on the basis of minimum amount of staple food alone. They need other necessities to ensure against malnutrition such as pulses, vegetables, milk and meat; they need potable water, sanitation, health care, proper accommodation and clothes, and a clean, healthy, peaceful and stable environment conducive to living. They need education and culture, and the satisfaction of working for their ever increasing material and cultural needs."*

Bibliography

Alam, Kousar J. : *Political Aspects of National Integration,* Meerut: Meenakshi Prakashan, 1981.

Almond, Gabriel A.: *Comparative Politics: A Developmental Approach,* Boston: Little, Brown, 1966.

Alva, Joachim: *Leaders of India,* Bombay, Thacker & Co., Ltd., 1943

Arabinda Poddar : *Bhagat Singh : The Political Personality*, Kolkata, Indiana, 2004.

Atri, Ajit : *Gandhi's View of Legal Justice,* New Delhi, Deep and Deep Pub., 2007.

Bapat, S. V.: *Tilak Sukti Sangraha,* A Kesari Prakashan, Pune, 1926.

Butalia, Urvashi: *The Other Side of Silence: Voices from the Partition of India,* New Delhi, Penguin, 1998.

Campbell-Johnson, Alan: *Mission with Bhagat Singh,* London: Hale, 1982.

Chatterji, Joya: *Bengal Divided: Hindu Communalism and Partition, 1932-1947,* Cambridge, Cambridge UP, 1994.

Chaudhuri, Nirad: *Thy Hand, Great Anarch! India: 1921-1952,* London, Chatto & Windus, 1987.

Dasai, M. H.: *Day to Day with Gandhi,* Varanasi, Sarva Sangh Pakistan, 1968.

Deutsch, Karl: *Political Community and the North Atlantic Area,* Princeton: Princeton University Press, 1957.

Ghoshal, U. N.: A *History of Indian Political Ideas*. London, 1966.

Haas, Ernst B.: *Beyond the Nation State,* Stanford: Stanford University Press, 1964.

Harrison, John: *The City in South Asia: Pre-Modern and Modern*, London, Curzon Press, 1980.

Hasan, Mushirul: *India's Partition: Process, Strategy and Mobilization,* New Delhi, Oxford UP, 1993.

Joshi, V.C.: *Bhagat Singh and the Process of Modernization in India,* Delhi, 1975.

Kenneth L.: *Ahmedabad: A Study in Indian Urban History,* Berkeley, University of California Press, 1968.

Krishna, B. : *Indian Freedom Struggle : The Pathfinders From Surendranath Banerjea to Gandhi,* New Delhi, Manohar, 2002.

Maheshwari, S.R.: *Public Administration in India*. The Higher Civil Service, Delhi: Oxford University Press, 2005.

Menon, Ritu and Bhasin, Kamla: *Borders and Boundaries: Women in India's Partition,* New Delhi, Kali for Women, 1998.

Menon, V. P.: *The Transfer of Power in India*, Bombay, Orient Longman, 1957.

Mosher, Frederick C.: *Democracy and the Public Service*, New York: Oxford University Press, 1968.

Nag, Sajal: *Nationalism, Separatism and Secessionism*, New Delhi: Rawat Publications, 1999.

Naik, J. P.: *Political Content of Education*, Socio Research Publications Centre, Calcutta, 1917.

Prasad, Lal Bahadur : *Indian Political System and Law*, New Delhi, Shree, 2005.

Singh, Balwant: *An Untouchable in the I.A.S.*, Saharanpur: Prem Printing Press, 1964.

Singh, Kirpal: *Select Documents on Partition of Punjab — 1947, India and Pakistan*, Delhi, National Bookshop, 1991.

Stanley A. Wolpert: *Bhagat Singh and Patel: Revolution and Reform in the Making of Modern India*, Berkeley, 1962.

Wolpert, Stanley : *Gandhi's Passion : The Life and Legacy of Mahatma Gandhi*, Delhi, Oxford University Press, 2001.

Yasin, Mohammad : *Indian Politics : Processes, Issues and Trends*, New Delhi, Kanishka, 2004.

Zaidi, A. Moin: *Evolution of Muslim political Thought in India*, New Delhi: S. Chand, 1975-79.

Index

J

K

L

M

N

P

R

S

U

V

W

❑❑❑